Fiction Rivals Science

Fiction Rivals Science

The French Novel from Balzac to Proust

Allen Thiher

University of Missouri Press
Columbia and London

Copyright © 2001 by
The Curators of the University of Missouri
University of Missouri Press, Columbia, Missouri 65201
Printed and bound in the United States of America
All rights reserved
5 4 3 2 1   05 04 03 02 01

Library of Congress Cataloging-in-Publication Data

Thiher, Allen, 1941–
    Fiction rivals science : the French novel from Balzac to Proust / Allen Thiher.
      p. cm.
    Includes bibliographical references and index.
    ISBN 0-8262-1357-X (alk. paper)
    1. French fiction—19th century—History and crictism. 2. Literature and
science—France. 3. Science in literature. I. Title.

PQ653 .T48 2001
843′.809—dc21

                        2001037033

♾ This paper meets the requirements of the
American National Standard for Permanence of Paper
for Printed Library Materials, Z39.48, 1984.

Designer: Stephanie Foley
Typesetter: The Composing Room of Michigan, Inc.
Printer and binder: The Maple-Vail Book Manufacturing Group
Typefaces: Palatino and Poppl Exquisit

For Irma

CONTENTS

ACKNOWLEDGMENTS   ix

ONE   *Introduction to Literature's Encounter with Science*   1

TWO   *Balzac and the Unity of Knowledge*   37

THREE   *Flaubert and the Ambiguous Victory of Positivism*   81

FOUR   *Zola's Collaborative Rivalry with Science*   125

FIVE   *Proust and the End of Epistemic Competition*   167

BIBLIOGRAPHY   211

INDEX   217

ACKNOWLEDGMENTS

I must first thank the University of Missouri, which, through the agency of its Research Council, provided a year of support during which I began research on this project in 1995. And I thank those in the Department of Romance Languages who have been supportive in many ways, from helping with the manuscript to listening and commenting on my ideas in various forums. I must also thank the staff of Romanistik at the Universität des Saarlandes who helped me with many details during my visit there in 1997. And finally, many thanks to those at Clare Hall at Cambridge University who gave assistance while I did some final research as a visiting fellow during the year 2000–2001. A good many individuals deserve thanks for ideas and criticism and other forms of help along the way. I name a few here: Uwe Dethloff, Sandy Camargo, Roger Shattuck, Noel Heringman, Audrey Glauert, and especially Irma Dimitrova, for her invaluable readings. Many thanks to Clair Willcox at the University of Missouri Press for sticking with this project even after it was criticized for not following current theoretical trends—which is certainly intentional on my part. And thanks to those anonymous readers who recognized that a book can be both scholarly and, hopefully, readable.

Fiction Rivals Science

ONE

Introduction to Literature's Encounter with Science

... à ce mot de science, je te vois bailler ...

[... at this word "science," I see you yawning ...]

—Stendhal to Pauline Beyle, December 31, 1804

HISTORICAL OVERVIEW

1654: Beginning of modern probability theory in Fermat and Pascal's correspondence, partially in response to questions about gambling.

1687: Newton's *Principia mathematica* sets forth his three laws of motion and creates celestial mechanics.

1697: Georg Ernst Stahl introduces "phlogiston" as the agent of burning, the first of four theories of heat to be debated into the nineteenth century (the other three being kinetic, caloric, and wave theories).

1713: Jacques Bernoulli's posthumously published *Ars conjectandi* contributes to probability theory with the laws of large numbers.

1724: Hermann Boerhaave, the best known doctor of the eighteenth century, proposes that heat is some kind of fluid.

1738: Voltaire publishes a work popularizing Newton, *Eléments de la philosophie de Newton.*

1739: Before becoming known for his *Histoire naturelle* (1749–1789),

1

Buffon translates Newton's *Fluxions* into French as part of a defense against Berkeley's attack on the calculus.

1743: Future encyclopedist D'Alembert publishes *Traité de dynamique*, using calculus for dynamics and rewriting Newton's second law as a problem in statics.

1768: Euler, the greatest mathematician of the time, begins *Lettres à une princesse d'Allemagne* outlining main physical theories of the eighteenth century.

1781: After early publications in natural sciences, Kant codifies Newton's epistemological revolution in the *Kritik der reinen Vernunft*.

1783: Stendhal is born. Hershel observes movement of sun through space and shows that solar system is moving in relation to stars. Lavoisier publishes critique of phlogiston theory.

1788: After years of elaboration, Lagrange's *Traité de mécanique analytique* uses the calculus, not geometry, to develop mechanics.

1798: Count Rumford demonstrates conversion of work into heat by measuring heat given off by cannon-boring.

1799: Balzac is born. Laplace begins publication of *Mécanique céleste*, five volumes of cosmology completed in 1825.

Part I: Thinking about Literature and Science

To write about literature and science of the nineteenth century requires the suspension of belief in what C. P. Snow described as an intellectual life made up of two cultures. Or, more precisely, it requires that one recognize that science and literature are distinct activities that have often entertained shared concerns in a common pursuit of knowledge. And an accurate historical perspective requires additional distancing: if the nineteenth century challenged the belief in two cultures, then the belief did not begin in the twentieth century. Pascal was already describing it, in the seventeenth century, when he discussed the opposition between the *esprit de finesse* and the *esprit de géométrie*. With these terms he named the mind seeking knowledge by critically using intuitive insight and the mind demanding mathematical formalism as the ultimate criterion of knowledge. These two types of mind characterize, respectively, the modern academic humanist and the contemporary scientist. The opposition of two types of knowledge—or minds—underwrites what many see as the institutionalization of two cultures in the modern university. However, this opposition must go back at least to the mathematically inclined Plato and his attack on poets in *The Republic*. And I would maintain, Pascal notwithstanding, that the opposition does not accurately describe the history of all the relations between literature and science. The point of this book will be precisely that nineteenth-century novelists in France wanted to overcome the distinction between two minds or two cultures.

It has become second nature for academic humanists to ascribe the opposition of the scientific and the literary mind to the inevitable history of our culture and usually to see therein a regrettable necessity. Humanists often point to the scientific revolution and decry it for bringing about the nonetheless necessary separation of two types of knowledge. But this projection upon history of the modern belief in two cultures is in part misleading. It reflects the contemporary fact that most professional critics and scholars of literature in Europe and especially the United States, for roughly the past century, have been attached to universities. Historically, however, most of the literary writers who have been the creators of literature have not had a professional allegiance to a department of literary studies, nor have these writers universally subscribed to the view that they must practice the pursuit of knowledge in some purely humanistic form. Writers have, historically speaking, rarely been academic humanists, and the enshrinement of the practice of literature in the university, as the case is today in the United States, is a rather novel historical experience, one limited to the twentieth century.

I stress this point, which a brief perusal of literary history quickly confirms, to bring up a second point. Most European writers, since the Enlightenment, have been keenly aware of what has been happening in the sciences. I would argue that much of modern literature has developed, especially from the eighteenth through the nineteenth century, as a response to the claims of science, specifically to the claims of science to dictate what can be known with any degree of certainty. In this period, in fact, many writers came to believe that they could rival science in proposing knowledge. This strikes me as a central feature of the French novel as it developed from Balzac through Proust. (I use the notion of development here with no reference to perfection of form, but rather to note that each generation of writers usually, but not always, capitalized upon what the preceding generations had done.)

During the preceding century, before the French Revolution, and during the heyday of the Enlightenment and its philosophical critique of tradition, rivalry is not the best way to view the relationship between writing and science. In the Enlightenment, the line of demarcation between literary writing and science was not entirely clear, and the same *philosophe* who in one moment was a creative polemist or an erotic novelist, might in the next moment be writing an epistemic discourse in the form of a treatise, a dialogue, or even a novel. Epistemic discourses were understood as part of that great realm called "natural philosophy"—science and philosophy as they were understood during the Enlightenment and which might include medicine, natural history, or metaphysics. Voltaire and Diderot offer many examples in their works of writers who believed that they could elaborate and disseminate knowledge on a par with any other thinker. As Ernst Cassirer put it in his study of the Enlightenment, the idea of the unity of reason and the idea of science itself were interchangeable.[1] However, if one looks forward, to a time after Proust and after the demise of the Newtonian worldview, one rarely discerns writers' feeling a sense of epistemic rivalry with science. As the twentieth century unfolded, relativity, quantum mechanics, neo-Darwinism, and molecular biology established a new cosmography and natural history that clearly concerned the writer, and many writers drew upon science in the twentieth century. But, in contrast to the Enlightenment, the twentieth century produced a cosmography in whose elaboration few literary writers have attempted to take part.

In brief, then, a series of transitions have led from the Newtonian revolution to Einstein's worldview, though—pace Foucault and Kuhn—few, if any, ruptures occurred along the way. I find no change in scientific thought during this period that was not well prepared for by many preceding shifts, theories, errors, arguments, and insights, all of which gave gradual birth to every theory from the new concept of energy to the idea that animals are the product of a long evolutionary history. But these transformations have been unceasing.

The transformation in mentality that occurs between the Enlightenment and the present can be underscored by comparing Goethe with Camus. Goethe expected his scientific work in natural history and optics to be taken as seriously as his poetry and theater. And they have

---

1. Cassirer, *La Philosophie des lumières*, trans. Pierre Quillet, 64.

been. In a novel like *The Elective Affinities,* Goethe could draw upon chemical theory to adumbrate a study of amorous affinities. In marked contrast, the young Camus, in *The Myth of Sisyphus,* dismissed modern physics as mere poetry—with the implication that science has little to do with the existential predicaments of modern life. Youthful Camus's novelistic practice largely confirms his lack of interest in epistemic issues that are specifically part of a modern scientific worldview. The world of *The Stranger* is not informed by any considerations of science, and Camus's "stranger" could be living at any historical period, however quintessentially modern many critics have found his anomie. (This lack of interest changed notably when Camus later made a doctor the narrator of *The Plague* and used a scientist as an exemplar of the ethically motivated rebel.)

It is true that a separation of epistemic discourses began during the Enlightenment, though clear lines of demarcation were not sharp before the end of the eighteenth century. At this time Newtonian dynamics received its canonical mathematical form, biology began to emerge as a new science, and medicine started to take shape slowly as an experimental discipline. Literature as a self-conscious economy of discourse emerged at roughly the same time, a process facilitated by a growing sense of difference among epistemic discourses, or a sense that different objects of knowledge demanded different types of discourse. In fact, literature began to mark out its own space during the eighteenth century when some writers undertook a moralizing discourse that was hostile to science. Swift's satire of the virtuosi and of mechanical philosophy in *The Tale of a Tub* (1704) represents a moment when science was contested by what one soon started calling, using an old word in a new sense, literature. Augustan hostility toward mechanical philosophy is, however, a minority phenomenon—even if satire became a dominant genre in the eighteenth century. After Swift, the claims of a too imperial science can also be reduced to naught by the wit of a Voltaire, the same Voltaire who wrote *Candide* and who was at the same time an ardent Newtonian (as were most Augustans). More typical is the French Enlightenment's reception of Newton and the new astronomy. Enthusiastic reception in France gave rise to a series of quasi-scientific works that, from Fontenelle's *Entretiens sur la pluralité des mondes* of 1686 to Diderot's various dialogues, incorporated the claims of science into the fabric of fictions or used fictions to enact thought experiments that seem to anticipate the playful hypotheses that Einstein and Bohr exchanged in making thought experiments to criticize each other. Literature and science were joined in these fictions, even when, as in Diderot's *Le Neveu de Rameau*, literature could contest science and science could mock literature.

To be sure, eighteenth-century fiction is not, despite the Enlightenment, entirely dominated by concerns with science. The influence of science on literature is also at times more subtle than is immediately evident. With regard to English fiction, one can consider in this light Ian Watt's suggestion that the development of realism in the eighteenth-century English novel owes much to learning how to do empirical assessment of evidentiary claims. Business and insurance companies used probability theory to make these assessments, which in turn developed a generalized sense of what is probable. In short, the rise of realism is tied up with the development of probability theory and with the ways that probable results are derived from probable causes. From Defoe on, representation of the real came to be understood as representation of the probable. I shall deal more with this question presently, for it ties directly into the later development of realism in France. On the Continent, much fiction in the eighteenth century was largely concerned with the improbable, for many French novels were allegorical works concerned either with erotic utopias or, much to the same effect, moralizing about the same eroticism. Science was not always of the greatest import in Enlightenment France, and developments in English fiction are as important for understanding the development of the French novel as any other source.

Formally and thematically, the modern novel came into existence in the nineteenth century when writers broke with the satirical and the moralizing impulses that characterized most serious eighteenth-century fiction. The modern novel broke with these impulses in order to invent a realism that was both a response to, and an attempt to rival, the claims to knowledge advanced by increasingly triumphant sciences. This response to science has rarely been critically recognized as an important component in the development of modern realism. In exploring this topic I will limit my concerns to the development of the modern novel in France and, specifically, to a study of four of the most important novelists: Balzac, Flaubert, Zola, and Proust. By considering these four and with a few considerations of Stendhal, my scope is sufficiently broad to make, in the course of this book, a case for a few general conclusions about the history of literature and science. However, these considerations are also sufficiently focused to allow a study in some depth of what I take to be the most important development in fiction after the Enlightenment. In France we can clearly see that the modern novel was born of a break with allegorical modes of writing. At the same time, the nineteenth-century novel continued the Enlightenment's affirmation of the Aristotelian axiom that literature serves knowledge. Novelists from Balzac through Zola largely accepted the Enlightenment belief that the same kind of rational constraints and possibilities govern epistemic enterprises, whatever may be the final discourse or formalism used to express the results of an epistemic inquiry. Knowledge is knowledge. This belief was essential for the development of literature's desire to rival science in the nineteenth century.

The Enlightenment belief in the unity of knowledge seems, by contrast, to have precluded a sense of rivalry, since Enlightenment thinkers largely accepted, usually with equanimity, that all discourses contributed to the same epistemic quest. The belief in the unity of knowledge is clearly set out, for example, in Voltaire. With scornful wit, Voltaire proposed as axiomatic the principle of epistemic unity as the self-understood necessary condition of knowledge. In the *Dictionnaire philosophique* he wrote, for example, under the entry on "Secte":

> Il n'y a point de secte en géométrie; on ne dit point un euclidien, un archimédien.
>
> Quand la vérité est évidente, il est impossible qu'il s'élève des partis et des factions. Jamais on n'a disputé s'il fait jour à midi.
>
> [There is no sect in geometry. You don't say a Euclidian, an Archimedian.
>
> When the truth is obvious, it is impossible for parties or factions to arise. Nobody has ever argued about whether there is daylight at noon.] (Edition of 1765)

Presumably from Voltaire's point of view, there should be no sects in literature or metaphysics. The Enlightenment impulse toward the universal had little need to accommodate sects, a characteristic for which it is harshly judged by today's multiculturalists. Confident that they knew the epistemic universals by which all deviations could be measured, Enlightenment thinkers were not usually given to celebrations of cultural relativity.

Yet, one may well ask if contemporary relativism is to be preferred to the Enlightenment's belief in the universal, or if the loss of belief in a universal culture is better than the pursuit of multiple singularities that makes up literary culture today. This fragmenting of knowledge has perhaps reached its limits in the postmodern relativist disbelief in anything but the claims of singular experience, at least insofar as the humanities are concerned. Reacting to this disintegration of the Enlightenment ideal, more than one contemporary has called for a reinstatement of some belief in epistemic universalism. Such, for example, is the sense of a recent work by Michel Serres, *Les Origines de la géométrie* (The origins of geometry), published in 1993. Serres celebrates the discovery of our multiple cultural legacies, but he also deplores the fragmentation of our culture—which, pushed to its logical extreme, would foreclose any entrance into any culture other than one's own. Serres proposes that we come back to the Enlightenment's finest universalizing modes of thought. Like the Voltaire of the *Dictionnaire philosophique,* he proposes mathematics as an example of a universal that no imperialist ideology has ever imposed on another culture at sword point, and for which no sectarian arguments are necessary. The multicultural origins of geometry are clear, even if before the modern era, Greek culture gave geometry greater development than did the succeeding empires that have come and gone in world history. Geometry, as Serres says, is a nonimperialist universal language. Serres is calling us back to an Enlightenment belief in the possibility of universal discourse that can promote communication between all people.

Something like this desire for a universal discourse caused literature to feel rivalry with science, for the separation of literature and science was already inscribed in the Enlightenment's division of knowledge into physical and moral knowledge. Enlightenment writers tried hard to unite their concern with these two areas in one rational and universal epistemic enterprise. Consider, without undue irony, the case of the French philosopher and mathematician Condorcet. Even as Condorcet was hiding during the Revolution from that embodiment of humane reason, the guillotine, he spent his last days meditating on the general progress the human mind had made in creating its systematic unity. Thus he wrote the *Esquisse d'un tableau historique des progrès de l'esprit hu-*

main (*Outlines of a Historical View of the Progress of the Human Mind*) to trace the epistemic unity of thought that philosophy, since Locke, had developed using analytical epistemology:

> This metaphysical method became virtually a universal instrument. Men learned to use it in order to perfect the methods of the physical sciences, to throw light on their principles and to examine the validity of their proofs; and it was extended to the examination of facts and to the rules of taste.
>
> Thus it was applied to all the various undertakings of the human understanding, and by means of it the operations of the mind in every branch of knowledge were subjected to analysis, and the nature of the truths and the kind of certainty we can expect to find from each of these branches of knowledge was thereby revealed.[2]

In Condorcet's summation of Enlightenment belief in the unity of mind, based on analysis, is expressed the belief that our intellectual, moral, and aesthetic concerns are, or can be, united. Condorcet's own fate may suggest some reason for hesitancy in affirming this belief. However, it is not clear that, without some axiom of epistemic unity, one can lay claim to knowledge in the humanist disciplines. The nineteenth-century writer's project is, to say the least, plausible.

Enlightenment rationalism declared every human subject to be a repository of reason and hence capable of acceding to all human values. The Enlightenment thus believed, in its optimism, that the human subject was capable of understanding the totality of our epistemic concerns. This belief contrasts radically with the negative side of the contemporary belief in two cultures, a belief that seems to justify that one create walls separating epistemic concerns from ethics and aesthetics. This is a serious issue. For example, the separation of epistemic rationality from ethical discourses can lead to the belief in the impossibility of communication between different cultures or social groups, as well as between science and the humanities. The horrors of the twentieth century have been ample witness to the harm wreaked by particularist thinking.

Without some epistemic axiom comparable to the Enlightenment belief in the unity of human knowledge, it seems to me that we declare the inevitable separation between thought about epistemic means and

2. Condorcet, *Selected Writings*, 226.

thought about human goals. In accepting the negative side of a belief in two cultures, we deny the grandeur of the Kantian vision of the Enlightenment, a vision that a postmodernist like Michel Foucault once highlighted for its potential for emancipation. (I intentionally call Foucault to mind, since, when not floundering on a cultural relativism that undermines itself, Foucault's work at its best also demonstrates the Enlightenment project in which scientific and humanistic concerns are united in a common project.) In Kant's work, epistemic unity is viewed as concomitant with moral autonomy, as Kant claims in his brief essay "What Is Enlightenment?": "Enlightenment is man's release from his self-incurred tutelage. Tutelage is man's inability to make use of his understanding without direction from another."[3] (Or in Kant's nongendered German: "Aufklärung ist der Ausgang des Menschen aus seiner selbst verschuldeten Unmündigkeit. Unmündigkeit ist das Unvermögen, sich seines Verstandes ohne Leitung eines anderen zu bedienen.") The goal of the Enlightenment was emancipation, and for Kant this meant a free subject empowered to use his or her epistemic faculties in every field of endeavor. Moreover, emancipation meant a critical mind that relied upon the epistemic unity of all discourses to liberate itself, as one sees in Kant's work itself. This may be utopian, but such an intellectual axiom allows every form of discourse to play a role in providing the knowledge that will lead to self-understanding and, hence, emancipation. I conclude this excursus by proposing that the history of Enlightenment literature and science demonstrates that the Enlightenment was emancipatory precisely to the extent that it united all discourses in a common project. This was a utopian ideal that we have perhaps all too easily given up. It is not clear to me that we are the better for having done so.

Since Kant, science, in all its multiple guises, has become dominant in providing the criteria for epistemic discourse: we rely largely upon science to tell us what we know. To the extent that literature has shared these epistemic goals, it has found itself eclipsed by science. This eclipse began with the German romantics, for whom it was an arguable question as to whether science's epistemic successes had been accompanied by human emancipation. The reaction against science was of little con-

---

3. Kant, *Foundations of the Metaphysics of Morals* and *What Is Enlightenment?*, trans. Lewis White Beck, 85. See also Kant, *Werke*, vol. 6, 53.

sequence in practical terms, though one can argue, with regret, that the irrationalities romanticism embraced eventuated in the nationalist political ideologies that ravaged the twentieth century. In any case, after the Newtonian revolution, and often against Newton, science made triumphant steps forward in explaining all manner of phenomena. After gravity and dynamics, physics offered ingenious descriptions of electricity and magnetism, then of heat and energy; chemistry suddenly found itself with a viable theory of elements and transformations of matter; and biology and geology took the shape that now gives full meaning to natural "history." Our cosmology and cosmography were transformed.

Science's successes were accompanied at once by a sense of triumph and a sense of fall as many writers, mainly novelists, believed themselves obliged to engage in an epistemic rivalry with discourses that purported to explain the world. Novelists who wanted to vindicate their claims that they, too, could offer knowledge often felt obligated in effect to be surrogate scientists. In some cases this move was empowering. The writer who could share the epistemic goals of science—a Balzac or a Zola—could participate with élan in the Enlightenment or, later, the positivist project of the development of knowledge. But some writers viewed science's success as actually entailing a lessening of the scope and certainty of knowledge. Such a writer—a Flaubert or a Proust—saw that it was incumbent upon literature to evolve strategies to compete with, or even to circumvent, science so that literature could lay its own claims to knowledge.

One intent of realism in modern literature, especially as found in the novel, was to endow the novel with the capacity to realize epistemic projects. After the work of scientists such as Newton, Laplace, Lavoisier, and Ampère, science could claim with much justification to offer the most certain, if not absolutely certain, knowledge of the world, and realism respectfully listened to what scientists had to say about what one could know about the world. From Newton through Lamarck and Cuvier, not only was science remarkably successful in imposing itself as the truth of the world, but it created a new world, a world with depths of time and reaches in space that overturned all traditional views of truth. The world the realist novelist sought to know was thus a world that science had discovered and situated within parameters that the novelist who wanted to be taken seriously was obliged to respect. Defining the real in terms consonant with scientific thought, realism proposed knowledge of a, if not the, new world.

The development of the novel is best characterized by historical continuity, especially when one considers how the novel was adapted to the transformations of our worldview. Nineteenth-century writers, like Balzac and Zola, were quite aware of participating in this continuity. These writers believed they were participating in the ongoing discovery of the nature of the world—the project of the Enlightenment as understood in Kant's broad sense—since it first began to develop during the Renaissance in the works of writers as diverse as Erasmus, Rabelais, Kepler, Galileo, Cervantes, and Newton. Balzac is still quite close to these thinkers in that he believed that the plurality of epistemic discourses could be united in the universal project of creating a totalizing discourse to illuminate the world. But this unity had already begun to go asunder toward the end of the eighteenth century when, as I suggested, the realms of moral and physical discourse about the world seemed increasingly separated. Moreover, novelists also confronted a growing paradox when they turned to the results of Enlightenment anthropology. Epistemic unity suffered when this anthropology insisted, on the one hand, upon the unity of human experience and, on the other hand, recognized the seemingly incommensurable diversity that characterizes the historical experience of all cultures. It was not at all clear how one could reconcile, say, Montesquieu's relativism with Condorcet's universalism.

Equally important for the development of the novel was the way in which historiography was beginning to undermine the continuity underlying the Enlightenment belief in epistemic unity. Historical epistemology laid claim to a qualitative knowledge of culture that stands in opposition, implicitly when not explicitly, not only to mere chronology, but, more importantly, to quantitative discourses. Enlightenment epistemology took the model proposed by Newtonian mechanics to be the pinnacle of knowledge, but historical epistemology proposed a new mode of knowledge whose basic ontology was not amenable to Newtonian analysis. These dichotomies did not initially prevent Enlightenment thinkers from continuing their claims to represent a universalism, but the growing separation of ethics, anthropology, history, and evolutionary biology from other epistemic discourses is a prelude to the sense of rivalry that novelists felt with science. From Montesquieu and Voltaire through Buffon and Lamarck, historical thinking became a new discourse. Novelists found themselves on the side of history, but this fact led to their desire to overcome the compartmentalization of knowledge that placed human concerns in a realm that might appear to have nothing to do with the objective knowledge science offered.

The conflict between quantitative and qualitative discourses was, and is still, central to our understanding of the relations between science and literature. The history of knowledge in our culture turns on the fact that, after Galileo proposed the first modern quantitative representation of nature, the representations of the world proposed by classical physics came to form the bedrock for our representations of reality. This was true during the Enlightenment, and it is remarkable that, even today, classical dynamics and astronomy often are the basis for describing what we take to be the real. After the work of Copernicus, Kepler, and Galileo, Newtonian philosophy gave us nothing less than the coordinates for constructing the coordinates of reality. Newtonian absolutes—space and time—became the public scaffolding for locating all that we take to be the real.

Part II: Background Reflections on the History of Science

In epistemological terms, the Newtonian revolution received its metaphysical imprimatur a century later in Kant's work, though that belated approval was hardly necessary for the mechanical model, derived from Newton's laws of motion, to sweep most epistemic rivals from the field in the eighteenth century. Kant codified in philosophical terms the ongoing scientific revolution that, from Copernicus, Galileo, Descartes, and Newton, had eventuated in the mathematical understanding of physical reality in works by Euler, D'Alembert, Lagrange, and Laplace. Coming after the revolution, Kant's work looked at and established the limits of empirical knowledge.

In Kant's work, the limits of knowledge are established in terms of a rationalist empiricism that separates the knowing subject from the realm of reality. By no great coincidence, it is also in Kant's work that the project of a universal ethics receives its most abstractly formal development. Kant universalizes ethics as a product of the rational subject. However, moral knowledge and empirical knowledge are also separated in Kant, and it seems to me that this separation is emblematic of a schism that brings the crisis of two epistemic orders to a head—even if Kant unites all knowledge, moral and empirical, in the rational subject. Kant's codification of the scientific revolution restricted our possibilities for knowledge of the world. In epistemological terms, he denies that we can ever know things in themselves, for we only know phenomena as they appear empirically to the perceiving subject. Except for the a priori certainties granted by mathematics and logic, our knowledge can only be obtained by the universal procedures of a rational empiricism that can speak with no certainty, for at best it can offer only probabilistic knowledge. In rejecting an ethics of particular cases as well as the possibility of certain knowledge, Kant's thought sets out the background for interpreting the next two centuries of estrangement between science and the humanities. Kant at once affirms the unity of the knowing subject while he severs it from the world that it should know, limits what the subject can know, and removes many of humanity's most important concerns from the realm of knowledge. The romantic attempt to overcome Kant and the limits on knowledge springs from a refusal of these severe limits; romanticism thus promotes new quests for knowledge, new forms of inquiry, and a desire to find enlarged epistemic discourses.

A second estrangement lies within the historical development of the sciences. This estrangement is in part the result of the hyper-evaluation of mathematics. Kant placed mathematics in the realm of the synthetic a priori, that realm where meaningful certain knowledge could be had by pure reasoning. Mathematical truths, in this regard, were therefore like ethical truths. In this respect, Kant's doctrine of metaphysical truths appears to be a last attempt to assure the epistemic unity of reason. His vision of unity has had little influence to counter the Neoplatonism that underwrites the doctrine of the primacy of mathematics, a doctrine often promoted by scientists since Galileo proclaimed that mathematics is the language of nature. Also since Galileo, many scientists have refused to communicate with a public that cannot follow the mathematical reasoning involved in the physical sciences. This refusal to translate quantitative formalisms into qualitative argumentation has a long tradition, beginning with Plato and renewed by Renaissance Neoplatonism before receiving impetus from Galileo (who nonetheless wrote in Italian for a general public). Then in the seventeenth century, refusing to render his own mathematical work clear to the understanding, Descartes purportedly wrote his work on geometry so that it could be understood only by those who could supply the proofs themselves. Comparably, temperamental Isaac Newton wrote the *Principia* so that those with only a "smattering of mathematics" could not challenge him. In other words, the equation of superior knowledge with mathematical formalism had become a well-established tradition by the time of the Enlightenment.

This legacy of Platonism has constantly weighed against any attempt to found an epistemic discourse that is not quantitative. Yet, it seems clear that mathematical discourse is not ipso facto a necessary or even sufficient condition to define what is an epistemic discourse. This is an important point for understanding the hubris of writers who thought they could rival science, and I should like to pursue it briefly. To this end I turn to physicist Joseph Schwartz and his very engaging book, *The Creative Moment*, published in 1992. Decrying the historical hyperevaluation of mathematics for an understanding of scientific procedures, Schwartz argues that if, by definition, mathematical formalisms are necessary for measurement, they are not necessary for understanding the relationships that science discloses. And the primary role of science is to reveal relationships. (Therefore, it seems rather perverse that such successful sciences as evolutionary and molecular biology have been under pressure to prove their epistemological worth by finding some kind of quantitative structure.)

In sciences that took shape in the nineteenth century, such as biology and geology, we clearly see the limits of the tradition of Platonism. Turning from Newtonian mechanics as the only model for science, nineteenth-century scientists began to think qualitatively, giving justification to nineteenth-century novelists who believed they could use the novel to offer knowledge in qualitative terms. Biology has been in the forefront of the rejection of quantification as the sole criterion for knowledge, a point well made by evolutionary theorist Ernst Mayr, who attacks contemporary prejudices in favor of Platonism in *The Growth of Biological Thought*. In criticizing the "essentialism" that has dominated Western thought since Plato, leading to the privileging of mathematics and physics as modes of knowledge, Mayr argues that only since Darwin have we been able to think in nonessentialist ways. Rejecting physics-envy with brio, Mayr claims, self-consciously echoing Enlightenment naturalist Buffon, that many subjects are too complex to be dealt with by mathematical treatment. Since Darwin, biology has been a science of populations, and not "classes." Thinking in terms of populations cannot lend itself to the "thinking of the physical scientists, whose 'classes' consist of identical entities, be they sodium atoms, protons, or pi-mesons." Biology thinks in terms of populations, every member of which is different from every other. Biology is knowledge about living groups—and so, may we add, are novels. And in anticipation of my later discussion of determinism, I note that Mayr offers a nuanced historical critique of the dominance of mechanical models for prediction. According to Mayr, biology thinks in terms of "stochastic processes, [that] even though making predictions probabilistic (or impossible) rather than absolute, are just as causal as deterministic processes."[4] This kind of thought marks the limits, if not the end, of the reign of classical Laplacian determinism and makes room for a recognition of the importance that classification and nonmathematical methodology can have for knowledge of the natural world.

If we can conceive of the history of epistemic discourses as something larger than the quest for quantification, then we can begin to see the role novels have played in the history of knowledge. The epistemic quest is a historical leitmotif that informs an ongoing dialogue between science and literature—including those nonmathematical sciences that have had to define themselves as separate from physics and without the aid of mathematics. For a study of literature and science, the points made by contemporary scientists like Schwartz and Mayr are singularly important in historical terms: the history of science and literature is a history of multiple ways of expressing epistemic relationships that may be variously disclosed by physics or biology, by medicine or psychiatry, or by literature and philosophy.

To be sure, I do not dismiss mathematics. Mathematics offers the most rigorous expression of epistemic relationships, provided that we define rigor as measurement and that these relationships lend themselves to some kind of recurrence. But our faith in mathematics should be tempered by the recognition that one has often been able to choose various formalisms in order to represent the same relationship. Newton chose geometry for the expression of his laws of motion. Later in the eighteenth century, Lagrange then developed differential equations to

4. Mayr, *The Growth of Biological Thought: Diversity, Evolution, and Inheritance*, 39.

represent the same relationships. Most of us can also use ordinary language to describe these same laws of motion. Mathematics has been essential for the elaboration of some epistemic discourses, but analogical reasoning has been essential for others—such as systematics, evolutionary biology, and poetry. I stress this point, for it must seem acceptable if we are to read nineteenth-century novels with a full sense of the *plausibility* of novelists' thinking that they could rival scientists. The history of the relations between science and literature has involved a quite reasonable quest for various forms of commensurability that can relate scientific, literary, and ordinary discourses. There is no pat formula for understanding these relations, for the rivalry with science, from the literary point of view, has been both friendly and hostile, vindictive and cooperative, and also pursued with a sense of superiority. After all, historically speaking, literature has probably made as many discoveries as so-called pure science (a purity discovered only fairly recently)—once we understand that discovery involves revealing relationships that are often translatable from one type of discourse to another. I suggest the dubious look at the work of poet-novelist-mathematician Raymond Queneau and his fellow experimentalists of OuLiPo, who have shown that literature can perform some of the same formal tasks as pure mathematics, which, for whatever it is worth, is often to express relations without content.

If we neglect Darwin for the moment and return to the eighteenth century, there is little doubt that, in the wake of Newton, quantitative science became increasingly the arbiter of the real, since science simply devalued any area of discourse that could not be described mathematically by rational empiricism. To describe the literary reaction to this devaluation, it seems accurate to argue that the beginnings of literary realism in the Enlightenment are motivated by the desire to find literary techniques that can rival, or at least imitate, the precision of scientific views in offering knowledge about what is the real. To this end, realist texts are obliged to enact fictions whose basic axioms are consonant with scientific empiricism. This is basically an epistemic matter, often restrictive in scope, for science often involves setting and settling what the limits of knowledge are. Realist works thus purport to embody epistemic principles analogous to those recognized by scientific epistemology. However, there is more than a rhetorical side to realism, and it would be a weak argument, typical of much recent literary theory, to say that realism is simply a literary construct. Realism constructs a known world that is consonant with the world we construct and know through science—and in which we sometimes think we live. Balzac, Flaubert, and Zola had few doubts about this proposition.

But these worlds are multiple, a demonstrated fact that, from *Don Quixote* through the Enlightenment and beyond, has underscored an interesting epistemological principle, at least from our contemporary viewpoint. Writers of realist fiction have constructed multiple worlds that nonetheless respect the constraints imposed by, say, the laws underwriting the Newtonian cosmos. In a sense, then, at least since Diderot and Sterne, realist novels have provided in advance a demonstration of the Mach-Duhem-Poincaré hypothesis. According to this principle, reality is so underdetermined that multiple hypotheses can explain the same phenomena. Since the beginning of the twentieth century, some variant of this hypothesis has been a dominant epistemological principle. The principle of underdetermination is one that most modern philosophers of science—a Popper, a Quine, or a Van Fraassen—would accept in some form or another. It squarely opposes the principle of "scientific realism," according to which there is one world "out there" having a structure that natural science reveals to an ever greater degree. Without paradox, I maintain that this twentieth-century antirealist hypothesis is, perforce, implicitly part of the credo that realist novelists have always accepted: reality is so underdetermined that an indefinite number of novels—or hypothetical models—can be elaborated to account for it. This hypothesis about hypotheses suggests that virtually any theoretical system will allow a thinker to gain some purchase on the real, and that competing systems or models may well have equal power in explaining it. In this regard realist, and many fantastic, novels have always had epistemological implications.

Historical considerations justify two observations that we can make to allay any paradox suggested here. First, from the Enlightenment through the end of the nineteenth century, the epistemology of scientific realism set the constraints for defining the limits of the real—in the face of vigorous romantic opposition. This realism finds its ultimate expression in the Newtonian-Kantian epistemological model with its belief in one geometry and one time scale that characterize a unique world that is the locus of reality. Second, it seems equally true that the development of realism in literature was in at least one sense opposed to constraints of epistemological realism in that the realist writer offered competing models of the real. Each literary model imposed itself on the strength of its own coherence. The multiple literary models that were all in some sense realist were implicitly (and at times explicitly) a challenge to the belief that there is only one order of the real. In this sense, literature has always been a rival to any system that would allow for only one order of the real.

A related historical point is in order to establish the context for reading nineteenth-century novelists in France. Of the greatest cultural significance is the fact that the constructs that science and philosophy had elaborated during the Enlightenment had become, by the time of the French Revolution, the basis for education. French education was using texts expounding Laplacian physics, for example, by the time Balzac and Stendhal were youths. The debate between quantitative and qualitative knowledge had also become part of the French educational program. Antimathematical views of science were promoted through the widespread teaching of Buffon's views of natural history. Though Buffon began his career by translating Newton, his subsequent views of natural history combined a Lockean nominalism, insisting that only the species has reality, with a type of transformationalism that recognized that current taxonomical families are "degenerate" forms of preceding taxa. Use of their ideas for educational purposes had made Buffon and Laplace into household names.

Recent intellectual history has created the impression that static structures determined mentalities in the eighteenth century, but this structuralism does not account for the dynamics of historical development. There was hardly a static moment in the propagation and modification of scientific doctrines as the eighteenth century codified Newton. The application of Newton immediately brought about challenges to mechanistic thought, and by the early nineteenth century a new generation of physicists had begun to find flaws in the completeness of the Newtonian system. And earlier, the adaptation of mechanical philosophy by various medical doctrines seemed complete when suddenly physiological vitalism challenged the medical belief that living organisms could be explained by the physiology of fibers. Medicine in the guise of iatromechanical physiology believed it could describe most illness as a result of a dysfunctional mechanism because our nerve or muscle fibers are out of kilter: fibers that could theoretically be described by the geometric disposition of the forces pulling the fibers. In their challenge to the mechanical model, vitalists noted nobody had ever seen a distorted fiber, and they challenged a priori Newtonian medical models in the name of a more thorough empiricism. It seems clear that the anti-quantitative theories of vitalist doctrines were more conducive to physiological research than mechanistic views, as is evident in the example of the physiologist Bichat (1771–1802). Refusing to use a microscope, the brilliant young vitalist physician founded histology and modern pathological anatomy by the systematic study and identification of tissues. Iatromechanical Neoplatonism made few similar contributions.

What strikes one today in looking at science and science education at the end of the eighteenth century is that Newtonian dynamics gave rise to a physics that is still essentially the basis of modern engineering, the classical mechanics deriving from Newton. But nothing else that students learned in 1800 seems quite modern, and it is important to see that often what we take to be modern is really only moving toward something that is about to seem even more modern. The history of science is invested, moreover, with a dynamics that allows for the coexistence of contradictory beliefs and systems. Buffon's natural history, with its suggestions of evolution, contains much that seems to point to the development of modern scientific naturalism, even though Buffon rejected Linnaeus and the work that founded modern taxonomy. Or, to offer another pointed example, medicine was largely medieval in spite of the patina of rationality offered by mechanistic philosophy—Galen and Hippocrates were still authorities well into the nineteenth century. Modern physiology, for example, only began to emerge when the next major medical researcher in France after Bichat, Magendie (1783–1855), undertook the quantitative experiments that founded experimental physiology. It may seem a mark of modernity that the protomodern psychiatrist Pinel (1745–1826) started keeping records to trace out the results of his "moral" cures of the insane, but Pinel's writings on insanity reveal a medical thinker for whom Hippocrates is more important than any modern scientist.

Modern chemistry cannot be said to exist until Lavoisier (1743–1794), soon to step up to the guillotine, discovered oxygen and laid the foundations for the systematics of a modern science. At the same time, separating itself out from natural history, biology was also coming into being—Lamarck (1744–1829) was about to invent the term for the

French—as was the case with geology and paleontology. The history of biology took perhaps its most decisive turn in Paris when in 1795 the extremely young Geoffroy Saint-Hilaire hired the brilliant zoologist Cuvier for the École Centrale and then the Musée d'Histoire Naturelle. Together, these two biologists epitomize the work that would give birth to modern zoological systematics, paleontology, and the continuing development of the transformationism that, with Lamarck's work, would lead to Darwin.

In the midst of this dynamic turbulence, in which a new world of thought was coming into being, Newtonian mechanics, armed with the calculus developed largely by French mathematicians, seemed briefly to offer what Mallarmé later dreamed of as an orphic explanation of the earth: the possibility that everything could be explained. For a brief moment it seemed that everything, from cosmology to mental illness, could be explained by attraction and repulsion as measured by mechanical laws of motion. This was a relatively short-lived moment of scientific euphoria, though we have seen this belief in a total theory repeat itself several times, most notably again toward the end of the nineteenth century when the hoped-for reconciliation of classical mechanics with the laws of electromagnetism and thermodynamics would explain everything; and again recently, in the late twentieth century, as we have pursued dreams of a "final theory." The orphic claim to explain the world through a single theory provides an important context for reading novelists who encountered science not merely as a discourse purporting to order various domains of our experience, but as a totalizing cosmography. I will offer a few comments on this Newtonian cosmography, since even after it was challenged in various quarters, it continued to offer a standard for defining what might be a totalizing vision of the real. And, for much of the nineteenth century, totalization remained an epistemological norm, or perhaps a dream.

Basic to this totalizing cosmography was the way space and time were absolute parameters measuring and hence defining objectivity. Perhaps we cannot imagine a "real" world without the scaffolding of public space and time. But only after Newton have space and time become absolute coordinates that figure the framework of the real—at least until the paper Einstein published in 1905 made time frameworks relative. In providing a metaphysical framework for Newton, Kant made space and time into fundamental categories of perception. Kant's metaphysics incorporates into his system the famous scholium at the beginning of the *Principia* in which Newton proposed his own metaphysics by noting that "Absolute, true, and mathematical time, of itself, and from its own nature, flows equably without relation to anything external" and that "Absolute space, in its own nature, without relation to anything external, remains always similar and immovable."[5] After Newton—and until Poincaré and Einstein—reality can be defined thanks to a solid metaphysical scaffolding that promotes quantification as a test of the real. The reality of space and time can be literally figured in terms of Descartes's analytical geometry. Space and time are identified with the coordinates of a Cartesian tableau, which means that these coordinates can be geometrically plotted. This operation makes the real definable through the exact parameters of geometric axes (or, later, through the calculus). Reality is figured through extended coordinates having a totally public existence. One consequence of this worldview is that any phenomenon not amenable to such localizing is declared a shadowy figment of myth, bad metaphysics, or, later, a fantasy of the romantic imagination.

There is a loss in this definition of reality, a loss paradoxically of the real world. In his classic *The Metaphysical Foundations of Modern Physical Science,* Edwin A. Burtt notes that, when Newton promoted Cartesian metaphysics, he brought about the final collapse of the medieval worldview. But Newton's work meant more than the abandonment of Aristotelian physics:

> Space was identified with the realm of geometry, time with continuity of number. The world that people had thought themselves living in—a world rich with colour and sound, redolent with fragrance, filled with gladness, love and beauty, speaking everywhere of purposive harmony and creative ideals—was crowded now into minute corners in the brains of scattered organic beings. The really important world outside was a world hard, cold, colourless, silent, and dead; a world of quantity, a world of mathematically computable motions in mechanical regularity. The world of qualities as immediately perceived by man became just a curious quite minor effect of that infinite machine beyond.[6]

5. Newton, *Newton* [selected writings], ed. I. Bernard Cohen and Richard S. Westfall, 231.
6. Burtt, *The Metaphysical Foundations of Modern Physical Science,* 238–39.

The triumph of Newtonian physics meant that the object of knowledge was no longer the immediately perceived world—even if the reality of the world was now a matter of public purview. The parameters of reality were in some sense *beyond or behind* what one immediately perceived: Newton's three laws of motion and the universal force of gravitation are not, after all, what one perceives when one looks at flora or fauna. Or as Newton specialist Richard Westfall has observed, "The [mechanical] philosophy was built on the premise that the reality of nature is not identical to the appearance our senses depict."[7] The real is at once public and invisible, quantifiable and yet in need of a demonstration of its existence. A paradoxical Platonism is at work here that would invite more than one romantic realist to believe that there was more to know than what the calculus promised, and not least of all Balzac or Stendhal.

In the eighteenth century Kant compounded this epistemological dilemma. Though he backed away from his early belief that only quantification results in knowledge, Kant did side with Newton against Newton's critics when he set out to prove that space and time are a priori particulars establishing the conditions of possibility for all knowledge. No experience, no perception, argued Kant, can be imagined separate from a subject situated in space and time. All experience *known* to be reality must be defined operationally in terms consonant with the abstract geometrical parameters of space and time—or the limit geometry of the only geometry known to Newton and Kant, Euclidean geometry. In effect, Kant accepted that physics, as guided by mathematics, was the supreme epistemic arbiter for the phenomenal world. By banishing the reality of the human subject to a noumenal realm, hidden behind phenomena, Kant presented writers and scientists with a challenge to look beyond his categories that limit knowledge to mere phenomena. All in all, the Newtonian world of abstract quantities created a situation against which biologists, geologists, and other scientists—as well as poets—have had to revolt to claim their epistemological autonomy. The recurrence of ideal mathematical entities is not a useful model for every epistemic discourse, be it biological or humanistic.

Plotting out time and space with the calculus, a Newtonian physicist like Laplace (1749–1827) believed that his equations could explain the entire world on the basis of the three laws of motion. (The skeptic might

7. Westfall, *The Construction of Modern Science*, 141.

point out that the framework provided by Newton's basic laws is supplemented by the metaphysical principle of causality or sufficient reason, and in the writings of Hume these doubts were sufficient, as Kant knew, to call the entire epistemic enterprise into question.) Practically, of course, one could only calculate probable and possible knowledge within the limits of empirical information. This is a new development in the history of knowledge: the epistemic restriction of what could be considered possible was ushered in by the development of the calculus of probability theory to which Laplace made notable contribution. After Pascal, Fermat, and Bernoulli, the development of probability theory meant that one could, in principle, picture a world populated only by knowable events, or a world from which ignorance was theoretically banished. The development of probability theory entailed that one could assign impossibility or null probability to events that heretofore might have had a claim to be known. And thereby the mathematical physicist banished the impossible from reality.

The possible and the probable are relative notions, and the meaning of probability is open to question yet today. But it is clear that the development of the concepts of the possible and the probable, during and after the seventeenth century, gave additional rules for constructing reality, especially when probability was calculated against the backdrop of the mechanically predictable universe of Newtonian forces and movement.

Of course, writers have always worked with some notion of the possible. The category of the possible was perhaps first defined by Aristotle, though the possible for Aristotle meant rather much the opposite of what it meant for the late Enlightenment writer who decided that what is possible is based on the probable. The possible is part of the essence of things for Aristotle—and hence has little to do with the absurd facts of history—whereas by the end of the Enlightenment, the possible is what can be circumscribed, through probability, as the empirically real. The development of the notion of the possible also meant that, by a kind of dialectical reaction, the impossible became an important category— for the impossible was not really a category of the understanding before the Enlightenment. But afterward, the impossible was cultivated by romantic writers from Tieck through Poe to demonstrate—to our horror and our delight—that the imagination was not to be limited by mere space, time, causality, and mathematical probability, those defining categories of rational empiricism.

The impossible emerged as a rational limit to the new epistemic categories of the possible and the probable. But it also defiantly emerged as the far side of the stochastic and aleatory notions of probability imposed by rational empiricism. For a proper historical perspective it is important to situate these latter categories in terms of their essential modernity. Probability theory first emerged with Pascal and Fermat in the seventeenth century. As Ian Hacking has argued in *The Emergence of Probability*, this sense of probability merged with the new mathematical sense of the aleatory to give us what he calls an epistemic sense of probability. No epistemic understanding like this had existed before in Western history. In the Middle Ages, the probable was frequently invoked, but this notion meant what was approved by the greatest authorities (and the probable held this meaning until, in the name of rational coherence, Pascal demolished it in the *Lettres provinciales* as part of his attack on the "probable opinions" of the Jesuits). With the development of the mathematical notion of probability, we can see that European culture also began to evaluate events in terms of evidential probability and possibility, so that after, say, the *Logic* of Port Royal, the probable was no longer construed as something that opinion approved as the *vraisemblable* [verisimilitude]. (This opens the way to the realism that Ian Watt describes.) It is clear from these very terms that developments in mathematics promoted the transformation of literary categories of understanding. Verisimilitude, in its modern meaning, can be traced back precisely to this moment when probability theory was developed and applied to commercial transactions.

Lorraine Daston has traced this development of probability theory in her *Classical Probability in the Enlightenment*, and the terms she uses also suggest the importance of probability for the development of the novel during and after the Enlightenment, for the very term *realist* has come to be bound up with the "probable." During the eighteenth century—which is to say before the development of postquantum, contemporary notions of the aleatory and the random—the very notion of a causeless event was inconceivable. Thus, knowledge of any event demanded an explanation that involved probable causes. Finding a cause became part of the ideology of common sense, which, as Daston puts it, meant that probability theorists in the early eighteenth-century defined their task as a mathematical description of good sense: "so long as reasoning by expectation was judged synonymous with good sense, expectation continued to play an important role in the calculus of probabilities." Since expectation is largely defined in advance by the social codes defining reason, probability theory was destined to confirm ideology, to which I add that probability became thus part of any code of realist representation.

However, by the end of the eighteenth century, the triumph of mechanistic philosophy and the development of new stochastic models, such as Bayes's rule for conditional probability, meant that probability increasingly dealt with induction based on inverse probabilities. Laplace, Condorcet, and later Poisson thus attempted "to codify the methodological intuitions of natural philosophers," or as Daston goes on to say, "A new model of causation took shape in their work, making it possible to conceive of a world in which macroscopic order was the product of microscopic chaos."[8] The mechanical order of the universe in its totality arose from the countless transactions that one could know with probability through the application of rational empiricism. Ignorance could be banned from a world in which mathematical models could predict with good probability the great patterns of the future produced by the microevents of the present moment. Statistical reasoning was coming into being. And, from a novelist's point of view, the absurd individual event could find meaning in a statistical totality.

In the latter nineteenth century these new methods for figuring probability would evolve to give rise to statistical mechanics as scientists attempted to reconcile thermodynamics with classical physics. But during the Enlightenment, probability was concerned only with classical dynamics and the use thereof for predicting the future on the basis of a present configuration of forces. The notion of totality is a key concept here. Laplace's often quoted commentary about the possibility of garnering total knowledge of the universe finds its full meaning when it is placed in this context. Filled with Enlightenment hubris about prediction, Laplace placed his description of how one might theoretically garner total knowledge of the universe in the most probable place—the introduction to his work on probability theory published in 1814, the *Essai philosophique sur les probabilités* (*A Philosophical Essay on Probabilities*):

> Nous devons donc envisager l'état présent de l'univers, comme l'effet de son état antérieur, et comme la cause de celui qui va suivre.

8. Daston, *Classical Probability in the Enlightenment*, 67.

Une intelligence qui pour un instant donné, connaîtrait toutes les forces dont la nature est animée, et la situation respective des êtres qui la composent, si d'ailleurs elle était assez vaste pour soumettre ces données à l'analyse, embrasserait dans la même formule, les mouvemens des plus grands corps de l'univers et ceux du plus léger atome: rien ne serait incertain pour elle, et l'avenir comme le passé, serait présent à ses yeux.

[We must thus envisage the present state of the universe, as the effect of its antecedent state, and as the cause of the state that is going to follow. An intelligence, which for one given instant could know all the forces which animate Nature, and the respective positions of the things which compose it, and if that intelligence were also sufficiently vast to subject these data to analysis, would comprehend in one formula the movements of the largest bodies of the universe as well as those of the minutest atom: nothing would be uncertain to it, and the future as well as the past would be present to its vision.][9]

Using the laws of Newtonian mechanics, human intelligence could in principle grasp what must occur in the universe and represent it according to the workings of a necessity that derives the future from the past. But lacking that knowledge, in practice human intelligence has developed probability theory as a substitute for total knowledge.

It takes but a moment's reflection to see that this description of total knowledge offers a model for the creation of the universe known by the omniscient novelist, that megaintelligence to whose vision past and future are present as one necessity. There is nothing "real" about such knowledge, but in the realist novel one finds an omniscient mind for which all knowledge is in principle certain. For what is most real is what a scientific mind has declared to be a theoretical possibility. And when the narrating mind waffles about its certainty, probability theory is there to justify the knowledge the narrator has, for probability theory works to fill in the gaps when causal connections are missing. Probability theory became a description of, if not a prescription for, a rhetoric of fiction. It promoted a new stance toward what constituted the real because probability itself redefined the relation of the self to what it could know as its world.

9. Laplace, *Essai philosophique sur les probabilités*, 2.

In his study of chance and gambling in the eighteenth-century novel, *Enlightenment and the Shadows of Chance,* Thomas Kavanagh has described the triumph of probability theory as a triumph of intellect over the menace that blind chance held for the Enlightenment ideal of a knowable universe. Probability theory produced a subject that could view itself as detached from the contingencies of history. In making its calculations, this subject constituted itself as a subjectivity, rather like the Kantian mind, that is always positioned by the present instance of calculation. As Kavanagh puts it, probability theory tended to obliterate the diachronic sense of the traditional subject that viewed itself as the continuation of an identity anchored in families, institutions, and inheritances, since probability theory "proposed a new form of subjectivity structured as the pure synchrony of rational individuals living within and carefully evaluating the complete paradigm of lateral options available at each successive moment of their lives."[10] I would only add that Kavanagh's description of probability theory, as it became formalized in statistics, has implications that seem more realized in the narrator we find in Balzac and Dickens than in their Enlightenment predecessors. But it is clear that probability theory transformed the knowing subject's relation to the world, and in a sense created that world by wresting it from chance.

Did any writer write a novel directly using probability theory? Probably not directly, though I will argue that Zola attempted to translate the statistical modeling of entropy into the distribution of events in some of his novels. But it seems clear that the new epistemic order, underwritten by probability theory, could escape no writer in a culture that used Pascal, Fermat, and the Laplacian worldview for pedagogical purposes. This guide to understanding reality was not entirely positive, in that probability imposes severe constraints on what can be represented and how it can be represented. Probability has a negative dimension: certain types of events are simply excluded from narration because they fall into the netherworld of the improbable, if not the impossible, for which no evidence can be reasonably adduced. Or if these improbable events are narrated, then they must perforce be designated as the improbable, which is to say, consigned to those realms of the unreal such as the fantastic, the insane, and the oneiric. The unreal, the improbable, and the

10. Kavanagh, *Enlightenment and the Shadows of Chance,* 22.

impossible haunt the literary imagination from the end of the eighteenth century through the present. These realms inhabit literature like the reverse mirror image of the realism that has dominated the development of the novel from *Don Quixote* on. In the nineteenth century these literary realms, drawn from the unfettered imagination, often acted as so many negations of the Newtonian worldview and the concomitant rationalism that became the dominant epistemic attitude. In the twentieth century these same realms became the favored haunts of literary explorers such as the surrealists or experimentalists like Borges or Robbe-Grillet. But from the end of the Enlightenment until the present, the exploration of the impossible has always predicated the probable and the possible—and in this sense every description of the impossible has had the effect of affirming the power of the probable to define what is reality.

A Test Case: Stendhal's Relation to Science

To bring some specificity to the preceding considerations about literature and science, I want to conclude this introductory chapter by considering the relation of science and literature in the work of the writer who, for many readers, is the first great realist. I refer to Henri Beyle, known usually as Stendhal. Stendhal presents the first interesting test case for my view that the modern novel in France arose in part as an epistemic rivalry in which literature wanted to compete in some sense with science. Stendhal appears at once to be a supreme literary rationalist and, at times, to affect a lack of preoccupation with science in his portrayal of aristocratic characters who seek to fulfill their needs in a world that is indifferent, when not hostile, to those needs. Stendhal is an ambiguous figure about whom contraries can usually be affirmed with equal ease, but, one thing is clear, he was always quite interested in science. In historical terms, he has been variously treated as a transition figure, the last Enlightenment rationalist, a major romantic novelist, or the first modern realist. Stendhal is a writer who combines at once the *moraliste* tradition of classical French letters, a rationalist view of knowledge inherited from Enlightenment science and philosophy, and the realist impulse that leads him to a near emulation of scientific method. He was, after all, a man who wrote that the love of mathematics is a love of what is the contrary of the subversion of truth. Or so says his alter ego in the autobiographical *Vie de Henry Brulard,* when he declares that mathematics is the opposite of hypocrisy.

The protagonist of his first novel, *Armance,* is at once a romantic destined to death and a student of chemistry—chemistry having become an avant-garde science by the end of the eighteenth century. And in Stendhal's final novel, *Lucien Leuwen,* Lucien, exiled in Nancy, finds that part of the ennui of life in the provinces of 1830 is to find there nobody, except the head of the liberal party, with whom to discuss Ampère and Cuvier, which is to say, the latest scientific developments in Paris. In these works, and others, it is evident that scientific pursuits were, for Stendhal, a proper activity for his elect, characterized by their nobility of heart. Stendhal's own involvement in science is best found in Stendhal's first clearly Stendhalian work, *De l'Amour (On Love),* in which, among other things, his desire to emulate Enlightenment science is transparent.

De l'Amour is part of the *moraliste* tradition, and by the *moraliste* tradition, I mean that semiphilosophical, semianthropological tradition of writings that, from Montaigne and Pascal through Chamfort and Vauvernagues, offer sharp observations describing the essence of humanity. These observations sometimes take the form of the essay, sometimes the brief narrative, or, at times, they are epigrammatic in their terseness. There is also a medical side to *moraliste* writing, which has its roots in antiquity, for these well-formed observations offer alternatively diagnoses and prognoses that point up a distant affiliation with the Hippocratic corpus of writings. Moreover, *moraliste* writings also offer descriptive norms by which behavior can be seen, by its very regularity, to embody a law. In *De l'Amour,* the law-giving side of Stendhal's desire to do science is found in his description of passionate love, a state that has usually been considered, when judged by reason, to be a deviant state. Stendhal takes this deviant state to be a form of regularity—not a singularity—that can be characterized as an extension of normal states or behavior. This epistemic description of love as a psychic phenomenon subject to law anticipates much in science, for Stendhal's work can be considered as a precursor to medical attempts to assign laws to neurological pathology and psychiatric attempts to understand pathological mental states.

In his treatise on love Stendhal wants to emulate science in that he wants to describe the phenomenon of love through a series of laws that frame, with scientific objectivity, phenomena taking place in the subjective world. That Stendhal is also performing therapy upon himself is hardly in doubt even upon a cursory reading of *De l'Amour*. But that insight is significant only if one understands that, with this therapy, the writer has transposed his own "data" and investigates his own states as if the data taken from these states belong to an objective world that the inquiring mind can order quasi-mathematically. This self-objectification is a fount of realist writing after the Enlightenment. In Stendhal's case there are also idiosyncratic components to his investigations and the captious way with which he at once calls upon science and criticizes it. It is not the least of Stendhal's contradictions—for which he, too, might be charged with the hypocrisy that he found denied by mathematics— that he denigrated science as antithetical to desire and aesthetic satisfaction. These denigrations notwithstanding, in *De l'Amour* he attempts to enroll science in the task of describing desire—under the pretext that he has found a description of the laws of desire in an Italian manuscript. With these mystifications, Kierkegaard is not far away—and neither is self-analyst Freud.

In *De l'Amour* Stendhal, the scientist studying desire, says that passionate love passes through a series of steps of which the most interesting is "crystallization." This stage is compared to the formation of crystals that occur when a stick is thrown into a salt mine and then withdrawn, after some time, shining with glistening "diamonds" that no longer allow the viewer to recognize the stick. Mineralogy suggests a method for psychology and a metaphor for objectively describing the transformation of the beloved by the psyche of the lover. Crystallization is the operation of the mind, as Stendhal puts it, by which the mind extracts, from everything that the beloved presents, the discovery that the loved object has new perfections. Stendhal draws upon a nascent scientific discipline to insert, in this work mixing a series of *moraliste* observations with narratives and psychological feints, a scientific paradigm for psychology. One might say that mineralogy plays the role here that classical energetics later plays for Freud, though that would only be partially right. Stendhal is consciously effecting a metaphorical transfer to move from an image borrowed from science to frame an invariant law of the psyche. (By contrast, it is never clear to what extent Freud was aware of his own use of metaphor.) Stendhal's law is scientific as an epistemic description of invariance, and it is literary insofar as it is a form of verbal creation using metaphor. Of course, insofar as metaphor is often at the basis of a scientific description, one can reverse the terms and say that a metaphor is striving toward objectivity and that invariance is being used as the basis for asserting truth in a literary text.

This metaphorical maneuver was a unique attempt on Stendhal's part to create explicitly a science of the psyche, though he did incorporate the "laws" he discovered into the construction of fictions like *Le Rouge et le noir* (*The Red and the Black*) or *Lucien Leuwen.* For example, in *Le Rouge et le noir,* beginning with the moment when Julien Sorel first encounters Madame de Renal, the reader sees that each character, going from surprise to surprise, moves toward that moment of crystallization described by the law of passionate love. As illustrated by the course of the love enveloping Julien and Madame de Renal, or Lucien and Madame de Chasteller, Stendhal's paradigm does not entirely eschew the iatromechanical mode of explanation favored by much Enlightenment medicine. The mineralogical causality presents an image of mechanical determinism, though the image of growth can also appear organic or vitalist. And vitalism remained an explanatory paradigm throughout the nineteenth century. In effect, Stendhal's law of crystallization appeals to more than one model. Relying totally neither on mechanistic nor vitalist explanations, Stendhal framed a "law" in *De l'Amour;* and then he implicitly demonstrated its application by finding it at work, so to speak, in the behavior of characters in two of his novels (or three novels, if one detects crystallization at work in *La Chartreuse de Parme*). What is noteworthy is that Stendhal performed an epistemic demonstration that used literature to promote knowledge.

The demonstration of a law offered by *De l'Amour* interests us for the way it shows that science could play a role in the development of realism, and all the more so in that Stendhal can also be considered the first modern realist in European fiction. Many critics have made that claim, not the least of whom was the great literary scholar Erich Auerbach. In his discussion of *Le Rouge et le noir* in *Mimesis,* Auerbach compares Stendhal's novel with works by his predecessors, with novels by Lesage or Abbé Prévost, with Fielding or Goldsmith, and even with the memoirs of Saint-Simon, and finds that Stendhal enters into his given "contemporary reality" much more than these writers, and more than Enlightenment luminaries such as Voltaire, Rousseau, or Schiller: "Insofar as the serious realism of modern times cannot represent man otherwise than as embedded in a total reality, political, social, and economic, which is concrete and constantly evolving—as is the case today of any novel or film—Stendhal is its founder."[11]

I quote Auerbach's judgment—to which I find myself somewhat assenting in spite of myself—since it points up what is at stake in the development of the modern novel in France. For Auerbach, and for much literary theory preceding him, the real was defined as something produced by a totalizing vision that was in effect the backdrop for epistemic judgments. The belief in a "total reality" is an a priori belief most readers cannot accept today—but I would also argue that Stendhal didn't really invoke that totalization either. Stendhal seems to believe more in the contrary of totalization, as one sees in his quite fragmented descriptions of social reality, perhaps the most famous of which is his description of the battle at Waterloo as seen by Fabrice del Dongo in *La Chartreuse de Parme* (*The Charterhouse of Parma*). In his enthusiasm for the glory Napoleon promised, Fabrice fails to see the Emperor, has his horse stolen from him, and discovers that war is essentially disorder and chaos. However, Auerbach's description brings to the fore an important part of what one means by nineteenth-century realism. Nineteenth-century realism (and this remains true of some contemporary literary theory) often embodies the belief that all phenomena can be coordinated in terms of a totalization. Totalization today, however, appears to be an a priori axiom that belongs to an outmoded epistemic economy. The belief in totalization is found in Balzac, not to mention Marx and Hegel, but it is not found in Stendhal, who is all the more our contemporary for that reason.

The issue of totalization needs some clarification, since it provides background for the epistemic ambitions of writers like Balzac and, to a certain extent, Zola. In the early nineteenth century the belief in totalization was buttressed by, when not derived from, the Newtonian worldview, especially as elaborated by mathematical physicists such as Lagrange and Laplace. Parallel to this development of a totalizing cosmology in science, proposing a model for the understanding of all phenomena in the universe, stands the desire for historical or metaphysical totalization found in Hegel, Schelling, and the Marx of historical materialism. Novelists have their place here, for a belief in totalization also underwrites some works of realist fiction. These works of fiction, as well as the works of philosophers, show homologies with the belief in total-

11. Auerbach, *Mimesis*, trans. Willard Trask, 408.

izing knowledge as formulated by Laplace when, as quoted above, he theorized the possibility of total knowledge that could be garnered by the application of the laws of Newtonian mechanics. Laplace anticipates the more grandiose moments of Hegel's world spirit—the famous *Weltgeist*—when the physicist, like some spirit larger than the universe, claims that a sufficiently large intelligence, in knowing, in one movement of mind, the movements of the largest bodies in the universe, as well as those of all the most minute atoms, would seize the totality of what is, past, present, and future.

The mathematical problems involved with Laplace's vision of totality need not concern us here, though the infinite number of equations necessary for such calculation might even cause God to order some new parallel processors. Rather—and here physics shares a problem with metaphysics and literature—the problem lies simply in the fact that there is no way to define the "things" that would be subject to Newton's laws. In our universe of shoelaces and cosmic dust, tea pots and solar systems, there is simply no criterion for how to frame a definition of the infinite number of points that might be subject to forces of attraction. The "atoms" of which Laplace speaks, and which would be the ultimate things subject to forces, are empty semantic categories necessitated by the a priori belief that, if there is a totality, there must be a totality of things—whatever they are. Atomism at this stage in its development resembles an a priori belief that knows that one must have something on which to peg forces—though there is no way really of defining the ultimate ingredients of the totalizing stew that Laplace believes in. One can compare in this regard Laplace with the Wittgenstein of the *Tractatus* who said propositions had to mirror atomic states of affairs—and who was then incapable of giving an example of what might be a real atomistic state of affairs that a proposition might mirror. There is no way of finding atomic states of affairs; there are no final building blocks; and the Wittgenstein of the *Philosophical Investigations* was among the first to recognize that there are no intrinsic boundaries setting off the things on which we peg our definitions.

Nineteenth-century metaphysics, as found in Hegel and Marx, presents an analogous a priori construction of the real in that nineteenth-century philosophy, wanting to emulate the physicists' totalization, declared history to be a totality, a *Ganzheit*. This totality is again a definition, a tautology, that declares that History is what has been, that is to say, by definition, a totality of states of affairs. Stendhal's older contemporary, Hegel, starts from this definition of the real—what has been is what has been—to arrive at the skewed vision of historical necessity in which the totality of what is, is because it is—from which he deduces that it must be so. Logical errors aside, in his totalizing, Hegel had a novelist's gift for presenting some concrete states of affairs to illustrate the totality. Rather than give every atomistic state equal weight—which a physicist must do—Hegel privileges those moments that keep historical forces going, such as Caesar's crossing the Rubicon in 49 B.C. to begin the civil war with Pompey, or the fall of the Bastille in 1789. As in a novel, the Hegelian version of total reality enjoys a number of privileged moments.

In that inversion of Hegelian totality called Marxism, the totality is as tautological as in Hegel, since the Marxist totalization is by definition the ensemble of all the forces that have gone to make up historical reality— which exists perforce through a circular definition. To tie his historical forces onto something, Marx defines his force carriers as those histori- cal classes whose warfare has been fueled by something like the dy- namics of forces that Newton found among the stars, though Marx is in- terested in successive states of disequilibrium that characterize humanity once it finds itself separated from nature. But this historical vision con- tains at once past and future; and the Marxist, like the Laplacian observ- er, claims to observe past, present, and future, as one great necessary to- tality unfolding through the play of forces that make up ultimate reality.

This excursus on the belief in totalizing knowledge—that Auerbach thought he found in Stendhal—sets the stage for the epistemic en- counter with science that underlies the development of the modern nov- el in the nineteenth century. At this point, however, I return to my par- tial disagreement with Auerbach, since it seems to me that Stendhal is more modern, or at least more our contemporary, than Laplace, Hegel, or Balzac. A novel like *Le Rouge et le noir* does not presuppose the possi- bility of totalization that one often finds in Balzac's novels or even in those of Zola. Stendhal's narrative structure typically aims at reporting the perceptions and reflections of characters engaged in the open expe- rience of daily life in society. Events exist as a function of perception, and, if we as readers want to peg forces on them that make up some pre- supposed totality, that is our privilege. But one finds little reference in the novels themselves to some a priori totality of which Julian Sorel's experience would be an exemplar. A literary scholar, Geoffrey Strickland, thus contrasts Stendhal's work with Balzac's: "Life as it presents itself to the man or woman with exceptional intelligence as well as strength and delicacy of character; that is the focal and developing pre-occupation in most of Beyle's stories and novels, and in all those we think of as characteristic. And this perhaps more than anything else is what distinguishes him from Balzac both as a novelist and as a histori-an."[12] In Stendhal's work the individual is the locus where one looks for the illustration of law. Stendhal believed in laws of passion and laws of intelligence, though they always functioned as modified by the individual's nature. In this regard Stendhal recalls Montesquieu and his attempt to define social and political laws as the function of the nature of a given society, but he also points to modern attempts to define the laws of individual development. He points to quite contemporary attempts of biology and psychology to find ways of understanding phenotypical development that somehow reconcile the invariant sameness described by general law with the empirical fact of individual difference. Actually, the idea of totality seems meaningless when applied to Stendhal's work, since his work dramatizes the workings of individual consciousness in interplay with the world. This is not to say that Stendhal could not make a good case for my thesis that the major novelists of the nineteenth century found themselves in rivalry with science. In a sense, this is very much the case. But this epistemic rivalry is not directly dramatized in works like *Le Rouge et le noir, La Chartreuse de Parme,* or *Lucien Leuwen.* With a reluctant modesty about his epistemic achievement, Stendhal knew that he would not be appreciated until late in the nineteenth century, and I would say that he probably underestimated the time it did take for him to become contemporary. Let us turn back, then, to a writer who is not quite our contemporary, that very nineteenth-century writer Balzac, that protean figure who in fact embodies the early nineteenth-century quest for knowledge and who, with the series of novels called *La Comédie humaine,* might even convince a skeptic that totalization is possible.

12. Strickland, *Stendhal: The Education of a Novelist,* 130. The works that could be quoted about Stendhal number in the dozens. Let me express here my debt to some of the major Stendhal scholars and their various works, such as Alain, Victor Brombert, Victor Del Litto, and the great Georges Blin, who first initiated me into serious thinking about Stendhal in his course at the Collège de France. Specifically with regard to this chapter, I call attention to Jean Theorides, *Stendhal du côté de la science* and Mario Bonfantini, *Stendhal e il realismo.*

TWO

Balzac and the Unity of Knowledge

Qui ne pardonnerait ce dernier plaisir à un homme de
science et de poésie?

*[Who would not forgive a man of science and poetry for this
last pleasure?]*

—Balzac, *La Peau de chagrin*

HISTORICAL OVERVIEW

1778: Mesmer arrives in Paris with his medical theory based upon animal magnetism, sometimes viewed as the precursor to psychotherapy.

1785: Coulomb publishes his research on the inverse square laws of electrical and magnetic attraction.

1789: After several years of research that included the discovery of oxygen and the development of chemical nomenclature, Lavoisier publishes his *Traité élémentaire de chimie* containing the law of mass conservation.

1801: Pinel caps neo-Hippocratic revival in medicine with *Traité médico-philosophique sur l'aliénation mental ou la manie*, often considered first modern work of psychiatry.

1800: Bichat's *Traité des membranes* results from research that founds histology and experimental physiology.

1809: In his *Philosophie zoologique* Lamarck proposes that species emerge from a gradual process of development going from the simple to the complex.

1811: Jöns Jacob Berzelius states that electrical and chemical forces are one and the same.

1812: Sir Humphry Davy publishes his *Elements of Chemical Philosophy*, the major work by this romantic scientist who refused Dalton's theory of atoms as basic elements.

1817: Founding paleontology, Cuvier develops Linnaeus's system of classification with *Le Règne animal*.

1819: Working after Young's experiments in light interference, Fresnel undertakes work on a wave theory of light, against Newtonian theory, reported in a *mémoire* to the Academy of Sciences.

1824: Carnot's *Réflexions sur la puissance motrice du feu* first describes the relation of work and heat later developed in thermodynamics.

1827: After Oersted's discovery of the magnetic field generated by an electric field, Ampère's work results in mathematical formulation of electromagnetism.

1829: Gustave-Gaspard Coriolis publishes *Du Calcul de l'effet des machines*, giving definitions of work and kinetic energy.

1830: Differences between antievolutionist Cuvier and transformationist Geoffroy Saint-Hilaire, a defender of the morphological unity of all living beings, result in public debate at the Academy of Science. Goethe writes a report on it.

1830: Stendhal publishes *Le Rouge et le noir*.

1831: Balzac publishes *La Peau de chagrin*.

Moral discourse, pornography, utopian eroticism—these are some of the genres found in the fiction of the eighteenth century. Enlightenment thinkers also used the novel to explore philosophical conundrums. Names like Richardson, Defoe, Montesquieu, Sterne, Voltaire, Diderot, and Goethe, among others, come to mind as illustrative of fiction's capacity to embody philosophical thought. My thesis in this chapter is, however, that the novel changed when Balzac transformed it into a more capacious epistemic discourse than philosophical allegory. Balzac understood this change as a challenge to science. He saw himself engaged in rivalry with the scientific discourses of his time at the same time that he saw his mission to be that of a collaborative critic. He understood his rivalry to engage not only the new totalizing discourses of

history and metaphysics, but also the new discipline of chemistry and
the older one of Newtonian mechanics, as well as disciplines such as
medicine, physiology, and biology that offer direct knowledge of life
forms, and hence of humanity. Most importantly, after the natural history of Linnaeus and Buffon, and with the work of Lamarck, Cuvier, and
Geoffroy Saint-Hilaire, biology was emerging as the totalizing study of
life forms as Balzac came to maturity. Moreover, geology and paleontology were taking their modern form; the story of the earth and its in-
habitants was becoming precisely that: a story conceived as a history, or
science as narrative.

The history of the novel, beginning with Balzac and, with some restrictions, Stendhal, is a tale of its reaction to, and interaction with, epistemic discourses as various as metaphysics, history, and natural science.
Here I place the accent on the most neglected feature of that story: the
novel's encounter with natural science. Only through successful competition with science, or so believed Balzac and a good many of his suc-
cessors, could the novel justify its claims to offer access to reality in ways
that might even be superior to scientific discourses with their claims to
represent the totality of knowledge.

Balzac endorsed the view that knowledge is ultimately granted by a
unified discourse. If reality is a single totality—a wistful axiom that contemporary physics pursues in its own way with its dream of a final, unified theory—it is not unreasonable to believe there should be a single,
totalizing discourse that offers knowledge of that reality. Or as Balzac's
alter ego scientist, Louis Lambert, says, "Aujourd'hui, la science est
une"—knowledge is one. In the context of Balzac's novel, this proposition is not, however, a straightforward endorsement of a nineteenth-
century version of the belief in a unified theory: Louis Lambert is a
scientist who goes mad pursing the axiom that "il est impossible de
toucher à la politique sans s'occuper de morale, et la morale tient à
toutes les questions scientifiques" [it is impossible to separate politics
and morality, and that morality involves all scientific questions].[1] Lambert goes mad pursuing the Enlightment dream of totalizing knowledge. And this madness marks a significant change of attitude about the
belief in the unity of all discourses that was characteristic of much Enlightenment thought. As we have seen, this unity is presupposed by

1. Balzac, *La Comédie humaine*, ed. Pierre-George Castex, vol. 11, 655.

Condorcet's attempt to figure physical and moral probability, and it underwrites Kant's view that pure reason can give rise to synthetic a priori propositions for both mathematics and morals. From a comprehensive historical perspective, it is clear that many Enlightenment axioms about knowledge continued in France, in science and history, well into the nineteenth century, and that romantics like Balzac and Stendhal, the romantics who invented modern realism, basically accepted the epistemic axioms of the Enlightenment. But Lambert's madness, perhaps like Faust's damnation before him, points to a certain loss of confidence. And, in the case of Balzac, it suggests that he sometimes accepted Enlightenment axioms the better to contest them.

Lambert goes insane in his quest for knowledge, and this insanity can be interpreted as a critique of the Enlightenment beliefs that Balzac acquired through his education. In his earliest essays, Balzac shows himself to be a Lockean nominalist, but he is also enough of a Cartesian (or Laplacean) physicist to believe that he could not affirm the existence of an eternal "principle" until "everything had been explained mathematically."[2] Locke, Descartes, Condorcet, and Malbranche, among others, provided a rationalist education for the young novelist growing up during the Empire. The other side of his education was provided by those eighteenth-century novelists, from Defoe through Richardson, who had produced a realist discourse more or less respecting the probabilistic knowledge that one supposedly garnered, through the senses, about everyday reality. Ultimately, however, at least to the contemporary reader, the realism of these novelists subordinates representation to moral discourse: epistemic interests are often sacrificed to more or less allegorical demonstrations. It hardly seem contestable that a reader has gained little knowledge, though much edification, when, after reading *Moll Flanders,* he or she can affirm that it is good to be virtuous when one is rich.

It is possible, of course, to argue that there is a moral dimension to Balzac's work—though that dimension is not so easily encapsulated as in a work by an English puritan. The difference between eighteenth-century fiction and Balzac's realism is evident, I think, in the way in which the moral dimension in Balzac is subordinated to an epistemic

---

2. Balzac, "Discours sur l'immortalité de l'âme," in *Oeuvres diverses,* ed. Pierre-Georges Castex, vol. 1, 545.

desire. Ethical judgments about the world, of which there are many in a Balzacian novel, are subordinated to the totalizing knowledge that the novel can offer in the first place. Knowledge precedes evaluation. In its most radical form, Balzac's desire to create an epistemic discourse results in what he called "philosophical" works, or novels that intend to promote the development of a unitary science or field of knowledge as Balzac conceived it. Viewed from this perspective, realism and metaphysical speculation can be seen as part of the same epistemic impulse in Balzac, for speculation is intended to promote epistemic ends. The quest for knowledge results in the realism of a *Père Goriot,* but also in the fantastic metascientific discourse of *Séraphita* as well as the extravagant allegory of *La Peau de chagrin.*

Although the Enlightenment framework sets out the most widely accepted criteria for what constituted the real and the knowable in the early nineteenth century, this framework was being challenged as Balzac was developing as a novelist. The latter part of the eighteenth century had already seen, in medicine and natural history, the vitalist challenge to the mechanistic paradigm. Vitalists postulated a life force that could explain human physiology and psychology, a life force that could not be described in mechanical terms. (Some literary romantics wanted to see in the vitalist challenge to the comprehensiveness of Newtonian mechanics a sign that physics and dynamics had no relevance for knowledge about life, but this was a minority movement.) The critique of the scope of Newtonian mechanics was hardly unique to vitalists. The challenge to its totalizing scope occurred in several quarters in the early nineteenth century. In the France of the 1820s, a critique of Laplacian physics was undertaken by physicists such as Ampère, with his work in electrodynamics, and Fresnel, whose renewal of a wave theory of light largely discredited Newton's particle theory. Fourier had begun the study of thermal conduction and was certain that heat was part of a class of phenomena that could not be explained by mechanical forces.[3] And Sadi Carnot had theorized that the amount of energy produced by a steam engine is dependent only upon the temperature differential between the beginning and end phase of its cycle. This principle was to lead to an understanding of heat as a form of kinetic energy. Carnot's thought about energy was not only a nascent revolution in science that

3. Stephen F. Mason, *A History of the Sciences,* 488.

demonstrated an area in which Newtonian laws of motion were not relevant, but, as we shall see, it finds pertinent resonance in Balzac's own way of thinking about forces in conceiving the causes of events in fiction.

The active critique of scientific disciplines found in Balzac's novels is part of an ongoing historical debate. Largely centered on Paris in the first decades of the century, this debate was promoted by scientists who felt too limited by Newtonian or Kantian metaphysics, or found simply that Newtonian explanations did not fit the data, as in the case of light waves and thermal conduction. In general terms one can say that the early nineteenth century witnessed a number of debates, by scientists as well as philosophers, concerning the frameworks that offered access to reality. In the context of these active debates, Balzac believed that he could actively contribute, in terms that were scientifically viable, to the solution of these debates—debates, for example, as to what constitutes mind, matter, and life forces. To take Balzac's epistemic quest seriously requires one to place these questions in the foreground of reading Balzac.

Balzac embarrasses some of his most partisan readers with his claims to have knowledge about, say, imponderable forces and spiritual fluids that, from the viewpoint of today's science, seem rather quirky indeed. But it seems to me that this embarrassment comes from having only a partial grasp of the conditions of possibility for knowledge in the first part of the nineteenth century—for Balzac is, often, no more quirky than mainline scientists of the time. Some of the "models" Balzac proposes for scientific understanding have disappeared—such as the physics of imponderables, mesmerism, and phrenology. Mesmerism and phrenology are, for example, historical oddities belonging to the realm of failed theories (though some revisionist historians want to see in these para-sciences the beginnings of psychotherapy or even of neurological determinism). Imponderables, on the other hand, were a rational solution to problems that could not be accounted for in other terms: before Carnot, nobody had found a way of measuring thermal energy, so heat seemed to be a weightless imponderable. (It required an "epistemological engine" like the steam engine to make this measurement possible.) A history of European culture—scientific and literary—should take into account the existence of many odd and unsuccessful theories, as well as the successful ones, for the history of culture is as much a history of the role of unsuccessful theories as of those relatively few that have survived. Moreover, unsuccessful theories often reveal that the line of demarcation between science and literature can be tenuous.

Literary history, I add, should certainly deal with these theories, and not only because they interested major writers like Balzac. Literature is concerned with impossible discourses as well as renditions of the possible. Literary historians can look upon failed scientific theories as a domain of the imaginary that, drawing upon Borges, one can call a realm of fantastic literature. One may speak of unsuccessful paradigms with regard to unsuccessful scientific theories—though I take my distance from the view that the history of science is punctuated by so-called paradigm shifts. Indeed, it seems to me that the history of most scientific disciplines is the history of a series of questionings and shifts that, over a period of time, has evolved continuously to such an extent that the early founding thought of a given discipline finally looks like a fantasy. Rarely does this evolution entail a dramatic rupture between one paradigm and another—though one can argue this point indefinitely. For example, Buffon's idea that animal families were created by degeneration from an original stock seems bizarre today, but it can be argued that this now "fantastic" idea generated a development that runs continuously from eighteenth-century natural history through Lamarck and Geoffroy Saint-Hilaire, then Darwin, to culminate in our own neo-Darwinian theories of evolution.

When historically situated, Balzac's interest in, say, animal magnetism is not simply eccentric, but part of his creative participation in the debate about imponderable substances and the nature of "immaterial" forces such as heat and electricity, for which there were several theories in the early part of his century. Imponderable substances—substances without weight—were put forward as an almost plausible theory with which one could explain everything—from the mysteries of electricity and magnetism, to the form heat assumed as a transferable substance called caloric—before energy was finally a received concept. (In fact, even at the end of the nineteenth century, one could find a few retrograde physicists who persisted in viewing the doctrine of imponderables as a plausible doctrine.) Balzac's relation to the sciences of his time is sometimes complex and subtle, sometimes bullying and full of braggadocio, but in the main it is not greatly out of step, for he constantly studied science of all sorts. Quite simply, Balzac wanted the novel to offer knowledge that could rival the sciences in their quest for totalization.

This enterprise meant that Balzac accepted some scientific models, rejected others, and considered all of them. His intent was really nothing less than a revision of science so as to bring it in harmony with the knowledge he could offer in the novel—in his creation of an epistemic totalization that was, by a priori definition, the ultimate goal of knowledge.

Balzac explicitly criticized scientific models for various purposes. However, most of his realist novels by and large implicitly accept the Newtonian-Laplacian worldview of post-Revolutionary science. Several of his "philosophical" works offer a critique of Newton and explore non-Newtonian theories of knowledge and the world. However, in such realist works as *Le Père Goriot* or *Le Curé de Tours,* Balzac does not challenge the materialist causality of celestial mechanics and terrestrial dynamics that Newton's French followers, such as Lagrange and Laplace, had succeeded in making into the dominant scientific model of the early nineteenth century—the model that served well into that century as an ultimate court of appeal for deciding what was knowledge of the real. This acceptance and criticism reflects historical struggles with Newton, as well as Balzac's own psychological make-up. He was educated in the mechanistic worldview, which sometimes caused him to believe that he himself was a victim of that "fatal" modern education in mathematics and science that the avowedly reactionary Count de Mortsauf deplores in *Le Lys dans la vallée* (*The Lily of the Valley*): "L'éducation modern est fatale aux enfants. . . . Nous les bourrons de mathématiques, nous les tuons à coups de science, et les usons avant le temps" [Modern education is fatal for children. . . . We stuff them with mathematics, we kill with doses of science, and wear them out before their time].[4] But Balzac could not overthrow the education that he criticized, for it gave him the grounds for criticizing the Enlightenment.

With this education, Balzac could stay abreast of contemporary scientific developments. For example, with regard to chemistry, Balzac knew quite well that Lavoisier (1743–1794) had given shape to modern chemistry with his work on elements and atomic weights; and that, during Balzac's youth, the atomism of Dalton (1766–1844) had taken chemistry a step farther toward a way of understanding the basic elements. Dalton's atomism had then been rationalized and given its modern

4. Balzac, *Le Lys dans la vallée,* 77.

symbolism by the Swedish chemist Berzelius (1779–1848)—whom Balzac literally memorized and rather much plagiarized for his own theorizing in his novel centering on research in chemistry, *La Recherche de l'absolu*. Balzac was equally as attentive to the way the foundations of modern biology were established in the Paris of his youth. A very young Geoffroy Saint-Hilaire (1772–1844), who became Balzac's friend later in life, was, in 1793, the first professor of zoology at the Museum of Natural History, and the zoologist Cuvier, for whom Balzac expressed great admiration, introduced comparative anatomy into zoology for the first time shortly thereafter. Balzac knew that their contrasting theories about the unity of nature came to a head in their public debate of 1830, a debate that can be taken as emblematic of the unsettled nature of the biological theory Balzac confronted and theorized upon just as he began to write *La Comédie humaine*. Balzac found himself drawn to the viewpoints of both scientists. In defending an evolutionary view of the unfolding of life forms, Geoffroy Saint-Hilaire proposed that all animals tend to repeat the same archetype, and that homologies of form demonstrate the principles of connection that all animals manifested. Cuvier denied evolution, maintaining that animal functions derive from morphology—a principle Cuvier put to use in inventing the science of paleontology. As we shall presently discuss, Balzac's own invention of character, his nonpsychological development of types, owes much to both scientists.

In brief, Balzac confronted a situation in the Paris of his youth in which Lavoisier's chemistry, the electrodynamics of Ampère, and Cuvier's biology were issues of public debate. Even an ancient discipline like medicine was receiving new foundations. Bichat, a model for Balzac's ideal doctor, had founded histology, and Magendie was undertaking the experiments that led to experimental physiology. (Medicine largely remained, however, an eclectic mixture of medieval humors theory, mechanistic explanation opposed by vitalism, and rudimentary physiology, for a modern theory of disease based on microbiology was some decades away—Pasteur was born in 1822.) In the context of this unique situation in which Paris became, for at least a generation, the world's most important center for scientific thought, it is not surprising that Balzac felt it incumbent to take part in scientific debates—for how else could the novel be transformed into something with an epistemic status that could rival the success of the sciences? Simply by being in the Paris of Magendie and Ampère, of Cuvier and Lamark, of Carnot and

Fresnel, a novelist alive to what was shaping the world was obliged to pay attention to the scientific theories transforming epistemic discourse—which included at the time controversial ideas, such as mesmerism and animal magnetism, that strike us today as failed theories. In résumé, the Paris of 1830, to name a symbolic date, was a place in which rivalry among various theories and epistemic models was intense. The totalizing worldview proposed by Laplacian-Newtonian mechanics came under criticism for its views of physiology, optics, and heat, but, for at least another generation, it remained a, if not the, fundamental model for understanding the world.

Balzac drew upon these debates for theories that he in turn translated into, and elaborated as, literary models. He used the nascent science of biology as well as the taxonomic tradition of natural history, arguably for the first time, as categories for understanding the human world. In his novels, Balzac wants to describe not just isolated classical "types" or *caractères* of the *moraliste* tradition, but related taxa that can be defined in terms of a totality of interrelationships. This is not to say that Balzac does this taxonomy systematically. Rather, taxonomy proposes an ideal model for understanding, drawn largely from nascent biology. Balzac theorized that, since human nature is encompassed by the presupposed totalization of knowledge, the nature of human society can be explained through its homologies with the entire natural world. This is analogous to an understanding of nature such as Geoffroy Saint-Hilaire understood it. But Balzac's totalizing synthesis also understands taxonomy in terms of morphological differences—whence Balzac's admiration for Geoffroy Saint-Hilaire's opponent, Cuvier. Balzac's totalization aims at reconciling the divergent theses of these adversaries by reconciling synthesis with analysis—to use the terms that Goethe used in his rather confused reports on the debate between Geoffroy Saint-Hilaire and Cuvier. Synthesis means linking characters in terms of totalization, whereas analysis led to characterization by means of the distinctive trait—traits drawn from Balzac's own ideas about the morphology of the human species.

In this description of the epistemic rivalry between Balzac and natural science, it is perhaps a bit misleading to maintain that Balzac was influenced by the biology that was being formulated in Paris by Lamark, Geoffroy Saint-Hilaire, and Cuvier. It is more accurate to speak of a convergence of theoretical interests in which Balzac found, in contemporary biology, analogies with his own epistemic vision. Early biology and Balzac's novels manifest the same concerns with vision, taxonomy, and figuring the relation of the particular to the whole—the *Ganzheit* that is the ultimate referent of early nineteenth-century natural philosophy. Balzac was in a sense predestined to get along with Geoffroy Saint-Hilaire and his historicizing the totality of life forces evolving and undergoing transformation in time. It is not immediately clear, in spite of my comment above, why Balzac honors so effusively the taxonomical observer that he found in the comparative anatomist Cuvier. Cuvier refused for religious, as well as scientific, reasons to accept transformism, but his work in paleontology was nonetheless crucial in proving that there have been successive extinctions of many species. Between Cuvier and Geoffroy Saint-Hilaire, biological science was historicized toward the past and toward the future, and in the two scientists Balzac encountered thinkers who, in different ways, placed individual species in contact with the totality of the biological and, for Balzac, the social sphere. Balzac admired both scientists for underwriting different aspects of his own totalizing theory in which society and nature are fused as a unity. If one wants to find a powerful source for this shared vision, one should look back to the naturalist Buffon, whose influence on both Balzac and Geoffroy Saint-Hilaire, though not Cuvier, is notable. Buffon promoted a nominalism in taxonomy that rejected Linnaeus and his taxonomy in favor of a view proposing the interconnected totality of nature and natural beings. According to the Buffon of the "Premier discours" of his *Histoire naturelle* (1749)—a major Enlightenment source for the belief in totalization—natural history is nothing less than the ever-ramifying story of everything that the universe offers us.

With these epistemic themes in mind, let us turn, first, to works in which Balzac explicitly deals with issues of knowledge, and then to examples of his realist work in which the novel is used as a vehicle for knowledge of the world. This division corresponds roughly to a difference between works that are metaepistemic and works, especially the realist works, in which the work itself embodies the epistemic project in the description of the world and the events that take place therein. The first Balzacian novel to illustrate this epistemic play is *La Peau de chagrin* (translated variously as *The Magic Skin* or *The Wild Ass's Skin*), an ironic allegory about knowledge that shows the critical distance Balzac could take from the sciences of his time. This relatively early novel was written in part after the debate between Cuvier and Geoffroy Saint-Hilaire and published as a book in 1831. In it, Balzac clearly manifests a desire to rival scientific discourse. He does so in the novel through an ironic critique of science's claims to knowledge. The overlap of the novel's creation with the debate of 1830 on the unity of nature is significant. It is quite likely that the open conflict of two major scientific minds gave Balzac warrant to consider himself capable of entering scientific debate and to criticize science while pursuing his own epistemic aims. When the experts disagree, then it is up the independent-minded individual to enter the fray, to weigh the evidence, and to criticize errors. (This is, I add, a relevant lesson for citizens facing the claims of genetics today.) This critical strategy is central not only to *La Peau de chagrin* but also to several successive early novels in *La Comédie humaine,* such as *Louis Lambert* (first version in 1832), *La Recherche de l'absolu* (first version in 1834), and *Séraphita* (1835). These are all works that explicitly enact critiques of science and procedures of knowledge. Taken together, they offer an overview of Balzac as self-conscious epistemologist.

The marvelous allegory of *La Peau de chagrin* introduces Balzac's epistemic critique in the guise of an exercise in aspect-seeing. Aspect-seeing, or seeing according to the perspective adopted on foreground and background, demonstrates that the very relativity of knowledge entails, as a consequence, that the novel must be considered an ideal vehicle for an epistemic quest. The relativity of knowledge allows the novel to rival science. (I use the notion of relativity here in its classical sense that, from Galileo through the nineteenth century, proposed that knowledge is relative to position.) Knowledge is relative to the perspective adopted by the observer confronting phenomena that may allow different explanations—and for which the novel is an ideal medium. At least two perspectives on the world are proposed in *La Peau de chagrin*. The novel's hero, Raphael, experiences a rise and fall that, on the one hand, may be explained by the natural forces that make him extremely lucky and then cause him to die from tuberculosis, or, on the other hand, the hero's death may be fatefully caused by a magic ass's skin that perceptibly shrinks each time it seemingly grants the hero one of his desires. So it is imperative, from a scientific standpoint, to explain why the skin shortens with each wish granted.

Raphael had himself been a Faustian seeker of knowledge whose passion for learning found expression in a treatise that he wrote offering a theory of the will. However, at the novel's outset, he is ready to commit suicide when he encounters a Mephisto-like antiquarian who gives him the wish-granting ass's skin. Raphael learns that he may anticipate that his every desire will be granted—except the desire not to desire. Balzac's allusion to Faust underscores the epistemic allegory here, since Faust's surfeit of knowledge leads him to desire to desire and thus to the infernal pact. Raphael's leap into desire suggests an allegory with a different epistemic slant. His is an allegory figuring the limits of desire that, when exceeded, portend the loss of the energy fueling desire. *Energy* is a term that is not quite yet in its place here, for the modern notion of the conservation of energy, or energy itself for that matter, was only first being theorized at the time that Balzac set out to write *La Comédie humaine.* Paralleling the development of the concept of energy, Balzac's allegory is about energy as the fuel propelling both desire and knowledge, so it is worth exploring analogies between the development of energy as a scientific theory and Balzac's literary knowledge of energy.

Balzac's contemporary Sadi Carnot (1796–1832) made one of the first modern attempts at theorizing energy in 1824, but his work on the "motive force of fire" went virtually unnoticed for another generation. Carnot died of cholera the year after Balzac published *La Peau de chagrin.* Remarkably, Balzac's concept of desire as energy strikes a coincident note with Carnot's view that heat energy is nothing other the motion of the particles of bodies, coincident in the sense that Balzac theorizes about "motive force" as something that can be defined as other than itself. This is analogous with the way Carnot was working toward the idea that heat and energy are interconvertible and equivalent.[5] It would be hyperbole to claim an exact correspondence here, but it is important to see that, in tying characterization to a force like energy, Balzac was participating in the search for new ways of theorizing motion and acts, and the power that lies behind them. Balzac was among the first to equate desire and what we now call energy, and he was among the first to relate desire and energy to the epistemic project itself: desire and energy are part of the knowing subject. In *La Peau de chagrin,* Balzac's allegory about knowing

5. My discussion of Carnot draws upon, among other sources, Mason, *A History of the Sciences,* as well as Cecil J. Schneer, *The Evolution of Physical Science,* and Emilio Segrè, *From Falling Bodies to Radio Waves: Classical Physicists and Their Discoveries.* I also recommend highly the ever useful Princeton *Dictionary of the History of Science,* ed. W. F. Byynum, E. J. Browne, and Roy Porter.

points up the limits of knowing, since to desire to know entails an expense of energy—as do all other forms of desire. Knowledge itself is the desire to go beyond what one can immediately see, which is the epistemic desire par excellence of Newtonian physics. But such desire leads to boundless expenditures of energy and, finally, death.

Balzac's epistemic allegory figures the limits of vision, though in rather comic terms. In *La Peau de chagrin,* an epistemic comedy is enacted in the way the supernatural seems to have become a part of the natural world. With the regularity of a Bergsonian comic machine, the magical shrinking skin is a diabolical causal agent, shrinking as energy is expended, that is as natural as death. From another perspective, however, the skin is simply one of those millions of things that one sees drying up and for which there is usually no explanation. Science is limited, since explanations are always relative to the epistemological framework involved. In his critique, Balzac makes a heavy-handed demonstration of the scientists' impotence to explain the shrinking of the skin, for it can be explained differently by every science, and thus seemingly by none. However, Balzac's demonstration seems less emphatic if we recall that, immediately before the novel was published, all of Europe had witnessed the edifying spectacle of two of the leading natural scientists of the time trying to destroy each other in their public debate of 1830: Geoffroy Saint-Hilaire and Cuvier had equally plausible theories about life and its variegated manifestations. With his shrinking skin, Balzac seems to imply that life, like any other magical phenomena, allows multiple and relative theories to explain it.

Most pointedly in the novel, then, Balzac undertakes a satire of natural history and medicine that shows the distance he could take from his masters and the confidence he felt in demonstrating the limits of received forms of knowledge. Toward the novel's end, when Raphael is near death from his successive wishes, he takes the skin to a zoologist who is classifying ducks in the hopes of producing a new species (a probable allusion to Geoffroy Saint-Hilaire's attempt to produce monster chickens by modifying their eggs). To explain the skin's shrinking, Balzac's zoologist uses rhetorical overkill with empty explanations drawing upon natural history, explanations that are something of a parody of Buffon's verbosity. These epistemic pirouettes leave Raphael with the opinion, reflecting what Buffon did hold in fact about Linnaeus, that all classification in natural history is merely a nominalist matter of nomenclature. The issue of aspect-seeing is central here: the naturalist sees the skin as an excuse for taxonomy, the harried romantic hero sees the skin as the central mystery of his expiring life.

Raphael goes to see a mechanical philosopher who views the skin as another illustration of the central mystery that mechanical philosophy has yet to explain: movement. And a mechanic sees the skin as a substance to be manipulated—something that he can't do. Nor can a chemist proceed to do much with the skin, although he views it as a substance to be decomposed into its basic elements, that is, until, confronting failure, he finally decides to view it as part of the class of things that one should not mention to the Academy.

Raphael takes his own decrepit body to doctors who view him according to the lights provided by their doctrines. Balzac does quick overviews, with comic overtones, of several reigning medical doctrines of the early nineteenth century. Each theory determines what one sees, since knowledge is relative to the perspective provided by an epistemic doctrine. A materialist doctor, representing the doctrines of the then-famous Broussais, sees only what Broussais always saw: general inflammation giving rise to monomania. A vitalist doctor, looking for the iatrochemist Van Helmont's mystical life force, the archea, finds in Raphael that the mind has attacked the epigaster, the locus of the life force. And a sceptic, closely resembling the experimental physiologist Magendie, is willing to experiment in order to see what will happen when Broussais's treatment using leeches or, alternatively, a "moral treatment," recalling the psychiatrist Pinel, have been applied to Raphael. These doctors are in turn commented upon by the ideal all-round doctor Bianchon, Balzac's own totalizing theorist. Bianchon explains that his colleagues' nosologies are so-many forms of aspect-viewing related to the three spheres of soul, body, and reason. This is a classical eclecticism that Greco-Roman medicine might have found amenable, though the final therapy is provided by Bianchon's reminder that at best one must trust nature—nature or that total curative agent that a Renaissance doctor like Rabelais, recalling Hippocrates, would have prescribed.

The novel's overview of sciences and medical doctrines presents Balzac's amused critique of any partial or relative vision that claims to understand human totality. However, this critique of science as partial vision risks turning against the novel itself, for what knowledge can the novel propose other than its own system of vision? And, moreover, even if one could be enlightened, can knowledge overcome the blindness of desire? Balzac represents this predicament in the novel itself. Raphael never achieves his quest to know what has befallen him or how to handle his desire. Rather, this quester for knowledge finds himself figured at the novel's end by a blind minstrel that he encounters on the route to Paris and in whom Raphael sees a fantastic image of his own desire. And a blind minstrel might well figure the novelist himself.

Raphael finally tries to elude desire and the quest. Most interestingly, before his death he tries to live like a natural being, like an oyster on a rock, making a fusion between himself and the totality of nature, becoming lost "in the sanctuary of life."[6] In this fusion he is "like a plant in the sun, like a hare in its lair" (282). But in this attempt to elude the quest, he undergoes an epistemic epiphany in which he seizes the plan of nature's organization. Every variety of life form appears as the development of a single substance. Lost in a dream of total science, Raphael has the impression that he is saved. Romantic biology is, however, therapeutic only in psychological terms, for Raphael awakes to hear another character describing his condition—and from this exterior perspective, it sounds as if he has an advanced case of tuberculosis.

Fleeing death, Raphael returns to Paris and tries to lose himself in slumber produced by opium, in a sleep without desire. But the renewed presence of the beloved Pauline renews his yearning. In his recognition of desire, he confronts the final flames in which desire consumes his energy. Raphael burns a fatal letter Pauline sends him, only to see in the ashes an "image trop vive de son amour et de sa fatale vie" [a too vivid image of his love and his destiny] reduced now to ashes by the loss of the energy that has fueled his quest (306). At last Pauline adventures to Raphael's bed where, igniting his last gasp of desire, she kills him. Raphael's knowledge of nature has not saved him, nor does it seem that knowledge of any sort could have enabled him to avoid destruction.

It remains an open question as to whether anyone could know what has been Raphael's destiny, other than the universal destiny of human desire and the depletion of energy expended in the service of that desire. Physics is related to physiology from this Faustian perspective. There is a clear intertextual relation between Raphael's desire and

6. Balzac, *La Comédie humaine*, ed. Castex, vol. 10, 282.

Faust's desire, as well as between Balzac's novel and the Faustian critique of an unbounded desire for knowledge. But Faust is not the only
scientist who stands as a patron saint to Balzac's project of seizing the
social world in *La Comédie humaine*. Balzac's title for his totalizing project recalls, with appropriate hubris, its intertextual relationship to perhaps the most impressive totalizing work of the Christian West, Dante's
summation of all true knowledge in the *Divina Commedia*. Like many a
scientist in the Paris that surrounded him—scientists who might be
likened to so many contemporary versions of Faust—Balzac could view
his own epistemic desire as excessive, and the warning written in San-
skrit on the ass's skin undoubtedly haunted him from the moment he
began *La Comédie humaine:* determine your desires by your life ("règle
tes souhaits sur ta vie"). *La Peau de chagrin* is a unique work in that it
proposes a critique of excessive desire that could put in question
Balzac's project of a totalizing natural history of society, as he phrased
it some years later in the "Avant-Propos" that he wrote in 1842 for *La
Comédie humaine.*

Balzac's belief in his understanding of epistemology, in 1832, was
nonetheless confident, and it is worth contrasting the critical doubts of
La Peau de chagrin with the confidence embodied in a published letter
Balzac wrote to a writer of fantastic tales, Charles Nodier. Writing
in effect a public manifesto in this admonishing letter, Balzac showed
that he was at once admiring of, and impatient with, contemporary science—and quick to make judgments. The infinite spaces of distant neb-
ulae that Herschel's telescope revealed were as much a cause of wonder
as the thousands of years that Laplace's calculations had added to the
world's age. But, Balzac assured, the time and space that we use for
knowledge depend uniquely upon human perception: and dream and
sleep show that one can travel outside of these coordinates. The fact that
all knowledge is relative to the subject is a cause for optimism as well as
for a belief that the subject can be liberated. Indeed, one day, Balzac pre-
dicted, some savant will explore sleep to show that, just as Cuvier and
Laplace "have torn facts from an ocean of thoughts," human beings possess the exorbitant faculty to annihilate, in relation to themselves, "space
which exists only in relation" to themselves.[7] In our present darkness,
however, humanity is obliged to accept the Newtonian-Kantian coordi-

7. Balzac, *Oeuvres complètes*, vol. 23, 177.

nates of time and space to find reality—while knowing that other worlds await the traveler who can enter the obscurity of dream, madness, and the fantastic. Magnetism and electricity, psychic or nervous fluids, the imponderables of late eighteenth century chemistry, these all suggest that there will be applications of science to create a new science of the human mind:

> Les bornes d'une simple lettre ne me permettent pas d'embrasser autrement que par l'énumération les magnifiques irraditions de cette science nouvelle; mais les prodiges de la *volonté* en seront le lien commun, auquel se rattachent et les découvertes de Gall, celle du fluide nerveux, troisième circulation de notre appareil, et celle du principe constituant de l'électricité; puis les innombrables effets magnétiques, ceux du somnabulisme naturel et artificiel dont s'occupent les savants de Danemark, de Suède, de Berlin, d'Angleterre, d'Italie, et que nient ceux de notre Paris.

> [The limits imposed by a letter do not allow me to grasp, except by enumeration, the magnificent radiations of the new science. But the prodigies of will power [*volonté*] will be what ties it to all others; and to which are linked the discoveries of Gall, that of nervous fluid, the third circulatory system of our body, and that of the principle constitutive of electricity, and also innumerable magnetic effects, such as those of natural and artificial somnambulism that are occupying scientists in Denmark, Sweden, Berlin, England, Italy, and whose existence our Parisian scientists deny.] (176–77)

Clearly impatient with the reigning empiricism of Parisian science, Balzac wanted to muster support for new theories that would displace the Kantian interpretation of Newton—as he shows in this letter to Nodier by twisting Kantian metaphysics so as to suggest the possible abolition of space and the willful freeing of the subject from the constraints of Kantian rationalism. Emanating from the subject, the new sciences of which Balzac is a herald should lend themselves to a unified science of the will.

A treatise on the will is supposedly written not only by the hero of *La Peau de chagrin,* but also by the hero of Balzac's slightly later work, *Louis Lambert.* This novel is a fictional biography that describes the failure to give birth to the new science that Balzac hailed in his letter to Nodier. *Louis Lambert* is an ambiguous metaepistemic work in that its hero, a savant whom the novel's narrator cannot quite understand, dies after a bout with insanity. Flaubert was duly impressed by this hero, in whom he undoubtedly saw a double, driven mad, as Flaubert noted, by thinking about intangible things.[8] Written with the sobriety of a biographical dictionary entry, *Louis Lambert* portrays the search for illumination as seen from without by a commonsensical narrator who can only surmise the inner mystical knowledge that Lambert has reached in his research. The novel's narrator is Lambert's best friend from their school days, a time when Lambert devoured every available source in an attempt to amalgamate religion, history, philosophy, and physics and thus arrive at a potential totality of knowledge. Lambert is rather like a schoolboy incarnation of some Hegelian world-mind whose development would ultimately result in the synthesis of all knowledge. Like young Cuvier, reconstituting a total organism from small fossilized remains, Lambert constructs totalities from traces of evidence (621). Presumably following in the footsteps of Swedenborg and Mesmer, Lavater and Gall, Lambert is a "chemist of the will" who wants to invent a new science. Hardly a Lavoisierian materialist, he wants to found his science on the fundamental axiom of human doubleness (622–23). This axiom is the basis for the prodigy's "Treatise on the Will" that an ignorant curate teacher confiscates.

As described by the narrator, Lambert could have become a Pascal, a Lavoisier, or a Laplace, but not due to the university studies that he later undertakes in Paris, which Balzac portrays as an intellectual desert. There, literature is taught by the repetition of tautologies, and science is fragmented into separate academies that have destroyed the dreamed-of unity of science that Lambert, before Balzac's Séraphita, hopes to formulate. Balzac was right historically in that Paris was indeed the place where empirically oriented chemists, physicists, and biologists were developing separate scientific disciplines that, in practical terms, did not rely upon a presupposed unity of science. The totalization Laplace's physics had proposed, for example, was foundering not only on its impracticality, but also on the development of disciplines, such as optics, electricity, and heat, that could claim their own autonomy vis-à-vis Newtonian mechanics. In a sense, then, Lambert's view of contemporary science is as "reactionary" as were Balzac's putative politics. (Or, if

8. Flaubert quoted in Balzac, *La Comédie humaine,* ed. Castex, vol. 11, 561.

one prefers, perhaps as "radical" as the Marx who also declared that there would be one science: "es wird *eine* Wissenschaft sein.")[9]

Like Hegel and Marx, Balzac defends a utopian view of science that would at once integrate literature and all epistemic discourses into a grand totality. And, so formulated, this utopian view condemns actual scientific discourse to the status of a fallen discourse that needs literature to supplement it as its totalizing other. This is one side of Balzac's attempt to compete with science, for he does indeed condemn theories that respect the narrow limits of rational empiricism. Yet, even the rather summary plot of *Louis Lambert* shows Balzac's critical self-awareness at work: Balzac's totalizing scientist, in his desire to encompass all of knowledge, goes insane, at least in the eyes of the world. Lambert could be viewed as a new kind of scientist in this madness, since, from Balzac's romantic perspective, madness liberates Lambert from the restrictive limits of space and time that prevent a total epistemic synthesis. But Balzac does not pursue this point here. Rather, Lambert seems to founder on the immensity of the task at hand, on the incommensurable distance between the real and the knowledge he can imagine. At times Balzac's utopian total knowledge is, like some Borgesian science, a form of imaginary totalizing knowledge that, because we can imagine it, serves to condemn real science and literature for their necessary partiality—when judged by the imagination.

Balzac's belief in, and desire for, the unity of knowledge finds correlates in the German *Naturphilosophie* that Schelling and Fichte underwrote, and, as I noted earlier, in the natural history of his friend, the zoologist Geoffroy Saint-Hilaire. Opposing Cuvier's rigid taxonomical separation of the animal kingdom into four orders, Geoffroy Saint-Hilaire argued, with increasing vehemence, for the unity of all animal orders as derivative from a basic model—what Raphael discovered in his communion with the totality of nature. The specifics of Geoffroy Saint-Hilaire's demonstration of what we call today homologies are less important for Balzac than the epistemic model that argued for connections underlying all apparent morphological differences in the animal kingdom. Balzac admired the genius with which Cuvier identified

9. I quote from the Habermas text, in which a contemporary neo-Marxist shows that he is unhappy that Marx actually believed in the totalizing thought that he held up as the epistemic ideal. From Jurgen Habermas, *Erkenntnis und Interesse*, 63.

species—Balzac's own concept of a social species defined by a distinguishing trait is closer, I think, to Cuvier than to Geoffroy Saint-Hilaire. But the utopian epistemic impulse is one he shared with Geoffroy Saint-Hilaire—and vice versa, since the scientist liked to quote Balzac's Lambert to the effect that science is one. Finally, of course, we see that Balzac shared the Enlightenment desire to unite physical and moral sciences with one total methodology. Balzac was not overly fond of mathematics, but he, like many others, was also enticed by the belief that one might find a moral calculus equivalent to the calculus of probabilities used by the physical sciences. For the early successes of probability theory promoted a belief in a total methodology that would produce the knowledge—the utopian knowledge—Balzac dreamed of.

There is, however, a dark side to the Faustian pact that underwrites Balzac's science. Opposing the utopian belief in totality is the belief that the desire to know is a destroyer of limits: Hence, the desire for knowledge brings about dissolution. Faustian desire refuses limits, a refusal demonstrated by the epistemic-erotic allegory enacted in *La Peau de chagrin*. That Balzac further developed this theme of destruction in *La Recherche de l'absolu* (*The Quest of the Absolute*, 1834) testifies to the ongoing rivalry he felt with the sciences, for in this novel Balzac rectifies the "mistakes" of contemporary chemistry while undertaking to show the hubris of modern research. In this "search for the absolute," Balzac portrays a demented chemist who, having nearly ruined his family with his exorbitant experiments, dies still believing that he can find the absolute. Through this portrayal of a chemist, Balzac intended to attack his rivals, the successful Parisian empirical scientists who were transforming chemistry as well as physics and biology and who, in their hubris, struck a Faustian note. *La Recherche* has also been read as a call for the creation of a latter-day alchemy. It is true that Balzac saw a line of historical continuity running from alchemy to the chemistry then being developed in the wake of Lavoisier's revolution in chemical theorizing. Balzac's chemist hero, Claes, is called an alchemist by the local folk who think, rightfully, he is insane in his obsession with research. However, historically speaking, Claes is working in the mainstream of nineteenth-century chemistry. He wants to decompose azote, or nitrogen. This experiment would show that the system of classification of elements, some fifty-three as Balzac got them from reading Berzelius, is not absolute, for any decomposition would suggest a more elementary substance than that of the atom. Claes, once a student of Lavoisier, wants to reduce the elements to an elementary unity. This desire for unity may have characterized his alchemical predecessors, and it also constituted a leitmotif in romantic biology.

However, with regard to chemistry, there was nothing intrinsically alchemical or even romantic about the early nineteenth century debate among chemists as to what might constitute an elementary substance. William H. Brock underscores, in *The Norton History of Chemistry*, the doubts that nineteenth-century chemists entertained about their science: "At the start of the nineteenth century several chemists, including Davy, found it impossible to believe that God would have wished to design a world from some fifty different building blocks. Their skepticism that Lavoisier had identified the truly elementary blocks was reinforced by Davy's experimental work in which he showed that several of Lavoisier's elements, including the alkaline earths, were not truly elementary." So the English chemist Davy, whose work Berzelius systematized, preferred "undecompounded body" to the term "element" and its suggestion of some ultimate nature.[10] The debate on the elementary nature of atoms was unfolding, and many felt doubts that anticipate what some contemporary physicists may feel about the proliferating particles that the standard model allows today in particle physics. Balzac wanted to participate in the debate about the foundations of matter by elaborating a critique of chemistry—through much cribbing from Berzelius. Through his portrayal of research, Balzac wanted to show that literature can at once participate in the elaboration of scientific discourse and, with its superior dramatic means, enact a critique of the scientific hubris that desires to go beyond limits. And if one inevitably thinks of Faust in this regard, it is because Faust is a constant model in the nineteenth century for pointing up the destructive side of epistemic hubris.

La Recherche de l'absolu is, however, more a realist work than an allegory, for Balzac wants to confront contemporary science by more or less embodying its research protocols in the novel. The novel's narrator self-consciously points this up when he says that he takes his epistemology from Cuvier. For this narrative undertaking, the narrator compares himself to an archeologist doing for society what the comparative anatomist does for nature: "Une mosaïque révèle toute une société comme un

10. Brock, *The Norton History of Chemistry*, 160–61.

squelette d'ichthyosaure sous-entend toute une création. De part et d'autre, tout se déduit, tout s'enchaîne. La cause fait deviner un effet, comme chaque effet permet de remonter à une cause" [A mosaic reveals an entire society just as the skeleton of an ichthyosaur presupposes an entire creation. In both realms all can be deduced, all is related. A cause allows one to guess an effect, just as each effect allows one to go back to a cause].[11] Balzac's narrator, perhaps not consciously echoing Laplace, invokes the principle of sufficient reason to explain his deductions about parts and the totality, for the epistemological principle that declares all has a cause underwrites the probability theory that is the basis for scientific rationality—including the reasoning behind such recently created taxa as the ichthyosaur. In Balzac's work causality also dovetails with probability theory to provide a model for aesthetic realism, since the narrator need only see what probability has produced to know what must be the case—and then proceed back to show what must be the causes. Through a slight of hand that Diderot's Jacques the fatalist would have approved, Balzac's narrator draws upon contemporary epistemology to justify his own procedures of representation.

As stated in the introduction, the development of realism is underwritten by the development of probability reasoning. Reasoning about the causes of events in a novel is analogous to reasoning from effects to probable causes (that form of probabilistic reasoning that led to the theory developed in Bayes's theorem about conditional probability). Probability theory underwrote a theory of rhetoric that could be used for writing fictions, for, in Laplace's terms, probability is the description of how psychological, as well as mathematical, certainty is induced, and the effect of certainty is what the rhetoric of realist fiction aims to create. In his *Essai philosophique sur les probabilités* (1814), Laplace is a conscious rhetorician when he claims that a *récit* or narration can always be constructed by probable reasoning from effects to causes, and that psychological certainty can be derived from a narrative line constructed by analogy with the probability of drawing lots. All this results in the assurance that the theory of probability is just common sense reduced to a calculus.[12] Conversely, this means that a calculus can be extended to a demonstration of common sense through narration. Laplace describes,

11. Balzac, *La Recherche de l'absolu*, 20. In his introduction to this edition, Raymond Abellio relates the novel to the development of science fiction.

12. Laplace, *Essai philosophique sur les probabilités*, 95.

really quite directly, how one can generate a narrative form, like a novel, narrating probable events.

Or, to reason like Cuvier and Balzac's narrator, what is the probability that a fossilized jaw bone belonged to a Marsupial species that is no longer extant in Europe? To make this kind of question into a generator of fictions entails that Balzac, as novelist, must link effects and causes, drawing upon effects that might plausibly be found before his narrator's eyes in the variegated undertakings of contemporary society. Here we see why the materialism of the Laplacian worldview is in fact the bedrock for Balzac's way of construing the arraignment of forces and probabilities in his realist works. The Balzacian realist narrator is often a version of the superior intelligence that Laplace placed at the center of the cosmos for the seizure of total knowledge. And if Balzac never challenges the theories of probability that found expression in Laplace's *Essai philosophique sur les probabilités,* this is because the Balzacian narrator implicitly, when not explicitly, appeals to Laplacian notions of probability to justify his knowledge of events and causes. From the perspective of Enlightenment mathematics, probability was a measure of ignorance of true causes. Conversely, the Balzacian narrator relies upon probability to establish the measure of his knowledge of the world. Balzac's narrator is not unlike the scientist whose impulse is to reduce the universe to a series of equations—working in effect toward the converse of a measure of ignorance. Given an "effect," the Balzacian narrator asks what probable causes can be adduced to explain, say, the presence of the "species" in question. The answer is a *récit,* to use Laplace's term, which is to say, a narration like *La Recherche de l'absolu* and all the other realist works that argue at once from the existence of the species back to probable causes and forward to the evolution of the type.

Balzac's chemist in *La Recherche de l'absolu,* Claes, is a type. Claes studied with Lavoisier, became a good father and respected citizen, and then neglected all his duties to pursue his passion for chemistry. If classified by nineteenth-century psychiatric nosology, he seems to be a monomaniac. Balzac introduces a bit of medical diagnosis to give an additional cachet of scientific authenticity to his character portrayal, though most monomaniacs did not pursue the absolute, and Balzac knows that the probable genesis of this type must be found in the historical context. The context is the scientific "mania" for knowledge that leads to the Faustian contract: Claes once met a Polish chemist who, Mephisto-like, awakened in Claes the epistemic mania that drives him beyond limits, to a death in which he "perhaps" found the key to the enigma of life: the absolute grasped by the bony fingers of Death.

Perhaps myth is always ready to invest realist narration. Especially when dealing with madness, reason seemingly must have recourse to myth, since myth is often the only means by which reason can represent its contrary, unreason or the irrational. In a sense, myth is the work of reason; indeed, it is an epistemic attempt to deal with what science cannot reduce to reason. In Balzac's novel, myth and a scientific hypothesis share common traits, or so it appears now that the nineteenth-century hypothesis about an absolute substance no longer has any currency as a theory. From today's perspective the absolute functioned as a myth, but it also generated theory. The hypothetical absolute is, in the Polish chemist's words, a substance common to all creations, modified by a unique force, though this unique force gives rise immediately to a mysterious "ternary"—the triadic substance Balzac saw characterizing everything from alchemy to Christianity. With his hypothesis about an absolute substance, Balzac's Claes joins in fact the post-Kantian search for what Kant said could never be known, the ultimate *Ding an sich*. Claes is seeking the ultimate inner substance behind all the variegated phenomenal manifestations that we can know, as subjects, looking at phenomenal objects unfolding in space and time. In this regard, romantic metaphysics and early nineteenth-century chemistry shared a common search.

Balzac wanted to foster this common search, since he thought that anti-Kantian metaphysics of the German sort should be melded with the positive sciences to produce the totalizing knowledge he sought. The recipe for this totalizing knowledge is expounded in Balzac's most explicitly "metascientific" novel, *Séraphita* (or *Séraphîta*, as this name is sometimes written). In this most theoretical of works, Balzac recast Swedenborgian cosmology to offer a critique of the claims of science, though a critique that should ultimately help science fulfill itself as a total explanation of the universe. *Séraphita* can be called a "mystical" novel, for the main character is an androgynous angel who reasons, however, more like an epistemologist than a seraphic being capable of revealing the hidden Kantian noumena. Religion is a matter of faith, s/he says, and, with that, s/he maintains that the question of religion, in epistemic terms, has been settled (which was Balzac's personal position in his letter to Nodier, as well as in his correspondence to Madame Hanska). However, Sériphita, like Balzac, also wants to show the inadequacies of any system of thought that might propose to replace religion, and by system of thought s/he especially has in mind the religion of science or reason that recent French history had elevated to a supreme position. S/he proposes, *al contrario,* the use of "mystical science" to complete the truncated knowledge proposed by unbelieving Parisian scientists (as Balzac also puts it in the *Préface du livre mystique*). It is dubious that, after the positivist revolution of the midcentury, anyone could ever speak of mystical science again—except from the margins of culture. In 1830 the notion was still polemical, though clearly a notion on the wane. But, fearing no polemic, Balzac wants to show that there is an epistemic relation that can mediate between mystical vision and knowledge in some nearly Kantian sense (which Kant would of course have denied). The most appropriate speaker for this mixed mediation is the creation who unites all opposites, the beautiful Séraphita-Séraphitus, a pre–pre-Raphaelite angel dwelling in an imaginary Norway, in an icy soul-scape that resembles a landscape of contrasts such as the painter Caspar David Friedrich gave us in his towering projections of the inner world. But the flora and fauna contained in this imaginary world are "real"—much as we see in mystical landscapes in early Renaissance paintings in which we recognize European birds and plants inhabiting a mystical, imaginary Jerusalem. The real and the revealed should thus complete each other, much as should natural history and mystical cosmology—or so Balzac hoped.

Swedenborgian cosmology, as recast by Balzac and explained by the novel's skeptical pastor, is less impressive than Séraphita's critique of science. Through this angelic character and the critique that s/he elaborates, Balzac wants to carve out an epistemic space in which his novels can take their place with other discourses of knowledge. In this move toward self-reflexive justification, *Séraphita* is an apology for those novels in which Balzac offers mere "realist" knowledge of the world, novels in which, from *Le Père Goriot* (1834) to *La Cousine Bette* (1846), there occurs, to say the least, no revelation of mystical science. In these realist works, one finds only the relative knowledge of ordinary causes and effects. Ordinary realism, like ordinary science, as Séraphita puts it, is simply a description of the fallen world. Realism relies upon the "langage du monde temporel"—language of the world fallen into time—and knowledge given by this language, s/he says, can only produce sadness. Hence Séraphita's claim that science is a melancholy state of affairs: "la science attriste l'homme."[13] To work within the confines of Newtonian space and time is, to paraphrase Séraphita, to exclude oneself from the realm of love—which certainly is the case in most of Balzac's realist works. Portraying far more greed than love, these novels describe a fallen world resolutely within the confines of Newtonian space and time.

Séraphita is an epistemological angel, reconciling all scientific and philosophical contraries, for s/he has read Locke, Buffon, Laplace, and Balzac's other favored scientific sources. S/he needs little mystical illumination for the epistemic views s/he defends. Séraphita's critique of science appeals to Lockean nominalism to show that the Newtonian-Laplacian worldview must lead, if one is logical, to a belief in the existence of things beyond the world of mechanical philosophy. As s/he explains knowledge to Wildrid, the young man courting her feminine side, true vision must represent the effects of moral nature as well as those of physical nature in their common and unified appearance. Though s/he seems to refer to mystical vision, Séraphita's terminology is couched in terms of causality that appeal to probability theory. Actually, s/he is more Laplacian than Laplace, since s/he claims that s/he carries within a mirror in which moral nature is reflected with all its causes and effects ["Eh bien, il est en moi comme un miroir où vient se réfléchir la nature morale avec ses causes et ses effets"] (795). In effect, s/he applies, like Laplace's hypothetical total observer, the principle of sufficient reason to all the phenomena in the universe, moral as well as physical. Since all has a cause, s/he sees that nothing is uncertain: past and present are present to the observer's eyes. Going beyond Laplace, s/he extends this abolition of uncertainty to the moral world, proposing thus to realize the Enlightenment's fondest hope of uniting moral and physical sciences—a project that theoretically, if not actually, underwrites Balzac's intentions for *La Comédie humaine*.

Séraphita wants to use science to combat the singleminded materialism and skeptical doubt that s/he finds characterizing the modern scientific mind (though s/he also is quite hostile to traditional theology). As a chemist and physicist, s/he defends the waning doctrine of imponderable forces in order to explain human thought on the model of

13. Balzac, *La Comédie humaine*, ed. Castex, vol. 11, 781.

magnetism. Magnetic force was construed as an imponderable substance united to a material body, and so, by analogy, one could argue
that immaterial thought is attached to the human body. As an epistemologist, s/he also claims that science's faith in mathematics shows that
even the most resolute materialists are willing to believe in abstractions—such as the infinite. Why then, s/he asks, do they doubt other abstractions, such as God, abstractions that exist, like the infinite, beyond
their comprehension?

Balzac is endorsing here a kind of Pythagorean philosophy of mathematics to maintain that Number, the source of the mathematics used to
describe time and space, is beyond knowledge and hence an object of
faith. Balzac's grasp of the infinite is not beside the point, since most
pre-Cantorian mathematicians readily admitted that the infinite was a
necessary concept, but not a comprehensible one. (The greatest mathematician of the early nineteenth century, Gauss, doubted that one could
speak of an actual infinite.) Moreover, Balzac's thirst for the unity of
knowledge must posit something like God, for, from the perspective of
this mathematical mysticism, God is the principle of unity that necessarily engenders the multiple. Using this kind of mathematical reasoning, Séraphita says that the multiple is derived from unity through
movement (819). And since number and movement are the basis for science and knowledge, one must conclude that Newtonian dynamics is in
some sense mystically grounded. Whether this theory can justify a leap
of faith is questionable, but it is of the greatest interest that Balzac wants
to demonstrate here that the crown of Newtonian physics—quantified
gravitational attraction and repulsion—can be used in all epistemic
quests, including the novel, once quantification is understood in analogical terms. And this generative principle implies that larger epistemic
ensembles—like a novel—may be more accurate than physics in its own
sphere. Or as Séraphita says with physics in mind: "Votre numération,
appliquée aux choses finies et non à l'Infini, est donc vraie par rapport
aux details que vous percevez, mais fausse par rapport à l'ensemble que
vous ne percevez point" [Your calculation, applied to finite things and
not to the infinite, is thus true relative to the details that you can perceive, but false relative to the totality that you cannot perceive] (820).
The totality is the backdrop that provides the criteria for truth and
knowledge, and this totality should thus be the ultimate object of
knowledge—at least when one is thinking like a physicist.

Thinking like a biologist, Balzac gives his nominalism expression in Séraphita's doubt about the possibility of quantification. This may seem contradictory in light of the above defense of totality, but let us consider what are the concepts that natural history, now becoming biology, imposes:

> Si la nature est semblable à elle-même dans les forces organisantes ou dans ses principes qui sont infinis, elle ne l'est jamais dans ses effets finis. Ainsi vous ne rencontrez nulle part dans la nature deux objets identiques: dans l'Ordre Naturel, deux et deux ne peuvent donc jamais faire quatre, car il faudrait assembler des unités exactement pareilles, et vous savez qu'il est impossible de trouver deux feuilles semblable sur un même arbre, ni deux sujets semblables dans la même espece d'arbre.

> [If nature is uniform in its organizing forces or in its principles that are infinite, it is never uniform in its finite effects. Thus you will never encounter anywhere in nature two identical objects: in the Natural Order, two and two can never be four, since one would have to bring together exactly similar unities, and you know that it is impossible to find two identical leaves on the same tree, or two identical examples of the same species of trees.] (820)

The doctrine of the absolute specificity of natural objects also holds for the moral world, says Séraphita, linking together once more, like Balzac's other post-Enlightenment narrators, the natural world and the human world. Séraphita's biological nominalism sounds somewhat backward looking, recalling the epistemology that led Buffon to deny any interest to Linnaeus's taxonomy. However, in claiming radical specificity for the individual, Séraphita's idea of privileging the individual also points toward the post-Darwinian thought about populations that modern evolutionary theorist Ernst Mayr has described. Such a privileging means that, for the naturalist and the novelist, knowledge demands the realization of a general taxonomy of the individual type. Balzac was convinced that this project could be realized in the novel through what he called, in his "Avant-Propos" of 1842 to *La Comédie humaine,* the description of the social species—by individualizing the type, and creating a type based on the individual.[14]

---

14. In his study of *Le Père Goriot,* Uwe Dethloff emphasizes the importance of the *Lettres à Madame Hanska* for understanding how Balzac viewed his work in this re-

Nominalism leads, moreover, to Séraphita's paradoxical denial that two plus two equals four. The naturalist in Séraphita denies the role of quantification in knowledge, at least as far as the individual is concerned. The description of an individual has the essential epistemic role, which in one sense denies that quantification is possible in every realm of knowledge, for one cannot simply add up unique individuals to have meaningful aggregates. Natural scientists were, and are, divided on the meaning of quantification, and I do not think any philosophically consistent explanation of what quantification is, or why it works, has yet been offered. In any case, in a context in which biology is defining itself as a science *not* based on physics, Balzac's epistemological angel knows well that her discourse will find acceptance among those for whom the basic unit of knowledge is the individual understood in its relation to the whole—such as for a naturalist like Geoffroy Saint-Hilaire, who maintained that connections or "analogies" exist among all vertebrates and perhaps invertebrate species.

Novels like *La Peau de chagrin* or *Séraphita* may be considered something like a preface to what most readers take to be Balzac's major achievement: the creation of a new type of realist novel. His early metascientific works, or the "philosophical" works if one prefers, are a complementary aspect of the totalizing that Balzac saw as his complete task as a novelist. Realism was conceived as a response to complete this totalizing, a totalizing that necessarily had to take account of the accomplishments of science. To this end Balzac created a type of novel that is largely consonant with the science of the early nineteenth century, which is to say that in his realist novels he created a novelistic form endowed with an epistemic dimension. The quest for the totalization of knowledge demanded that Balzac in fact call upon science for the epistemic coordinates for defining the real. In incorporating into fiction these coordinates—such as those of Newtonian cosmology and dynamics, the taxonomical understanding of biology, or then-nascent en-

---

gard. Dethloff quotes Balzac: "Aussi dans les Etudes de moeurs sont les individualités typisées; dans les Etudes philosophiques sont les types individualisés. Ainsi partout j'aurai donné la vie—au type, en l'individualisant, à l'individu en le typisant" [Thus in the Studies of mores are individuals typed, and in the Philosophical studies are types individualized. So everywhere I will have reproduced life—in the type by individualizing it, in the individual by making a type of it]. See Uwe Dethloff, *Balzac: "Le Père Goriot": Honoré de Balzacs Gesellschaftsdarstellung im Kontext der Realismus Debatte*, 37.

ergetics—Balzac made the scientific understanding of reality a ground for the practice of fiction. In brief, Balzac's use of science to define the real was part of a programmatic effort to demonstrate that the novel as a genre can propose knowledge. Balzac's enthusiasm for his own research program may seem dated today, but it seems incontrovertible that, with this program, the novel became an instrument for defining the real—an instrument that even some of today's postmoderns still respect whenever they acknowledge that the novel offers access to, and hence knowledge of, reality that no other discourse offers.

Balzac published *Séraphita* in the same year as *Le Père Goriot* (translated sometimes as *Old Goriot*). For many generations of readers, it is of course *Le Père Goriot* that represents, to the extent any single work can, the novel that invents the axioms for the modern novel. Coming after Balzac's metascientific works, *Le Père Goriot* is, perhaps with *Eugenie Grandet* (1833), a test case for his desire to rival science by offering knowledge of human society now conceived as a branch of natural history. But the novel also reflects an understanding of basic physics and dynamics. Balzac's use of the novel for purposes of epistemic investigation means that a full reading of a realist novel like *Le Père Goriot* must be attentive to the several epistemic discourses Balzac calls up, combines, and juxtaposes to produce what aims at being the unique exemplar of a partial totalization of reality. In the interest of clarity, then, let me offer a brief recapitulation of the epistemic frameworks presupposed by Balzac's realist works before turning specifically to *Le Père Goriot*.

Newtonian dynamics was still the dominant science in the 1830s, and it is hardly surprising that Balzac respects a Newtonian framework to frame the configuration of forces present in the novel. In the broadest sense, the framework is set up by the parameters of public space and time within which one can plot out the movement of the characters as so many bodies in motion. Within this framework Balzac takes into account the evidential probabilities determining the possibility of events. Of some historical interest is Balzac's frequent suggestion that the chemistry of imponderable substances might explain the human consciousness portrayed in the novel. Far more important, however, is the attention Balzac gives to types or species as they are shaped by a historically determined milieu to which these human types struggle to adapt. As a naturalist observer, Balzac was keenly aware of the way species do or do not adapt to their milieu, a milieu undergoing constant modification in time. The possible and probable extinction of types is a recurrent theme in Balzac's work. (For example, in *Le Père Goriot* survival is a leitmotif in the consciousness of a survival artist like Vautrin or an *arriviste* aristocrat like Rastignac.) Cuvier's vision of successive extinctions is an accepted fact for Balzac's natural history of the human animal.

Balzac scholar Madelaine Fargeaud-Ambrière even speaks of the mathematics of Balzac's science.[15] By this comment, I understand that, in Balzac's post-Enlightenment mind, much that he describes should be amenable, theoretically at least, to some potential Laplacian quantification—which throws light on a good many of Balzac's analogies. This attraction to mathematics brings up an interesting caveat about epistemic paradox when reading Balzac. In spite of Séraphita's paradox, Balzac could hardly deny the epistemic power of mathematical discourse. When thinking as a social physicist, neither Balzac nor his angel could deny, on its own terms, the Laplacian belief in the finality of mathematical explanation. Only when thinking as a biologist or historian does Balzac push forward the recognition that the historization of knowledge entails the rejection of the epistemic primacy of the quantification of experience. Historical knowledge is of a different order of being from mechanical or systemic quantification, a fact to which history and nascent sciences like evolutionary biology, paleontology, and geology have all attested. Balzac, moreover, often seems to want to combine metaphorical quantification and a description of the unique history of a living being. Such contradictory tensions underlie what can appear to be a paradox involved in the attempt of Balzac's realism to seize individual types. These tensions generated by apparent paradox—that an individual can be a type—point up how directly Balzac was enmeshed in the epistemological debates of nascent scientific modernity. True, the paradox later finds a solution in Darwin, in a theory that allows individual difference to generate changes in populations, but that lessens none of the interest one takes in Balzac's attempt to represent the relation between a type and his truly individualized characters.

15. Fargeaud-Ambrière, "Balzac, Homme de science(s)," in *Balzac, l'invention du roman*, ed. Claude Duchet, 54. Fargeaud-Ambrière has done much useful work on Balzac and science. In addition to the many other scholars I have used here—Pierre Barbéris, Philippe Bertault, Albert Béguin, Geneviève Delattre, Ernst Robert Curtius, etc.—I call attention here to two especially useful books on questions of Balzac and science: Moise Le Yaquanc, *Nosographie de l'humanité balzacienne*, and Per Nykrog, *La Pensée de Balzac dans "La Comédie Humaine."*

Balzac theorized his views about type and individual in his novels, some ten years after *Séraphita,* in 1842 when he wrote the "Avant-Propos" to *La Comédie humaine.* This document is of first-rate intellectual interest for what it tells us about Balzac's conception of his work's relation to science. Unabashedly explaining his competence to rival biology, he spells out in this forward how he could apply Geoffroy Saint-Hilaire's notion of the "unity of plan" of natural beings to his literary work, since "There is only one animal. The creator having used only one and the same pattern for all organized beings."[16] Saluting Geoffroy Saint-Hilaire as the victor over Cuvier on this point, Balzac goes on to explain that differences in form are due to the milieu in which the species develops, and, most importantly, society is the milieu that creates the specific differences that constitute the various "species" of humanity. Using the technical term *milieu,* Balzac links his writing here with the epistemic project of Geoffroy Saint-Hilaire and implicitly with Lamarck, and more distantly with Buffon—for he claims to have understood that society resembles nature before knowing about the debates that culminated in the polemic of 1830. The separation of nature and culture that Rousseau had proclaimed is in effect dismissed by Balzac, since society functions as a natural milieu in which adaptation leads to new species.

In his "Avant-Propos," Balzac not only plays with the idea that the notion of species, as used by natural history, can be applied to society since one finds there "social species." He also resolutely endorses the transformationist view that allows types or species to change—in Balzac's world, grocers can become peers of the realm. Balzac is thus claiming for fiction the capacity to participate in the great taxonomic endeavors that, from Linnaeus to Cuvier, were mapping the natural world. Moreover, what was (and is) a hypothesis for the natural world—the transformationist origins of species—is more of a demonstrable fact in the social world: transformations of society exist as documented history. The recent work of a historical novelist like Scott, Balzac suggests, demonstrates that the historical dimension of knowledge can be fully incorporated in the novel through its investigation of transformations of the social milieu.

What is innovative in Balzac is that he is writing a discourse in which

16. Balzac, *La Comédie humaine,* ed. Castex, vol. 1, 8.

human beings are squarely recognized as part of the animal kingdom. In other words, there is no ontological break between the natural realm and the social realm. Even the most atheistic philosophers of the Enlightenment had not usually been ready to embrace such a complete naturalism—say, the atheistic doctor La Mettrie who, in describing "machine man," still wanted to consider "man" the pinnacle of creation. In spite of his atheistic belief in mechanical physiology, La Mettrie unwittingly slipped God back into the human machine when he proclaimed that humans have a unique capacity for language—in the form of that logos that is the *arche* of theology. By contrast, the more or less Christian Balzac depicts, in *Le Père Goriot* and many later novels, a world in which human beings belong to Cuvier's *embranchement* of vertebrate beings. They share the analogies that Geoffroy described as characterizing all other animals, for humans and animals are all zoological beings differentiated in terms of a common plan that unites them in what biologists today call homologies. Their "morphology"—to use the term Goethe had recently invented—is shaped, moreover, by the natural forces of the milieu Balzac studies with such great detail. And finally, Balzac's fiction coincides with nascent biology in his search for the type, or the singular, real specimen that is the basis for the naturalist's creation of a taxon—something like what later biology came to call the holotype, the single specimen chosen to be an exemplar for a new species. Balzac clearly believed that the ontology of fiction and of natural history coincide in this epistemological quest for the unique individual that is nonetheless the type for a species.

Such types are found in the realist works like *Le Père Goriot*. Dedicated to Geoffroy Saint-Hilaire, though several years after its original publication in 1835, this realistic novel might be taken as the antithesis of *Séraphita*. It contains no fantastic elements, no androgynous angels making metascientific perorations. Moreover, it contains hardly any metascientific discourses justifying the unitary materialism Balzac thought would explain mental and physical phenomena. The novel simply demonstrates that unitary materialism, and thus contains nothing that the atheistic scientific community could not accept. It is a novel rigorously situated in the here and now of physical space, an ordinary epistemic space, open to every investigator interested in the quotidian. The novel's title outlines its limited subject matter, relating the demise of a single human being, in this case, a once prosperous pasta manufacturer who allows himself to be exploited by his two greedy and vain daughters. Balzac could not limit himself to a single case study, and the work does introduce other major characters, such as Rastignac, a prototypical impoverished member of the provincial nobility whose education takes up much of the novel. This education consists largely in discovering the unscrupulous nature of the struggle necessary to succeed in a world in which, as old Goriot says, money is life. Another important character is the unscrupulous swindler and convict Vautrin, a philosophical villain whose cynicism is almost unbearable. These characters recur in other novels, though the recurrence of characters is of lesser interest than the way Balzac invented, in these characters, the individual type.

The novel is constructed to elicit knowledge about these types and the milieu in which they have developed. Though composed of four titled sections, the structure of *Le Père Goriot* can be divided into three parts. In the first section, the introduction, Balzac's narrator describes the milieu, set in Paris, that is first centered on the Vauquer boarding house. The narrator begins by framing a series of questions that are so many requests for knowledge. This section sets out an epistemic demand for answers that can elucidate these implicit and explicit questions. The novel's second part, comprising the sections called "L'Entrée dans le monde" and "Trompe-la-mort," answer these questions by tracing out the trajectories of the characters encountered in the boarding house in which the questions were first generated. Answers to these questions take the reader into other milieux, most notably that of the hereditary aristocracy and the newly created aristocracy of the moneyed elite. The final structural movement coincides with the last named section, "La mort du père." This section works out, with geometrical precision, the final movement leading to the father's demise—emptied of all force and all his wealth—and traces the general geometry of rising and falling that the various characters undergo in struggling in a milieu in which only the crassest instincts have survival value. Most notably, the young pauper aristocrat, Rastignac, discovers that his ascension has only begun.

In *Le Père Goriot*, the narrator offers a plot organized as so many microsequences. These sequences are narrated in response to a desire for knowledge that might explain various puzzles and enigmas brought about when an observer looks at the world. Balzac begins the novel, for instance, with the famous demonstration of how one goes about describing a social milieu with his depiction of the Vauquer boarding house. The narrator proposes a model of homological description in which, as he puts it, the character of the landlady explains the boarding house, and the boarding house implies the existence of the landlady. Typed as resembling all women who have known misfortune, Madame Vauquer is nonetheless an individual specimen. She has adapted to the milieu that has shaped her: "L'embonpoint blafard de cette petite femme est le produit de cette vie, comme le typhus est la conséquence des exhalaisons d'un hôpital" [The pale portliness of this little woman is the product of this life, just as typhus is the result of the exhalations of a hospital].[17] Mixing medical discourse and natural history, the narrator invents a composite epistemic discourse that wants to explain type, milieu, and phenotype through their interaction.

Metaphorically at least, the narrator is a natural historian when he explains why most of the boarders cannot answer the questions raised by father Goriot's curious presence in the boarding house: "Les vieilles gens dont la curiosité s'éveilla sur son compte ne sortaient pas du quartier et vivaient dans la pension comme des huîtres sur un rocher" [The old people whose curiosity was awakened by him never left the neighborhood and lived in the boarding house like oysters on a rock] (54). These mollusk-like characters do, however, have epistemic desires and can want to know. For example, characters invent explanations of Goriot's presence in the boarding house so that finally Goriot is typed— wrongly—by an employee of the natural history museum as "un colimaçon, un mollusque anthropomorphe à classer dans les *Casquettifères*" [a snail, an anthropomorphic mollusk to be classified among the *Casquettiferous*] (55). Balzac's playful invention of taxonomy shows the distance he can take vis-à-vis the scientific discourse that he adopts at the same time he satirizes it. There is something intrinsically comic about the fact that this Parisian biotope is also the biotope to which must adapt the scientists who produce the concepts that should describe the scientists who live in it, in Paris, that unique milieu for *homo scientificus*.

Buoyed by these epistemic explanations, plot is generated by the narrator's playing with the readers' probabilistic expectations. Opening *Le Père Goriot*, a knowledgeable reader automatically questions the proba-

---

17. Balzac, *Le Père Goriot*, 29. This edition has a useful preface by Félicien Marceau.

bility of finding a rich old man, one moreover visited by two beautiful young women, in a less than elegant boarding house. To explain his presence, and even more so that of two beautiful young women, probability theory demands that one be able inductively to offer probable causes for these seemingly improbable events. The entire novel is, in this regard, a kind of inductive demonstration of probable causes. Few earlier novels rely so overtly upon inductive strategies to motivate narration (except parodistically in works by those writers like the Diderot and Sterne to whom Balzac duly pays homage). Balzac's strategy in creating plot is not to use "suspense"—that baroque device that poses an enigma or problem to be resolved and then titillates the reader by keeping the resolution at bay. Rather, Balzac's narrator sets out his inquiry as one that is to be solved by ferreting out probabilistic causes—and this inquiry in turn becomes an education for Rastignac as the young noble undertakes the quest that gives the data needed to elucidate the mystery. In his need to survive, if not to conquer, Rastignac is an epistemic quester possessed by a "furieuse envie de savoir la vérité"—a furious desire to know the truth (75).

Rastignac has to know the nature of the milieu to which he must adapt, and, in seeking this knowledge, he discovers what will best facilitate his quest: a knowledge of probabilities is necessary for survival. Like a Dante with a perverse Virgil, Rastignac has been preceded on this quest by the criminal Vautrin, the savant who already knows the milieu and how it can destroy those who don't know it. The notion of milieu here acquires the biological sense of an environment to which specific species adapt. The milieu found in the natural history incorporated in the novel is quite precisely a *bourbier,* or a mire, in which, as the ever knowledgeable Vautrin says, those who get filthy while in a coach are honest people, whereas those who get filthy on foot are scoundrels (76). Vautrin's quick lesson in basic social taxonomy is the best preparation that Rastignac receives to acquaint himself with the milieu frequented by the elegant women, whom one would normally not expect to be connected to old Goriot. But plot unfolds and demonstrates that the improbable can be shown to be probable, and that the complex workings of the milieu make these relations possible. Beautiful aristocratic women can frequent a run-down boarding house when they are exploiting a father who lets himself be bled by them.

Motivated first by the desire for knowledge, Rastignac finds that his desire transforms itself into a desire for what knowledge and power can obtain. Rastignac is set on a trajectory that, in terms of narrative geometry, aims at ascension. In Balzac's work, ascension describes metaphorically a successful quest, in conventional terms, but it also figures the expenditure of force. As Newton teaches, to rise is to exert force against opposing forces as dynamics. Rastignac's quest for knowledge and for social success is threatened by his own contradictory desires and the force they demand. Or perhaps one might say that he wants to catapult himself up by using contradictory forces for which there is no vector resolution. Balzac uses a mathematical image to describe the threat to Rastignac's ascension: "Rastignac résolut d'ouvrir deux tranchées parallèles pour arriver à la fortune, de s'appuyer sur la science et sur l'amour, d'être un savant docteur et un homme à la mode. Il était encore bien enfant! Ces deux lignes sont des asymptotes qui ne peuvent jamais se joindre" [Rastignac resolved to open two parallel trenches in order to pursue his fortune, he would rely upon science and love, he would be a savant doctor and a man of fashion. How childish he still was! These two lines are asymptotes that can never join up with each other] (118). By dispersing his energy along two asymptotic lines, his twin projects will not come together like intersecting lines. Each project would be like a straight line approaching the tangent of a curve, coming closer and closer to the points of the curve as it approaches infinity, but never reaching it. This is an analogy Balzac uses several times in his work. Desire is geometricized as an infinite undertaking. And it can never join the trajectory of force moving knowledge, since knowledge follows a different, Faustian line, one also moving like an asymptote toward the infinite. Behind these metaphors stand undoubtedly Fichte's thoughts on the infinite as the object of all human quest. (Balzac recommended Fichte to Nodier with enthusiasm.) But we also recognize here Balzac's concept of energy and his attempt to plot the vectors in the expenditure of energy.

Balzac is romantic in many respects, and in this regard we might speak of romantic physics: desire and knowledge can be represented as vectors of a potentially infinite expenditure of energy, to use a technical concept not yet available to Balzac. Desire and knowledge cannot be reconciled, since the infinite is incomprehensible, and perhaps they can never even be realized. What could it mean to find an infinite force to motivate them? In *Séraphita* the infinite confounds knowledge by imposing upon knowledge a recognition of its limits. Perhaps like desire, knowledge is condemned to failure, for there can be no infinite expenditure of energy in the service of either. Just as the engineer Carnot relied upon the axiom that there can be no perpetual motion machine to demonstrate the nature of the expenditure of energy, so Balzac accepts as axiomatic that all energy is limited, and thus knowledge and desire are limited. The finite nature of energy sets the limits of reality. This is a bedrock axiom of realism, for Balzac and for today.

Mathematics is a frequent source for the figures and images that stage Balzac's world for epistemic purposes. Mathematical metaphors work well for the geometry figuring desire and the plot that results from it. However, Balzac's desire for quantification is sometimes contradictory, for the historical knowledge that underwrites the Balzacian novel is not amenable to the application of mechanical dynamics. In spite of his own historicizing of knowledge, Balzac, like a literary Laplace in quest of totalization, accepts the a priori possibility that most experience could conceivably be measured and quantified in some sense. This belief surfaces throughout the realist novels, as in the following passage in which a Newtonian concept of force is combined with a belief in the materiality of an imponderable such as human thought. Passages such as these present not just metaphorical fioriture, but sum up Balzac's somewhat contradictory worldview about a possible quantification, if not an exact vector sum, of all the forces in the world: "Pendant ces huit jours Eugène et Vautrin étaient restés silencieusement en présence et s'observaient l'un l'autre. L'étudiant se demandait vainement pourquoi. Sans doute les idées se projettent en raison directe de la force avec laquelle elles se conçoivent, et vont frapper là où le cerveau les envoie, par une loi mathématique comparable à celle qui dirige les bombes au sortir du mortier" [During those eight days Eugene and Vautrin had remained silently in each other's presence as they observed each other. The student wondered in vain why. Probably ideas are projected forward in direct proportion to the force that conceives them and go to strike where the brain sends them, according to a mathematical law comparable to the one that directs shells when they are shot from a mortar] (139). Like Goethe experimenting with the chemical notion of elective affinities, Balzac is trying here to conceive something like an algorithm to express the interaction between character types as they engage in their struggle for mastery. The image of the cannon shot is of course a metaphor of struggle and combat, but the metaphorical quantification of struggle is part of the attempt to measure ineffable or imponderable substances—like human thought or, equally as interesting, force and power. From a broader historical perspective, the attempt to understand force has been part of the larger European quest for rationality since Machiavelli as well as Galileo. Beginning with these thinkers evolved the idea that power and force, in their respective domains, are ultimate realities behind all phenomena. Balzac brings to the novel an epistemic concern in which the metaphorical notion of power links up with the non-metaphorical use of force as a way of defining the real, for the notion of force can be used for a quantitative expression of individual relations in the material world. Marx was not wrong in his judgment that Balzac, for all his contradictions, is more in contact with historical reality than any other novelist in the first half of the nineteenth century: Balzac well understood that the multifaceted concept of force was a notion that provides for a definition of the real in diverse contexts. Marx wanted to do the same thing for the "forces" of history (though by the end of the century Hertz thought that force had been so overextended as a concept that it should be banished as a foundational concept in physics).

Balzac's attempt to understand force underlies the development of the narratives in his novels. Larger narrative patterns are motivated by Balzac's desire to link dynamics to the unfolding of events. Each character is pushed forward by his or her energy, pursuing a trajectory that unfolds in terms of sequential events. Balzac's understanding of force is in this regard modern: force is a vector with both magnitude and direction (I say modern because the vector notion is only implicit in Newton's earlier definition of force). For example, in *Le Père Goriot,* Goriot himself follows a line of development that ends in a depleted state of energy—to use a concept that, I recall, was being invented as Balzac wrote the novel. By contrast, the vector of a character's development can take an upward movement, as in the case of Rastignac, and perhaps Goriot's ambitious daughter Delphine. But Goriot's trajectory is most clear: once he has given up every material possession that could benefit his daughters, once all his energy is expended, he dies. With no money, he has no energy, for money, by his own definition, is the essential force in this milieu. Another nascent capitalist, the criminal Vautrin is at least momentarily stopped in his trajectory, since the opposing force of the police neutralize his upward ascension and prevent him from becoming a rich slave owner in the United States. He is literally and figuratively arrested in his ascension in *Le Père Goriot*.

Goriot's daughters are threatened with a fall once the force propelling them is met by a counterforce. At the novel's end, when neither daughter comes to her father's funeral, it is an open question as to whether they can continue upon their path in society. Rastignac's first move after the funeral is to accept the challenge of struggle among competing forces in society. He will remain Delphine's lover, which suggests that, whatever be the outcome of his struggle, he believes he can gain a boost in force by attaching his trajectory to hers. By contrast, the failure of the force of desire is clearly illustrated in the moving example of Rastignac's cousin, Madame de Beauséant. Upon being betrayed by her lover, who prefers a rich marriage to fidelity, she decides to spend the rest of her life in seclusion. Her choice to abandon society for "exile" in Normandy is equivalent to expending one's force. There is a rich overdetermination to these trajectories: Madame de Beauséant's move reflects at once the classical moralist's belief in the ravages of passion and the modern epistemologist's view that all conflicting forces must eventuate in a vector resolution in which weaker forces are annulled and absorbed by greater powers.

In résumé, then, what strikes the literary historian upon considering Balzac's tempestuous encounter with science is the way in which he naturalizes Laplace's physics and probability theory. He embodies theory in the fabric of his novels in ways that had not occurred in literature before. Linear dynamics and the calculus of probability are intrinsic to the figuring of experience in Balzac, for events are determined in terms of vector relationships that link up as causal chains. Finally, in Balzac's realist work we find a world of probable forces unfolding causally in terms of the materialism that Marx, among others, wanted to make into the hallmark of historical totalization.

To conclude these considerations, let me adduce another example of the way in which Balzac's energetics is the basis for his realistic plot development, especially with regard to how his characters interact in a determined milieu. Balzac often conceived of the milieu as a closed system in which each character's force can only be augmented or diminished by clashes with other characters to whom energy is transferred or from whom it is extracted. In their own way, works like *La Peau de chagrin* and *La Recherche de l'absolu* illustrate this principle, though an even more pointed example of contrasting vectors can be found in a realist work like *Le Curé de Tours* (The curate of Tours, though, curiously, the title is left in French for the one translation I have found). Energetics is placed in the foreground in this novel narrating a struggle for power between two priests, albeit one of the priests is too naive to be aware that a struggle is taking place. The central character is a curate, Father Birotteau, who does not realize he is being dispossessed by Troubert, an ambitious priest who desires to ascend in the church hierarchy. The ascent of the power-obsessed, yet ascetic Troubert is exactly balanced by the decline and fall of the hedonist, though well-intentioned curate Birotteau. In his ascent, Troubert strips Birotteau of all his possessions, deprives him of all resources, and leaves the poor priest at the end of the novel exiled, across the river from Tours, in a village. From this vantage point the once happy Birotteau is reduced to contemplating in anguish his beloved cathedral, now seen in the distance, as upwardly rising Troubert leaves to occupy a bishopric. The gain and loss of energy is symmetrical. One priest is empowered to move up to become a bishop, and the other loses all energy to end disenfranchised in exile. Or to express this movement in terms of more classical dynamics, the chiasmatic resolution of forces follows rigorous geometry: Troubert's ascension is proportional to Birotteau's decline. And in the most palpable realist terms, the transfer of power as energy can be measured by the loss of possessions, of place, and even of flesh. The once portly priest Birotteau becomes sickly and emaciated after he loses his position and possessions. With no energy, bereft of all force, he collapses immobile in his exile.

Newton knew that he had not explained motion, that he had simply described it in quantified terms as a product of forces that are amenable to public purview. At times a literary Newtonian, Balzac also believed that motion remained the great material mystery. He intuitively sensed that something like the concept of energy would remove some of the mystery. His own vector geometries show that he conceived of the energy available in the social milieu to be finite, mobile, and subject to transfer. In this sense he seems to be groping, like Carnot and others at the time, for a theory to explain force and movement. With these themes in mind I want to conclude with a bit of speculation. I recall that Carnot was working out, in the 1820s, the principles that would later be the basis for the laws of thermodynamics, for entropy and the conservation of energy. Although Balzac probably did not know that Carnot had published the beginnings of a theory of thermodynamics in 1824 in a small book called *Reflexions sur la puissance motrice du feu* (*Reflections on the Motive Power of Fire*), it is clear that Balzac shared the same concern about energy that, in Carnot's work, was leading toward a kinetic theory of heat and energy. In his encounter with the science of his time, in his desire to compete with science on its own terrain, Balzac applied a concept something like energy to character development, an application that is fundamental to the development of the novel. In this sense it seems justified to compare Balzac's development of literary form with the development of Carnot's work in thermodynamics. One led to literary realism and the novel as we understand it; the other led to the second law of thermodynamics and the concept of entropy, breaking the visegrip of mechanistic philosophy.

Of course, neither Balzac nor Carnot are a permanent stopping point in our intellectual history. A generation after Carnot's death, the first law of thermodynamics reformulated his work in the principle of the conservation of energy. But the second law of thermodynamics then proposed that this energy, in its distribution, would tend toward equal distribution, and hence all things would run down. The process of time is the inevitable increase of disorder. This interpretation meant the end of the reign of classical dynamics and its laws of equilibrium, for the order of the world, once seen as based on synchronic processes, must have an inevitable historical dimension. Or as Cecil J. Schneer puts it in his classic *The Evolution of Physical Science*, "Processes, even mechanical processes, were now seen to change with time. There was an evolution, not merely to living things as Darwin had asserted, but even to the inorganic world."[18] After Balzac and Carnot, the next generation formulated that entropy, a measure of unavailable energy, is the most probable process of any system.

With the understanding that entropy is also a measure of the necessary dissolution of energy, the nineteenth century's project of epistemic totalization came to an end, for the concept of entropy undermines the very idea of the closed system, with that fixed totalization of which Laplace, Hegel, and Balzac had dreamed. Any system is necessarily an open system, evolving through time, as energy is displaced. Totalization is irrelevant for describing those random entropic processes by which

18. Schneer, *Evolution of Physical Science*, 202.

the lowest level of energy of a system is in the long run the most probable. So Balzac's energetics is homologous to an early stage in the development of the concept of energy, when one thought as much in terms of forces as in terms of energy. What Balzac developed was the idea that the vector array of forces, describing the way in which the powerful were rapaciously destroying the weak, was as evident as the earth's attraction to the sun. This naturalizing of social forces in the Balzacian novel makes of Balzac one of the great contributors to knowledge in the nineteenth century.

THREE

Flaubert and the Ambiguous Victory of Positivism

L'esthétique attend son Geoffroy Saint-Hilaire, ce
grand homme qui a montré la légitimité des monstres
. . .

*[Aesthetics is waiting for its Geoffroy Saint-Hilaire, that
great man who justified our interest in monsters . . .]*

—Flaubert to Louis Colet, October 12, 1853

HISTORICAL OVERVIEW

1821: Flaubert born. Amici working on achromatic microscope.

1822: Magendie confirms Bell's work on nerves by showing that spinal nerves have separate paths controlling movement and sensation.

1826: Comte begins his *Cours de philosophie positive,* mainly published 1830 to 1841, a work crowning humanity's coming of age with the age of science.

1826: Baer studies follicles and discovers the mammalian ovum.

1830: Lyell's *Principles of Geology* sets forth the principle of uniformitarianism, the doctrine that geological change occurs slowly according to long-lasting processes.

1833: Müller begins publishing his *Handbuch der Physiologie des Menschen,* confirming each nerve responds to a stimulus in a specific way and suggesting that human beings perceive only the effects of their sensory systems.

1835: Dumas appointed to position at the École Polytechnique where he develops his theory that organic compounds exist as types.

1839: Schwann, working with the botanist Schleiden, lectures on cellular theory in research on microscopic structures of animals and plants.

1841: Remak describes cell division and works throughout decade, with Müller, to develop modern embryology.

1850: Helmholtz, studying physiological optics and color vision, invents the ophthalmoscope, this after formulating the first concise law of the conservation of energy in 1847.

1855: For work on gastric juices and hormonal functions, physiologist Bernard takes Magendie's position at the Collège de France.

1857: Flaubert publishes *Madame Bovary*; Baudelaire, *Les Fleurs du mal.*

1858: Following Schwann, Virchow decrees every cell is derived from a preexisting cell and says that disease originates in single cells, thus founding cellular pathology.

1859: Darwin publishes *The Origin of the Species by Means of Natural Selection.*

1865: Pasteur studies silkworm disease and conceives that microorganisms are agents of pathology. Bernard publishes *Introduction à la médicine expérimentale.*

1881: *Bouvard et Pécuchet* posthumously published.

It is a critical truism that Flaubert's work is fundamental in the development of the aesthetic goals of modern realism. Flaubert is undoubtedly the most important novelist for the development of the modern novel's rhetoric, especially in his use of indirect discourse and irony. In Balzac's wake, Flaubert is equally as important for his inscribing a rivalry with science into his work, though it is an indirect rivalry, one matching in subtlety the effects of his rhetoric. But the role that Flaubert's encounter with science played in developing modern realism has not been given due recognition: foremost among Flaubert's goals was the creation of a novelistic form that could offer revelation of essential kinds of knowledge that, from his viewpoint, could rival the truths science offers. This belief is more problematic for Flaubert than Balzac. Balzac thought he could put fictional discourse on a par with scientific discourse. He believed the novel could compete with science on science's own terrain. This was not such an obvious proposition for Flaubert. This doctor's son who became the patron saint of the modern novel was nearly overwhelmed by the claims of a triumphant, positivist science that believed it alone was destined to provide answers to all the meaningful questions humanity could ask. Flaubert was not altogether sure that science was wrong.

Flaubert's ambiguous sense about literature's relation to science is revealed, outside of his literary works, in comparisons he made in which he likened art to science, foreseeing that art would come more greatly to resemble science as art "perfected" itself.[1] The terms here suggest that Flaubert, at times, took science as the measure of progress and saw that literature needed to come up to these standards. One may suspect the presence of the paternal influence in these judgments. As his biographers often stress, Flaubert's boyhood milieu initiated him into science. However, his interest in science lasted all his life; Flaubert's correspondence reveals his unflagging interest in scientific matters. In his correspondence to George Sand, for instance, he showed his interest in modern biology. Flaubert found, he said, that Haeckel makes Darwin clearer than Darwin himself does in his own works.[2] Like many up-to-date Europeans, Flaubert relied upon Haeckel, Darwin's indefatigable European champion, and Haeckel's interpretation of evolutionary theory, even after they had read Darwin. Other key sciences for Flaubert were of course medicine and physiology. His father and brother were both doctors—and his correspondence documents in rather amusing ways how he used his brother to garner information, say, for the operation on the clubfoot in *Madame Bovary*. Flaubert had friends among the scientific community, including, interestingly enough, the son of one of the last scientists to try to defend spontaneous generation against Pasteur. In brief, Flaubert was constantly in contact with science, both as an omnivorous reader and through the cultural milieux he frequented in Normandy and Paris.

Only two of Flaubert's novels, *Madame Bovary* and *L'Education sentimentale,* have played an important role in shaping the rhetoric of mod-

1. See, for example, Flaubert quoted in René Descharmes, *Autour de "Bouvard et Pécuchet":* La littérature prendra, de plus en plus, les allures de la science.—Le grand Art est scientifique" [Literature will take on, more and more, the appearance of science.—Great art is scientific] (94). Writing in the 1920s, Descharmes, like many later modernist critics, apparently thought that, for Flaubert, this prediction merely meant that art should be impersonal.

2. Alphonse Jacobs, ed., *Gustave Flaubert-George Sand: Correspondance,* 474–75.

ern fiction. However, several of Flaubert's other works offer a full measure of how a defensive epistemic rivalry underpins his creativity. In this regard, rather eccentric works like *La Tentation de Saint Antoine* and *Bouvard et Pécuchet* present the contradictory scope of Flaubert's epistemic struggles, and perhaps failure, to make of literature a place of privileged knowledge that would not be beholden to medicine or physics. *La Tentation de Saint Antoine* is an allegory in which Flaubert seems to have wanted, at least when he first wrote it, to exorcise the temptations of science and knowledge. But in the final version he ended up affirming the power of science to replace religion with a microscope. It is, to be sure, one of the most bizarre works of the nineteenth century. In his last work, the unfinished *Bouvard et Pécuchet*, Flaubert used nearly Voltarian satire to neutralize the claims of any form of epistemic discourse. He undertook this paradoxical attack on knowledge by a dialectical demonstration of the futility of all epistemic discourse—though this project necessitated that he attempt to master all of science. Between these two works dealing explicitly with science and knowledge, Flaubert wrote the consummate realist novel, *Madame Bovary*. Or, more precisely, Flaubert began *La Tentation de Saint Antoine* before he wrote *Madame Bovary*, but finished it later, in 1874, before he began *Bouvard et Pécuchet*. I stress this chronology to point up the continuity of Flaubert's concern with epistemic issues, as well as the near impossibility of assigning any orderly development to it.

With this chronology in mind, I want to discuss the full scope of Flaubert's rivalry with science by first dealing with the two explicitly, if eccentrically, epistemic works. *La Tentation de Saint Antoine*, an allegory about knowledge and knowing, can open this discussion, since it presents Flaubert's first explicit confrontation with science; then we can turn to Flaubert's final statement in *Bouvard et Pécuchet*. This unfinished final novel sketches out Flaubert's encyclopedic solution to the challenge of finding the form for what appears to be the ultimate destruction of knowledge. In a farcical description of an epistemic quest, his last novel proposes a satire of knowledge by trying to incorporate all forms of knowledge into the novel itself. When set between the extravagant quest for knowledge portrayed in *La Tentation*, and the satirical destruction of knowledge in *Bouvard et Pécuchet*, *Madame Bovary* stands out as an extraordinarily inventive realist solution to the problems posed by the possibility of a fictional epistemic discourse when scientific positivism was increasingly triumphant. Published in 1857, *Madame Bovary* is consonant with the scientific and positive discourses of nineteenth-century France—though at the same time hesitatingly contestatory of positivist claims that only positive science can offer access to knowledge. In a sense, this novel rivals positivism by incorporating the positivist observer into the text. And by "positivism" I mean not only Auguste Comte's philosophy and his narrative about humanity's coming to epistemic maturity in the nineteenth century; I also mean the positive epistemology of medicine, physics, and chemistry, of which Claude Bernard's thought can be taken as representative. *Madame Bovary* illustrates that the novel can embody the determinism that positivist medicine declared to be a necessary condition for knowledge of the human condition. And so in *Madame Bovary* the experimental gaze of doctors like Magendie and his pupil Claude Bernard became the basis for the rhetoric of fiction. But let us first look at Flaubert's saint before dissecting his fallen woman.

Flaubert's *La Tentation de Saint Antoine* is closer to Goethe's second Faust than to any novel written after it. The work reflects Flaubert's confrontation with the biological and medical community, though it can also be read as Flaubert's vision of how historical science had brought about the death of the gods. The surrealist tapestry that this novel weaves, largely in dialogue, presents Saint Anthony in a fourth-century desert. Flaubert's original idea for the work was apparently inspired by a Brueghel painting in Genoa. However, the iconic springboard was not simply the excuse for a historical re-creation, such as in the case of a historical fiction like Flaubert's own *Salammbô*. One is hard pressed to see a historical creation in *La Tentation,* unless the exploration of a historical hallucination from within can be called a historical inquiry. In form, this novel is really closer to theater, the *Gesamttheater* of a Wagner, or, more precisely, the type of theater of the psyche Goethe created in *Faust* I and, especially, in *Faust* II. And if Flaubert worked on this psychic panorama off and on for all his life, one may suspect that it was because he, like many of his contemporaries, was subject to Goethe-envy.

Our earlier comments on Faust and Balzac point up that Goethe-envy is an aspect of epistemic rivalry that Flaubert was hardly alone to suffer. Sufferers thereof were legion. Goethe-envy is a syndrome that casts much light on the way the rivalry with science was experienced by nineteenth-century writers. Goethe's life and work presented that tantalizing Enlightenment example of a writer who could make original contributions to science and, from science, draw original inspiration for literature. Of course, it was easier to imitate Faust than Goethe himself, and so Goethe-envy can be described as a peculiar nineteenth-century syndrome that led writers to be vicarious epistemic questers in an imitation of knowledge-sated Faust, especially by incorporating the Faustian attitude toward knowledge into their works. The writer suffering Goethe-envy proclaimed a desire to master all of art and science. Then, having supposedly mastered all knowledge, with the supreme Faustian gesture the writer declared that he was beyond all striving for knowledge, for it had been a fruitless task. The epitome of this attitude is found in Mallarmé's opening line from "La Brise Marine": "La chair est triste, hélas! Et j'ai lu tous les livres" [The flesh is sad, alas! And I have read all the books].

In Faust was reflected an ideology, when not a philosophy, that permeated the positivistic nineteenth century. Faust is—to paraphrase the Rimbaud who brought the vision of Faust to a violent culmination—the supreme savant, or seeker of knowledge whose desire for *voyance* flounders on the impossibility of finding knowledge that could transfigure desire. Throughout the nineteenth century, moreover, the sober protocols of scientific methodology increasingly seemed remote from science's putative desire to master the infinite; this distinction was hardly lost on Flaubert, the creator of prosaic Charles and Emma Bovary. The positivist was quite attuned to how the overblown quest for the infinite invariably ends up in a tawdry drama of regret, tears, and suicide—the conclusion of *Madame Bovary* that indirectly mirrors the conclusion of Goethe's first *Faust*.

In *La Tentation de Saint Antoine,* Flaubert directly developed successive versions of his own *Faust*. His final version is one portraying, and perhaps affirming, the ideology of triumphant science. Part of this triumph was due to the development of archeological knowledge that had transformed the European understanding of history—and the history of knowledge—since Goethe had conceived his Faust. An appreciation of the feats accomplished by historical science underlie Flaubert's ambiguous attitudes toward science. Archeology had retrieved a historical past whose beliefs had been killed by the critical spirit animating this same science. Flaubert's ambivalence about this achievement permeates much of his work. Ambivalence aside, he had to rely upon modern critical history and archeology for the knowledge incorporated into his *Tentation,* a novel depicting, among other things, the proliferating doctrines of early Christianity. The novel's historical decor, set in a fourth century reconstructed by scientific inquiry, is the backdrop against which Flaubert dramatizes the supreme temptation, which, in this Alexandrian drama, is the temptation to know. With the advent of knowledge, as the Bible showed us even before modern archeology did, the illusions of innocence wither, for innocent belief cannot withstand the criticism of scientific knowledge. In this novel Flaubert seems at times wistful when recalling that, what Eve had begun, with her desire for knowledge, the Enlightenment had continued: the destruction of paradise. Flaubert is not gleeful about the fact that post-Voltarian modernity, and its application of science to everything, had brought about the death of those desert gods who once protected humanity as it wandered in ragged ignorance.

Flaubert's Saint Anthony wanders alone in the desert, trying to avoid the usual temptations and remain ignorant while meditating on his past accomplishments. His mind is nonetheless full of the competing discourses that, in his century, claim to grant knowledge of the world. At the end of the novel's first section he undergoes a hallucination, one originating, we are told, in the saint's epigastric region. This ironic nod to classical medical theory borrows from Van Helmont's vitalist theory, according to which the archea or life force is lodged in the epigastrium (a doctrine that Balzac also treated with heavy hand in *La Peau de chagrin*). To describe "medically" the saint's madness, Flaubert inscribes a traditional medical analysis into his text, though it is an anachronism that Flaubert uses ironically, perhaps directed against his own temptation to believe that physiology can describe the mind's functioning. This and other allusions to the history of medical doctrines also show, with ambivalent irony, that the historical mind can recuperate all previous scientific theories as so many fantastic hypotheses demonstrating the historicity of knowledge. It requires then only one more ironic step to conclude that these past hypotheses also suggest the probably fantastic nature of what we presently take to be knowledge. One effect of *La Tentation de Saint Antoine* is to imply, without affirming, that a complete collection of the knowledge of all that humanity has deemed to be knowledge would largely be a collection of such fantasies—such as the hallucinations of a Saint Anthony.[3]

In his hallucinations, Anthony resists knowledge. For example, by flagellating himself, he resists the blandishments of the Queen of Saba, who would initiate him into all the mysteries. This resistance to the supreme temptation of knowledge comes to an end when Anthony encounters Flaubert's version of Mephistopheles, the diabolical tempter who can grant every wish in exchange for one's soul. In Flaubert's novel Mephisto shows up in the guise of Hilarion, first appearing as a dwarf, before growing, like modern science itself, into a giant. Confronted by this overpowering figure, Anthony lets himself be embarked on a quest for knowledge—which in this case encompasses an overview of all the competing heresies of the ancient world.

Peter Starr has pointed out that Hilarion, the name of Anthony's tempter, suggests the naturalist Geoffroy Saint-Hilaire (though the name is also redolent of the fourth-century scholarly bishop of Poitiers, the Saint-Hilaire who used his pen to defend orthodoxy against Arianism).[4] The onomastic overlap points up that Flaubert's Mephisto—a twerp who grows quickly into a giant—is a quite nineteenth-century tempter. He is a scientist capable of discoursing on all the luxuriant growth of doctrines and gods that human history has produced. With his Hilarion, Flaubert, the novelist acting as an encyclopedic cultural historian, satirically emulates the naturalist and his belief in the unity underlying all the differences of the natural world by cataloguing the cultural doctrines of the antique world, though it may appear that their commonality lies in their all mutually contradicting each other. Flaubert undertakes a summing up of doctrines of knowledge that existed before modern science replaced religion as the arbiter of knowledge. Like a sci-

3. In his own slightly demented way, novelist Raymond Queneau, a twentieth-century admirer of Flaubert, took inspiration here for research that was supposed to result in an encyclopedia of demented knowledge, an "encyclopédie des sciences imprécises," or a collection of systems and theories that the mad and the eccentric have succeeded in having published. Parts of this "research" in insane science were incorporated in Queneau's novel *Les Enfants de Limon* (1938), and much of it went into André Blavier's book compiling works of madmen who have published, *Les Fous littéraires*. See note 8 below.

4. Peter Starr, "Science and Confusion: On Flaubert's *Temptation*," in *Gustave Flaubert: Modern Critical Views*, ed. Harold Bloom, 199–218.

entist, the novelist is an archeologist listing all the cultural forms—religions and gods—that have disappeared now that archeology has reduced them to lifeless objects of the scientist's epistemic catalogue.

Flaubert's archeologist in the novel, something of a double for the novelist himself, is Hilarion, the Mephisto-like tempter who brings to an end Anthony's attempt to avoid the temptation of knowledge. Anthony's temptation can be read as the dialectical opposite of Faust's attempt to embrace all temptations. With the skill of a diabolical logician, Hilarion condemns Anthony's quest for innocence through ignorance by pointing out that ignorance is in itself sin, for ignorance is the froth of pride. Flaubert's Hilarion is a dialectician who shows that the Christian defense of ignorance is a subtle form of self-gratification:

> Tu te prives de viandes, de vin, d'étuves, d'esclaves et d'honneurs; mais comme tu laisses ton imagination t'offrir des banquets, des parfums, des femmes nues et des foules applaudissantes! Ta chasteté n'est qu'une corruption plus subtile, et ce mépris du monde l'impuissance de ta haine contre lui! C'est là ce qui rend tes pareils si lugubres, peut-être parce qu'ils doutent. La possession de la vérité donne la joie.

> [You deprive yourself of meats, of wine, of steam baths, of slaves, of honors; but you allow your imagination to offer you banquets, perfumes, nude women and applauding crowds! Your chastity is only a more subtle corruption, and your scorn of the world simply the impotence of your hatred of it. That's what makes your kind so lugubrious, perhaps because they doubt. The possession of truth brings joy.][5]

Mephisto's claims for joy are unusual in Flaubert, though perhaps we can read here an exposition of what Nietzsche called "the gay science," or a joyous will to truth that recognizes truth as a will to illusion in the name of life. Flaubert uses his Faustian framework to portray the early Christian impulse to denial as life-destroying while suggesting that the same impulse to destruction lies behind the science that allows the critique in the first place. This double aspect is found in much of Flaubert's work: the possession of truth gives joy, says Hilarion, though joy is only an illusion fostered by the science whose will to power, as Nietzsche was

5. Flaubert, *La Tentation de Saint Antoine*, 76. See note 9 below.

to argue, disguises its destructive impulse by calling the truth good. Flaubert's overlap with Nietzsche is considerable, and it is useful to keep in mind Nietzsche's critique of science to grasp one aspect of Flaubert's reaction to science. Especially in *La Tentation* is the destruction of religious illusion dramatized as a result of science, though science may be merely another illusion. The destruction of illusion is undertaken by that *Wissenschaftler* Hilarion, the scientist as devil whose promise of joy appears self-defeating at best, at least until the end of the second version of this bizarre work.

Hilarion offers Anthony an overview of knowledge as provided by the theories and doctrines of gnostics, heresiarchs, Church fathers, and others. Anthony's resistance to knowledge weakens progressively. He sees that Tertullian may attack knowledge, but most praise the knowledge that they can offer, especially those specialists in gnosis like Manes or Basilides. The magician Apollonius of Tyana, who knows all the gods, rites, and oracles, overtly scorns Anthony's religious need for ignorance and his need for illusion and describes him in terms that are full of contempt: "Il croit, comme une brute, à la réalité des choses. La terreur qu'il a des dieux l'empêche de les comprendre, et il ravale le sien au niveau d'un roi jaloux!" [He believes, like a brute animal, in the reality of things. The terror he has of the gods keeps him from understanding them, and he drags his own down to the level of a jealous king!] (143). This scornful jeering, coming from a Platonist magician, is a prelude to the comprehension of the gods Hilarion then offers Anthony. Setting out an extraordinary parade of deities, Flaubert celebrates the leitmotif of the death of the gods by showing them in their demented splendor. Blame for their demise is laid upon the shoulders of the sadistic scientist, Hilarion, who gloats in the gods' abjection (182). With some anticipation of *Bouvard et Pécuchet*, Flaubert stages a Rabelaisian satire with this encyclopedic parade of deities whose penultimate god is Crepitus, the god of the fart. Upon his demise there remains only the Lord of Hosts, and, upon the extinction of his voice, all is silence. The only remaining god is science—or the devil himself—triumphant in his will to power after his victory over the gods.

Hilarion then shows Anthony the universe of the new science—new since Copernicus, Galileo, and Newton. Thoroughly indoctrinated, Anthony now scorns his former ignorance as he flies off into the infinite universe that Hilarion describes with a mixture of Newtonian mechanics and Spinozist ontology. Good and evil are perceptions relative to the observer and have no meaning in the infinite expansion that must be logically characterized as one Substance—Spinoza's "Natura sive Deus." Moreover, Hilarion initiates Anthony into epistemology by explaining that the knowledge a subject has must be necessarily deformed because that knowledge must be garnered through the viewing lens of the individual self: "Mais les choses ne t'arrivent que par l'intermédiaire de ton esprit. Tel qu'un miroir concave il déforme les objets;—et tout moyen te manque pour en vérifier l'exactitude" [But things come to you only through the intermediary of your mind. Like a concave mirror it deforms objects;—and you have no means by which to verify its exactness] (148). Through these conceptual pirouettes, Flaubert's devil challenges empiricism, which is to say, the epistemology of the realist novel. If, as he claims, the observer is always a deforming mirror, then how can the self have any purchase on the objective world, how can knowledge be obtained by the utter subjectivity that informs every act of perception? It might seem impossible for knowledge to exist if it is impossible to strip away prejudice and become the neutral eye of pure objectivity.

In his final diatribe against the possibility of knowledge, Flaubert's Hilarion sounds much like Balzac's Séraphita, since he, too, finds that knowledge founders on the infinite: "Jamais tu ne connaîtras l'Univers dans sa pleine étendue; par conséquent tu ne peux te faire une idée de sa cause, avoir une notion juste de Dieu, ni même dire que l'Univers est infini,—car il faudrait d'abord connaître l'infini!" [You will never know the universe its full extension; consequently, you cannot have any idea about its cause, or have an accurate notion about God, nor even say if the universe is infinite,—since you'd first have to know the infinite!] (148). With that, after proclaiming that perhaps all is illusion, that illusion is the only reality, Hilarion disappears, abandoning Anthony to his own devices. The epistemic devil invokes the infinite as an epistemic impossibility that throws doubt on the possibility of any totalization, and with this doubt, on any knowledge whatsoever. *La Tentation de Saint Antoine* plays with the concept of totalization, here taken parodistically to its extreme limit. Flaubert's irony is underscored by the fact that this claim is bandied about by a devil named Science who boasts that his desire is without limits (141). Totalization founders on the infinity of desire, and the infinite desire for knowledge, which renders totalization impossible.

The theme of the infinite found in Faust and again in Balzac's *La Peau de Chagrin* returns to challenge the idea of totalization each time it appears in the nineteenth century. Tied up with desire, the infinite is also a very mathematical notion that plagued cosmology from the moment Pascal formulated that we are stuck between the infinitely small and the infinitely great—or between two contradictions that no amount of knowledge will ever eliminate. Pascalian faith is not, however, the solution Anthony turns to.

Awakening from his voyage to find his heart dry, Anthony is tempted by suicide and sex, by destruction and fornication—or by the Devil in his "double aspect" (207). After his fall from flight, Anthony should be at his nadir; but in a surprising move, Flaubert reverses field. Anthony suddenly becomes a biologist when he ponders the much debated question of nineteenth-century biological inquiry: to wit, if there is only one unique life substance, why are its forms so varied? This question brings back natural history as the novel's epistemic focal point, for Anthony undergoes a hallucination in which various monsters appear, from the sphinx to the unicorn. With this parade of monsters, Anthony's tetralogy mimics the results of research undertaken by Geoffroy Saint-Hilaire and his son Isidore, those genial hybridizers who produced monsters to show that deviant morphology is subject to the same natural laws as normal embryonic development. By its very deviation, the monster is actually testimony to the singular and regular plan that presides over the elaboration of varied forms that are different, and yet the same by analogy (or, in today's terminology, by homology).

The doctrines of physiologist Claude Bernard, the patron saint of experimental medicine, are also to be detected at this point when Anthony becomes a scientist. Bernard declared that the "unnatural" and the "abnormal" were no longer categories one could use to describe natural phenomena: all processes of organic development are ruled over by the same invariant regularities described by physico-chemical laws. Ergo, whatever the result of any pathology, nothing is abnormal when observed by the experimental scientist who always finds the same "normal" laws at work in producing morbidity. Monsters are the normally abnormal.

Anthony also appears to have become a physiologist at the end of the final version of this wacky drama about the quest for knowledge. Looking through a microscope—or something like it—Anthony, the scientist, loses his fear when he sees life being born at the cellular level. He sees that all forms are related as matter. At this, he rejoices and even wants to enter into other life forms, to go into each atom, and to become matter. Anthony's exultant materialism seems now to fly in the face of the desire for death he first felt upon finding himself alone in the universe. It is difficult to reconcile his two desires, one for death, the other for entrance into the eternity of matter's unending transformations. One wants to patch together the book's ending by saying that perhaps Flaubert was unsuccessful in creating some irony at the end that would meld together disparate ideas. A vision of a Spinozist acceptance of death was probably at the origins of his first version of Saint Anthony, and in the final version it is up to the reader to reconcile it with Anthony's positivist vision of matter. Saint Anthony's joyful discovery of the post-Virchow doctrine that all life forms share the same form—i.e., cells—is also difficult to reconcile with the appearance of the face of Jesus in the middle of the sun at the drama's end. (Virchow's doctrine that "omnis cellula e cellula" received published form in 1858.) Perhaps Flaubert wanted to equate Helios, the sun, with the quest for knowledge, a Greek leitmotif—while ironically attempting to show that Christianity was one last manifestation of the Greek desire for knowledge or for logos. However, that reading is a great deal to ask from one line coming at the end of a parodistic and sometimes incoherent work.

Most critics read a victory of positivist medicine in the work's finale, and this interpretation is consonant with one of Flaubert's stances toward science. In his reading of the conclusion, for example, Maurice Nadeau sees no significance in the appearance of Christ to Anthony, the scientist, since Christ's appearance is simply a "historical truth" that is part of the "truth of Anthony's character."[6] Arguing that the real issue is elsewhere, Nadeau sees Flaubert coming to accept a nature philosophy of the sort propagated by Haeckel, Darwin's disciple in Germany. Flaubert's acceptance of positivism is shown in the way that truth is found, not in materialized spirit, but in a spiritualized matter. Faith has been replaced by a knowledge of cells, and physiology has replaced theology and metaphysics. From a different perspective, as Sartre and oth-

6. Nadeau, *Gustave Flaubert, écrivain*, 268. In his interpretation, Nadeau leans on the fact that Flaubert wrote to one of the Goncourt brothers the rather positivist statement: "[L]a cellule scientifique rend la foi inutile." (271) [The scientific cell makes faith useless.]

ers have argued, Flaubert's father, the positivist doctor, finally triumphed in Flaubert's mind over Flaubert's mother and her Spinozist pantheism, the pantheism of which Flaubert was a proponent in his letters to Louise Colet in the 1840s. Whatever may be the proper biographical perspective, it is true that, by roughly the mid-nineteenth century, physiology was triumphant as a paradigm of new understanding. With the founding of what Claude Bernard called experimental medicine and the introduction of a rigorous deterministic view of physiological functions, experimental science was transforming medicine.

In fine, at the end of *La Tentation,* science is clearly the arbiter of what constitutes knowledge and the real, both within the text and, perhaps by implication, in the historical world to which the novel is addressed. It is not clear if one is to be happy with this historical world or not. Nevertheless, the novel has traced out the history of knowledge leading up to the positivism of the historical moment. It has traced the way to the historical science of which Flaubert made copious use when he literally transposed archeological descriptions to create his gods and monsters. *La Tentation* is a compendium of the received scholarship of his day. Like some Hegelian world spirit, the novel speaks of its own historical science in order to talk about the historical world of both the fourth century and the nineteenth century. The reference to the nineteenth century is clear insofar as Anthony becomes a scientist worshiping the physiological discoveries that have put the physico-chemical nature of life on view. Science is thus incorporated into the novel as the main theme, indeed as the drama, of the work. Whatever be the quirkiness with which Flaubert treated these motifs, *La Tentation de Saint Antoine* is clearly beholden to the epistemic discourses of the mid-nineteenth century in a fairly straightforward way. The saint becomes a scientist. And such has been the march of history, or so Flaubert seems to say. If Flaubert undoubtedly was much more attracted emotionally to sainthood—as witnesses the tale "Saint Julien l'Hôpitalier"—intellectually he could not reject triumphant positivism. Art needed religion, but Flaubert's intellect condemned the needs that Flaubert profoundly felt and for which he tried to substitute an art consonant with what his intellect could respect. Art must be more like science—while respecting the artist's need to reveal the ideal. These issues will concern us again, in a different shape, in *Madame Bovary.*

Science is also the dominant theme in Flaubert's last work, the unfinished *Bouvard et Pécuchet*. Flaubert left this work incomplete at his death in 1880, a few years after he had finished his final version of *La Tentation de Saint Antoine*. The parodies of *Saint Antoine* give way in this last novel to a clear-cut satire that demonstrates that Flaubert could never totally accept the victory of science—even if writing this novel meant that he had to master virtually every epistemic discourse that the first half of the nineteenth century had produced. So on the one hand, his encyclopedic satire is an oblique homage to science, but, on the other hand, it also bears witness to a rivalry that imposed on Flaubert the need to encompass all knowledge and then go beyond that knowledge by destroying it through satire. Faust would have a last laugh at science's expense, as it were. *Bouvard et Pécuchet* is thus a quasi-Faustian, and satirical, monument to the power of research—ineffectual research in the case of his characters, but quirkily awesome when envisaged from the viewpoint of how much research Flaubert undertook himself.

To create his novelistic encyclopedia, Flaubert brings together in the novel two middle-aged copy clerks, Bouvard and Pécuchet, and allows them to acquire enough money so that they can purchase a farm in Normandy. Here they want to pursue, unsystematically, what Stratton Buck concisely calls "all the sciences and disciplines of human culture."[7] Each attempt they undertake in the pursuit of knowledge results in practical disaster and theoretical confusion. By the end of the novel as Flaubert left it, the reader has, thanks to the hapless clerks, surveyed agriculture, chemistry, anatomy, physiology, medicine, hygiene, astronomy, paleontology, geology, archeology, historical science, literature and aesthetics, political theory, political economy, sex, gymnastics, spiritism and magnetism, magic, philosophy, pedagogy, phrenology, religion, music, and urbanism—to offer, in the order of presentation, a not all-inclusive list.

Typically, Flaubert proceeds dialectically in the work in that he sets forth one opinion about a body of knowledge and confronts it with a conflicting opinion so that the competing claims of different doctrines cancel each other. This procedure is not without historical precedent. It is, for instance, rather much like what the doctor magus Agrippa von Nettesheim did in the early sixteenth century when he set out to demolish science in his equally wacky encyclopedic review of knowledge, *De incertitudine et vanitate scientiarum et artium, atque excellentia Verbi Dei*

7. Stratton, *Flaubert*, 115.

declamatio (1530). Creating a collage of conflicting opinions *Of the Vanitie and Uncertaintie of Artes and Sciences,* Agrippa demonstrated, to Rabelais's delight and Montaigne's chagrin, that there are conflicting opinions on any subject of knowledge one wishes to name, astrology or baking, medicine or magic. In a sense, then, Flaubert renews the Renaissance genre of the anatomy of knowledge that proposes to demolish certainty through dialectical idea-bashing.

There is a difference between Agrippa and Flaubert, and this difference between the Renaissance and the nineteenth century points up some problematic issues in Flaubert's novel. Agrippa takes on a demonstration of the futility of knowledge seemingly in his own name, whereas Flaubert presents the hopelessness of knowing by showing how hapless are his benighted characters. Moreover, science, for the Renaissance writer, has no privileged status, and his use of contradiction is essentially a rhetorical ploy—it has no ontological weight, since contradiction is merely a property of language. (Contradiction has so little weight that Agrippa could totally contradict his attack on knowledge by publishing in 1531 *De Occulta Philosophia,* a work that positively affirms alchemy as supreme knowledge.) For the Renaissance, contradiction was largely a rhetorical category, and, to the extent that the quest for knowledge was not animated by the new critical spirit, knowledge was largely a question of manipulating texts to quote authorities.

A nineteenth-century author, however, confronts science as a practice that cannot be put into question. The basic propositions of Newtonian dynamics, for example, are unassailable by anyone who cannot propose a successful counter-theory. And whatever may be his attitude about science at any given moment, Flaubert knows this. Knowledge may be misused and abused, and in the case of Flaubert's puppet-like—and very likeable—characters, knowledge is constantly misapplied with catastrophic results. Bouvard and Pécuchet are much like belated Renaissance compilers of discourse, or copyists for whom copying is access to science. They manipulate discourse, but with no criteria for judgment, and it is their comic lack of criteria that produces the satire demonstrating the futility of science and knowledge.

Flaubert loads the deck historically to create this satire. He situates his characters sufficiently early in the nineteenth century so that he can refer to scientific disciplines that lend themselves more easily to denigration. Bouvard and Pécuchet have no easy criteria for judgment, at least in part because Flaubert loads them down with scientific models largely from the early and mid-nineteenth century, many of which were already historically dated or even antiquated by the time Flaubert was writing the novel in the late 1870s. Bouvard and Pécuchet begin their quest for knowledge in the 1840s, before Darwin and Pasteur's work had transformed biology and medicine. With the historical distance he granted himself, Flaubert needed not worry about the triumphant scientific paradigms that were sweeping the field of all competition—such as atomic theory after Mendeleyev, microbiology, field theory, or even the experimental medicine Flaubert held in awe. He thus avoided all theories that had displaced the debates about the sciences and parasciences in which Bouvard and Pécuchet had become involved. And one may ponder the fact that Flaubert ended his Alexandrine drama about Saint Anthony with reference to contemporary science while avoiding reference to it in a satire taking place in the early nineteenth century.

To illustrate this latter point, let us consider the involvement with chemistry that Bouvard and Pécuchet pursue. First initiating themselves into the arts of food preparation, they manage to conserve foods that promptly rot, and then they set up a distilling apparatus that equally promptly blows up. Perhaps, they decide, this is due to their lack of chemistry. But which chemistry? Embroiling themselves in the debates of the 1840s about chemical theory, Bouvard and Pécuchet learn that atomic theory is hardly settled, and that organic chemistry is divided between those who use the law of equivalencies and those who use atomic theory.[8] Having run up against this conflict between theories, which roughly reflects the debates at the time between chemists like Berzelius and Dumas, Bouvard and Pécuchet are perplexed. What criteria do they have for deciding which theory is correct? Bouvard and Pécuchet decide to drop chemistry altogether after encountering a village doctor who blames chemistry for its bad influence on medicine— the pre-Pasteurian medicine that this country eclectic practices. (One detects a historical irony here since it was a chemist, Pasteur, who transformed the practice of medicine).

Turning from harmful chemistry to beneficent medicine, Bouvard and Pécuchet begin to study a new science and start looking at anato-

---

8. Flaubert, *Bouvard et Pécuchet*, 82. This edition has Raymond Queneau's important essay on Flaubert.

my books. In their quest for medical knowledge they then purchase anatomical medical models that unfold to reveal the hidden world of human viscera. One model offers a literal revelation of viscera, which attracts a mutinous crowd that believes a cadaver is being sequestered in Bouvard and Pécuchet's house. From this experience Bouvard and Pécuchet learn what it means to bring learning to the countryside and so "took up the ambition to suffer for science" (85). Flaubert's own favored *Dictionnaire des sciences médicales* becomes their favored work, which in turn leads to their desire to practice their current favorite science, though not before they first master the intricacies of physiology. And so it goes.

A résumé of "plot" in the novel is a résumé of an encyclopedia of arts and sciences available in the 1840s, arranged by thesis and antithesis, but accompanied by no dialectical synthesis to bring about knowledge at a higher level. One could say that the satire is based on a dysfunctional Hegelian model, and so it is hardly surprising to learn that, in their study of philosophy, Pécuchet explains that, according to Hegel, the rational is the real, and that the real is found only in the idea, and that the laws of mind are the laws of the universe—a state of affairs Bouvard can only pretend to understand. But Bouvard might well take solace in the fact that his existence is proof that the Hegelian system doesn't work. As Flaubert amply demonstrates, the laws of the mind seem to have little to do with the universe.

Interpretations of the intent animating the novel's critique of knowledge in *Bouvard et Pécuchet* vary greatly. Though clearly a satirical work dealing with knowledge, *Bouvard et Pécuchet* provides a litmus test for readers and critics' feelings about science. Those many humanists who feel the onus of reproving science for its epistemic imperialism find in the novel a portrayal of the bankruptcy of science and scientific rationality. That minority of readers and critics who, like novelist Raymond Queneau, feel an affinity with scientific rationality find in Flaubert's encyclopedia a satire of the abuse of science—and perhaps a defense of skeptical rationality. From Queneau's perspective, for example, Flaubert's rage against *bêtise*—or cosmic stupidity—can be put in the service of science, for the satire underscores the dangers run by those who seek knowledge "without method" (11). I point out these opposing viewpoints about this extraordinary satire, since both seem legitimate, depending upon the framework one selects for reading the novel. In a sense, Flaubert's own ambiguities about science and literature allow one to affirm both sides of the opposition. Feeling the sting of competition with science, Flaubert could not passively accept the triumph of science, but his intellect allowed him no choice. Nonetheless, at the end of his life he decided to lampoon science by writing a novel that encompasses the range of possible knowledge available in France for the decade of roughly 1840 to 1850. In his satirical depiction of knowledge, literature might somehow appear superior to science, or perhaps superior to the misapplication of knowledge. Fiction can portray the debacle of the application of science in the lives of two comically mediocre men as they go about their unending epistemic quest. At least through this portrayal, some kind of victory emerges for literature, as a form of consciousness if not as an absolute.

The importance of this victory, however minor, in Flaubert's work is crucial for understanding the history of relations between science and literature. Flaubert's encyclopedic satire foreshadows confrontations yet to come both in and out of literature. *Bouvard et Pécuchet* broaches the epistemological problem of the foundations of knowledge that many modern theorists see originating in Nietzsche. But in Flaubert's novels we already see a critique take shape that eventuates in philosophers of science like Foucault, Kuhn, and many lesser constructivists, deconstructionists, relativists, and others who believe that all knowledge is arbitrary in its very foundations. It is noteworthy that, after Flaubert and Nietzsche, the postmodern critique of knowledge is often an essentially literary critique, for it sees in every truth claim a form of fiction. And, as hostile critics of science point out, there is something naive about a truth claim that is not self-conscious of its arbitrary or fictional status—in the way that many literary fictions are. In their exemplary naïveté, Bouvard and Pécuchet might seem to be exemplary scientists, and the novel in which they appear to be a critique of epistemological naiveté.

This question of the novel's self-consciousness brings up the recurrent question of the self-reflexivity of a truth claim that acknowledges that it is a fiction, and I allow myself an excursus here on issues that concern both how we interpret Flaubert and how we deal with the relation of literature to science. The epistemic claim that knowledge is fiction is also a claim to knowledge. This claim is linked in turn to the problem of justifying the knowledge that allows a theorist to declare that he or she knows that knowledge is unfounded, for what are the foundations of the claim that knowledge has no foundations? Reflecting upon Nietzsche's claim that truth is an illusion, we want to know what truth underlies the illusion that proclaims truth to be an illusion. In short, all antifoundational positions are subject to the self-denying demonstration of their self-referentiality, for does one want to claim that the truth that truth is an illusion, is also an illusion?

From this perspective perhaps only a fiction is capable of demonstrating the fictionality of truth, if the self-destructive self-referentiality can be neutralized by irony. For this reason, then, we might understand why *Bouvard et Pécuchet* continues to offer the tantalizing example of the fiction that denounces knowledge or truth in fiction through the staging of the impossibility of knowing more than the impossibility. Irony notwithstanding, the reader is entitled to ask what one is to make of the claims of a satirical novel that demonstrates the putative futility of all the arts and sciences and their claims to order the world and produce truth. Does Flaubert's demonstration of the confusions of knowledge about, as well as through, literature undermine the claims to knowledge in literature? To interpret *Bouvard et Pécuchet* as a demonstration of the futility of knowledge would imply that this literary demonstration itself is futile, which would mean that this literary demonstration can only serve to designate its own failure.

I do not mean to bring up this problem in the spirit of a facile deconstructionism that works with the axiom that all literary language is self-referential, for I hardly wish to suggest that all literary language designates only its own deferral of ungrounded meaning. It seems obvious that much literary use of language, like any other use of language, is not self-referential. It is true that self-referential features often accompany literary texts as part of the procedures and techniques that allow the enactment of the fictions and are part of the rhetoric of some fiction. This self-referentiality is part of the self-consciousness by which fictions designate their consciousness of their own status—as fictions—but this hardly undermines meaning. On the contrary. And implied self-consciousness about a fiction's status as fiction does not imply that fictions cannot also have many other functions, for it is simply quite true, as numerous examples in the history of literature demonstrate, that an epistemic quest can be undertaken in a fiction.

The postmodern desire to read every text as a demonstration of its own aporias will automatically result in a failure to see how seriously Flaubert challenged scientific epistemology on its own terms. Conversely, such reading leads to the failure to see how he accepted scientific epistemology, especially in *Madame Bovary* and *La Tentation de Saint Antoine,* as the only possible way to make truth claims. Even a reader like Michel Foucault, who took critical distance from the wiles of deconstruction, gave in to the temptation to turn Flaubert into a demonstration of futile self-referentiality. With his own program for demonstrating the arbitrary foundations of epistemic discourses, Foucault was drawn to *Bouvard et Pécuchet* and its implicit questioning of the status of a literary discourse that portrays the failure of science in its claims to knowledge. The novel appealed to Foucault's desire to turn every epistemic discourse into an autonomous discourse grounded only in itself. His interpretation is noteworthy for an understanding of the contemporary failure to have any positive agenda for reading literature. Foucault viewed *Bouvard et Pécuchet* as a metademonstration of the futility of any discourse. At the end of the novel—as we learn from the notes Flaubert left on his death—the two copyists, who have by now failed at all the arts and sciences, would go back to their first occupation. They become copyists again. They cease attempting to apply the knowledge found in the texts they read. With this proposed ending in mind, Foucault turns the novel into the following kind of self-reflexive demonstration:

> Ils renoncent (on les contraint de renoncer) à *faire* ce qu'ils avaient entrepris pour devenir ce qu'ils étaient. Ils le sont purement et simplement: ils font fabriquer un grand pupitre, double, pour renouer avec ce qu'ils n'avaient cessé d'être, pour se remettre à faire ce qu'ils avaient fait pendant des dizaine d'années,—pour copier. Copier quoi? des livres, leurs livres,tous les livres, et ce livre, sans doute, qu'est *Bouvard et Pécuchet:* car copier, c'est ne rien *faire;* c'est *être* les livres qu'on copie, c'est être cette infime distension du langage qui se redouble, c'est être le pli du discours sur lui-même.

> [They give up (they are obliged to give up) *doing* what they had undertaken in order to become what they were. They become it purely and simply: they have a great writing desk built, double size, to take up again with what they had never ceased to be, to begin again to do what they had done for years,—to copy. Copy what? books, their books, all books, and this book, doubtlessly, that is *Bouvard et*

Pécuchet: for copying is *doing* nothing, it is a way of *being* the books
that one copies, of being this small distension of language that dou-
bles itself, of being this fold of discourse in upon itself.][9]

With his usual interpretive seduction, Foucault demonstrates here how
to detach language from the world: copying is not an act, it is simply
auto-replication in which the Word duplicates itself, folding back upon
itself, designating itself as a copy of itself. From this perspective, *Bouvard et Pécuchet* is the library of Babylon, and Flaubert's now postmodern rage destroys science by burning it up with all the books in the library—the library of the encyclopedia of misapplied knowledge.

But this postmodern anger with knowledge is really Foucault's, however much it overlaps the regret Flaubert felt about the demise of art and
religion. Foucault's is the anger of a generation that felt deceived in the
twentieth century by science and raged against it for not offering the absolute that Marxist science once promised, but failed to deliver. Flaubert
may have shared a nostalgia for eschatological visions, but Flaubert's
anger was against *bêtise,* a nearly metaphysical concept that, for Flaubert, replaced the theological notion of the fall after the fall of theology.
The Jansenist background, ever central to French culture, offers an appropriate context for understanding Flaubert, since Flaubert, not unlike
Pascal, was wedded to science in spite of himself: science could offer relative knowledge in a fallen world in which only ignorance, if no longer
sin, is an absolute. In this fallen world, however, one could not find the
absolute knowledge of which Flaubert dreamt in anger and nostalgia—
for he dreamt of an aesthetic and epistemic absolute that would, like
Mallarmé's Book, offer redemption through the kind of revelation that
the Middle Ages once believed in. Flaubert was ironically aware that
only a metaphorical devil can keep such an impossible idea alive—
Hilarion was always ready to prod Saint Flaubert into dreams of the absolute. Bouvard and Pécuchet show the reader where such dreams can
lead.

Flaubert's metaphysical pessimism corresponds to what some, more
historically inclined critics have seen in his various works as an entropic vision, or a vision reflecting consequences that one can deduce from

9. Flaubert, *La Tentation de Saint Antoine,* 32. This edition is prefaced with Michel
Foucault's essay on *La Tentation.*

the second law of thermodynamics. To evoke entropy is to suggest that his work somehow reflected the developments in thermodynamics to which I referred in discussing Balzac and energy, especially the doctrine according to which disorder is the most probable state of any system. It is true that Flaubert's works offer a relentless demonstration of how things go sour and come apart and that the passage from the ordered to the random is usually the most likely course of events. If dissolution is a leitmotif in Flaubert, and even if disorder may well appear to be the most probable state of affairs, I do not want to argue that Flaubert's rivalry with science led to direct emulation of physics, however much increasing disorder manifests itself as the most probable tendency in works like *Madame Bovary, Bouvard et Pécuchet,* or "Un coeur simple"— the latter story providing a textbook demonstration of the random passage from order to disorder. Or the reader wishing to contradict me and find entropy in Flaubert might turn to a passage from *L'Education sentimentale,* that education in loss in which Frédéric goes to the palace at Fontainebleau only to discover that the meaning of time is dissolution:

> Les résidences royales ont en elles une mélancolie particulière, qui tient sans doute à leurs dimensions trop considérables pour le petit nombre de leurs hôtes, au silence qu'on est surpris d'y trouver après tant de fanfares, à leur luxe immobile prouvant par sa vieillesse la fugacité des dynasties, l'éternelle misère de tout;—et cette exhalaison des siècles, engourdissante et funèbre comme un parfum de momie, se fait sentir même aux têtes naïves.

> [Royal residences contain in themselves a special melancholy, which is probably due to their oversized dimensions for their small number of inhabitants, to the silence that one is surprised to find there after so many fanfares, to their motionless luxury that proves by its age the transience of dynasties, the eternal misery of everything;—and that emanation of the centuries, numbing and funereal like a mummy's perfume, imposes itself even on the simplest minds.][10]

This description of the eternal misery of everything certainly sounds like a consequence of the second law of thermodynamics (even if entropy as a concept is not directly amenable to intuition by simple hearts).

10. Flaubert, *L'Education sentimentale*, 323.

But there is an overdetermination at work here. Flaubert's own invert-ed theology of humanity's constant fall also underlies his portrayal of the ongoing loss of energy leading to the disorder and dissolution that characterizes much of his work. I think that the specialist in naturalism, David Baguley, is probably closer to the truth when he says that Flaubert is at the origins of the type of naturalist novel in which "the determin-ing factor of deterioration is . . . generalized as the insufficiency of hu-man life itself, trapping the individual in the snare of routine existence and its sordid compromises."[11] In this type of naturalist novel, of which the prototype is *L'Education sentimentale,* Baguley finds a static, circular, or repetitive form conveying a vision derived more from Schopenhauer than from science. If an entropic vision is present in Flaubert's work, and an interesting argument can be made in favor of that interpretation, then it also coincides with his anger about a world that constantly deviates from ideal order. Perhaps much can be known about this world, Flau-bert seems to affirm with deliberate ambivalence, but it will never find a place in the totalizing encyclopedia of our Faustian dreams.

The contrary of those dreams are found in Flaubert's realism. In de-veloping this realism, Flaubert was concerned with science, though not so much with specific issues of science such as entropy, energetics, or bi-ological determinism that we find in the satirical encyclopedia under-taken by Bouvard and Pécuchet. Rather, in Flaubert's realistic work his rivalry led him to endow his fiction with the shape of science. Flaubert's realism mimics scientific objectivity in order to decry science, as well as art, as they unfold in a fallen world of random processes. This mimicry is especially true of *Madame Bovary,* the novel in which Flaubert invent-ed the rhetoric of the modern realist novel, partly in expiation for his youthful dreams of Saint Anthony and fantasies about an absolute epis-temic revelation. But his rhetoric also aims at giving the novel the shape of science through its narrative objectivity. In the novel Flaubert sets up a central conflict so as to dramatize a fallen world in which science and art are wedded, literally and figuratively, and not at all successfully. Sci-ence and art—illustrated by the undertakings of quasi-doctor Bovary and his almost romantic wife Emma—are as little applicable to the fall-en world in *Madame Bovary* as they are in the encyclopedic farce enact-

11. Baguley, "The Nature of Naturalism," in *Naturalism in the European Novel,* ed. Brian Nelson, 22.

ed in *Bouvard et Pécuchet*. But in *Madame Bovary*, an awareness of the fall is made transparent by a usually omniscient narrator who sees the world in every detail and from whom nothing is hidden. The narrator is in effect a surrogate scientist granted a quietly diabolical vision that goes beyond the powers Balzac granted his often garrulous narrators— for the world is quietly transparent to Flaubert's narrator. He is present often only through a persistent irony that Balzac never granted his intrusive and judgmental narrators. In *Madame Bovary* Flaubert grants his scientist-like narrator omniscient presence so that the novel achieves the shape of the absolute epistemic discourse of which Flaubert had dreamed, and which he could only find by creating it in a fiction.

In Flaubert's view, science aims ideally at an absolute epistemic discourse, and art at an absolute ideal structure. It might not immediately appear that these two are reconcilable, especially from Flaubert's perspective. He often tended to view these two absolutes as rivals, like two perfect deities who must struggle to eliminate each other in a universe in which perfection is defined as oneness. But the ideal includes knowledge, and Flaubert, desirous of creating an ideal art form, had to integrate epistemic discourse into his work. Thus, in *Madame Bovary*, he borrowed from scientific procedures to create a new rhetoric of fiction: he created a narrator who is analogous to the objective viewer posited by science. The omniscient—and hence diabolical—narrator is *par excellence* the neutral viewer who can entertain phenomena with an objectivity denied normal mortals. Interestingly, and perhaps contradictorily, Flaubert's narrator objectively describes a fallen world in which an ideal viewer has no place, since the ideal of true knowledge is an impossible dream in this world. The irony created by this procedure often erodes the supposedly neutral stance of the objective viewer. Frequently, irony erupts in the novel to undermine the belief that objectivity is meaningful, even if the reader must accept the objective truth of the narrator's language. The shape of science is, to say the least, often bent by the irony that undermines it, though never destroys it, in Flaubert's most realist work.

The necessity of irony for the creation of the novel's total vision is testimony to the limits of objectivity. Yet, the fact remains that Flaubert's narrator, by his very viewing stance, pays homage to the scientist posited by Laplacian physics. Or, in terms of then more-recent science, Flaubert's narrator seems to take cues from Claude Bernard's scientific doctor: he is the experimental observer who registers the workings of the physico-chemical world. We might say that Flaubert's narrator looks upon a series of chemical processes with all their attendant consequences for adultery in small French towns. Paradoxically, then, Flaubert's objective viewer is there to register the failure of objectivity, as found in science, embodied in Charles; and the failure of the ideal, in art, as represented by Emma. The novel records the failure of art and science in a work of art—and so science and art are thus perhaps reconciled in the knowledge of their mutual failure. With its self-consciousness, if not self-reflexivity, the novel demonstrates itself to be a superior form of discourse in that it can offer knowledge of the failure of all other discourses. Again it may appear that Flaubert's triumphant rivalry with science undermines itself from the outset, since the failures that the novel registers include art as well as science—and the triumph of its form is also a triumph of epistemic vision.

From the time of Henry James through the essays of later critics like Percy Lubbock and Auerbach, and finally coming to fruition in the writings of modern narratologists, Flaubert's rhetoric in *Madame Bovary* has received voluminous commentary. Critics and theorists have generally emphasized the way in which Flaubert created a new means for representing perception. Auerbach noted that Flaubert's narrator has the power to enter into the perceptual world of the characters and, with regard to Emma, "bestow the power of mature expression upon the material which she affords, in its complete subjectivity."[12] To which I add that this power is the scientific dream, at least the dream of a certain science, that desires to master subjectivity and study it as an objective given. This is achieved, as Georges Poulet observed, through the creation of "a general coherence, due to the fact that objects, taken as simultaneous or in succession, are always tied together by the unity of a perceptual consciousness [*pensée perceptive*], and that this consciousness itself is always preserved from dissolution into successive states through the objectivity of the universe with which it never ceases being in contact."[13] Perception is defined as consciousness of the exterior world, which means that consciousness can be defined through the world of

12. Auerbach, *Mimesis,* trans. Willard Trask, 427.
13. Poulet, "La Pensée circulaire de Flaubert," in *Flaubert, Miroir de la critique,* ed. Raymonde Debray-Genette, 105.

things. Things can be objectively studied. Through this relationship, consciousness becomes potentially an object for science's epistemic investigation as well as the subject of the ideal structure created by a work of art.

Flaubert refused conventional rhetorical technique, and so narratologist Gérard Genette claims that Flaubert initiated the modern novel by refusing the novel—through a "déromanisation du roman."[14] Genette's theory of the novel at one time opposed proper fiction, with dramatic and narrative interest, to something that isn't properly fiction. This is a narratologist's opposition that one can accept only with reservations— since it implies some essence of narration that stands opposed to other discourses, say, objective description. If we accept Genette's distinction of pure narration and description, then we can say that Flaubert, in his desire to rival with the absolute discourse proposed by positivist science, created a fictional discourse offering a pseudoepistemic certainty. Hence the recourse to description. Flaubert undertook this in opposition to traditional narrative discourse that clearly separates world, the observed, and the observer in such a way that plot serves as the center of interest. The opposition between epistemic discourse and narrative discourse is, however, what the scholastics called a distinction of reason, and it is clear that some epistemic discourses involve narration—consider the "history" of the earth or the "story" of evolution—and vice versa. I make this point to argue that narration can be knowledge, and that description can exist as part of the narrative project as characters undertake actions in their world.

Having set up the distinction between narration and description, narratologists are usually obliged to abolish the distinction when they attend to the workings of Flaubert's rhetoric. Flaubert's objective narrator offers a discourse that aspires to (fictional) certainty by positing a world whose valid description is guaranteed by the narrator's presence—a presence that borrows its criteria for certainty from the epistemological doctrine that makes direct observation a criterion for truth. Positive science guarantees the workings of the text by defining the foundations of knowledge in this tightly circular way. Moreover, epistemic mimesis is also guaranteed by the way that Flaubert's description is anchored in a narration that illustrates the causal connections obtaining in the fallen

14. Genette, *Figures*, vol. 1, 243.

world that we, fallen readers, may also believe we share with the text.

Some readers fail to see beyond the explicit treatment of science within *Madame Bovary*, and thus they find in the novel a harsh critique of the pretensions of science. That the novel satirizes science in presenting Charles and the village pharmacist Homais is clearly the case, but this satire is underwritten by a narrative stance derived from scientific epistemology. Flaubert's ambiguity is not given its proper due when a critic hostile to science confuses Homais's viewpoint with the novel's viewpoint, as in the following example:

> In the Flaubertian text science does not constitute a system of truth that explains the world. . . . It is at best simply the pretentious labeling thereof; like M. Homais it sticks on labels, confects packages. Struck with classifying mania, it makes order, it names, it spells out. . . . The discourse of science resembles the house of squire Homais: a ruffling of texts that protect against the real, while proclaiming one's mastery of it.[15]

What the critic describes here is science in the fallen world inhabited by the inept Charles Bovary and the would-be scientist, the braggart pharmacist Homais. But the satire of these inept scientists is provided by a rhetorical structure in which the narrator can objectively judge these buffoons because he incarnates a positivist worldview that defines the reality these characters transgress in their pretensions and stupidity. It is in light of this worldview that the fall of scientific discourse in Charles's world is measured. The narrator's stance is not to be confused with the acts and attitudes of the characters he describes, characters who illustrate the misfit between claims to knowledge and the world, much as in *Bouvard et Pécuchet*. Moreover, the fall of scientific discourse, its dysfunctional application by Homais and by Charles, is complementary to the fall of art, as embodied in Emma's romanticism and in the misuse of literature and art that eventually results in her suicide. Emma's abuse of art leads to dysfunctional behavior, though most critics are hardly tempted to read a total condemnation of literature in her failures. Her attempts to live poetry are as deficient as Charles's attempt to be a "representative" of science. It is true in simple terms that science should

---

15. Françoise Gaillard, "L'En-signement [*sic*] du réel," in *Production du sens chez Flaubert*, ed. Claudine Gothot-Mersch, 206.

stand in opposition to Emma's romantic sentimentalism, albeit that, in Flaubert's novel, the would-be scientist and would-be artist of life are also united in their common ineptitude.

In brief, the thematic role of science—especially its lack of congruence with the world in the novel—needs to be read against the backdrop of the positivist narrator whose gaze is something like that of an ironic clinician. Against this backdrop one has the perspective from which to consider Emma, art, and the dialectical relationship Flaubert presents between science and art. If the narrator is positioned much like a neutral, if ironic, scientist, it is noteworthy that the narrator presents himself to the reader at the novel's outset as if he were going to be an important character, even perhaps a friend of Charles. Flaubert opens the novel with Charles's first entrance into a schoolroom in which the narrator is apparently sitting, though the narrator makes no further allusions to his own presence for the rest of the novel. The narrator, once having introduced himself as a presence, needs no longer to call attention to his voice, the voice of the objectivity that penetrates the characters like an x-ray. It is as if Flaubert, with older forms of fictional discourse in mind, had felt the need to situate his narrator before granting him the absolute presence that informs the novel. The narrator must first be situated in the fictional world before he can transcend the world and become the only access to this world. Proust, as we will see, was most attentive to this feature of Flaubert's novel.

The narrator immediately draws attention, at the novel's beginning, to the incongruous hat Charles brings in with him. The hat seems to spell out the life of failure that awaits the schoolboy. Attention to symmetry demands that one note that, if the novel begins with Charles's absurd appearance, it ends with Homais's triumph in bourgeois society. The novel is framed, at its beginning and its end, first by Charles's fruitless initiation into schooling and knowledge, and then by Homais's final triumph through learned pretense. Knowledge seems dysfunctional from the beginning, set in a rowdy school, to the end, when a charlatan triumphs through his uses and abuses of science.

The opening scene, describing the incongruity of hat and pupil, anticipates the misfit between Charles and life that characterizes him throughout the novel, in his uselessly seeking knowledge and in his failure as a doctor. His anomalous hat preludes to his lack of academic, professional, and personal success. Charles's failure in learning and science is, moreover, one in which his father, a surgeon's assistant, preceded him. The only thing at which his quasi-doctor father was successful was dissipating his wife's fortune. There is in this portrayal a hint of genetic determinism behind Charles's incapacities. If Charles is determined by his inheritance to fail, it is not the least of Flaubert's ironies that he should draw upon the nineteenth-century medical version of genetic determinism—a genetic determinism without genes—to show that medical science is useless in the novel's fallen world.

The gap between the official world of science and Charles's world is clear when Charles, having been withdrawn from an elite secondary school, a *lycée*, and setting about to become a low-ranking health official, an *officier de santé*, studies such courses as anatomy, pathology, physiology, pharmacy, chemistry, botany, clinical practice, and therapeutics, "without counting hygiene and medical material, all names whose etymology he was ignorant of and which were so many doors to sanctuaries full of august darkness." In short, "il n'y comprit rien" [he understood nothing].[16] His only hope of becoming a second-rank doctor is to memorize by rote all the answers to the examiners' questions. He becomes a machine for regurgitating discourse, and the world of scientific discourse, that world of texts and treatises about the real, remain hermetic to this medical practitioner.

Charles manages to start a practice by marrying a widow with money. He meets the future Madame Bovery when he is called to set a fracture for Emma's father. How good Charles's fortune is, is relative to one's assessment of his future, but he is fortunate in that the father's fracture is as simple as the medical neophyte could possibly hope for. This case is, I think, Charles's first, and last, significant success. He remains a medical ignoramus, but not without sources of knowledge at hand. Flaubert's works are full of allusions to books and texts associated with knowledge, or with the various forms of the aesthetic ideal. In Charles's life, the world of science remains locked up in the *Dictionnaire des sciences médicales*, the medical encyclopedia whose pages remain uncut in his office. (Notably, his only attempt at reading them comes at the end of the novel when Emma is dying of the poison she takes.)

Flaubert adroitly compounds the discomfitures of the country doctor in many details. For example, when the country squire Rodolphe brings his servant to be treated by Charles, it is the servant who prescribes his

16. Flaubert, *Madame Bovary*, 43.

own treatment. He wants to be bled—in this self-prescription he is asking for the panacea of the leading French doctor of the time, that sincere charlatan Broussais, who made bleeding into a universal remedy in the first part of the nineteenth century. The servant is bled, passes out, and is followed by Charles's assistant for the operation, Homais's servant Justin, who also collapses at the sight of gushing blood. So it is sturdy Emma who must remove a blood-filled basin, and, as she does, her body's movements reveal the "inflexions of her corsage" (160). The narrator objectively notes the movement of Emma's body, but, so does Rodolphe. Inept medical practice is linked by the narrator's perception directly to the revelation of Emma's body, to the vision of possible seduction, and thus to the series of catastrophes that brings Charles to unhappiness and Emma to her end.

The disparity between Charles's capacity and what his scientific profession demands is nearly total—as is the gap between what Emma desires and what Charles can offer her. This misfit is established in the first part of the novel. Then, to complete the portrayal of science and its dysfunctional role in Charles and Emma's world, Flaubert sends the couple to live in a second village, Yonville, where they meet, in the novel's second part, that inimitable scientist, the fraudulent pharmacist Homais. Homais allows Flaubert to widen his scope, for Homais embodies all the beliefs of the Enlightenment that, for Flaubert, had become the clichés of bourgeois rationalism. Homais is a Voltairian deist whose basic credo is, as he vaunts it, belief in the laws of physics (112). Flaubert develops a satire through this character that is close to what he later does with Bouvard and Pécuchet. For example, upon visiting a *filature,* or spinning-mill, Homais wishes he had his own *canne métrique.* He wants a measuring stick so that he can measure everything around the mill. It appears that quantification, mindless quantification, is the ultimate test of knowledge for this caricature of the Laplacian scientist. With this portrayal of Homais, a self-proclaimed voracious consumer of epistemic discourses, Flaubert parodies his own desire to master the epistemic ideal, which would be mastery of the totalizing encyclopedia. In self-praise Homais vaunts in fact his mastery of the encyclopedia, declaring to mother Lefrançois, when she questions his competence in agriculture, that, as a scientist, he is empowered with universal knowledge:

Certainement, je m'y entends, puisque je suis pharmacien, c'est-à-dire chimiste! Et la chimie, madame Lefrançois, ayant pour objet la connaissance de l'action réciproque et moléculaire de tous les corps de la nature, il s'ensuit que l'agriculture se trouve comprise dans son domaine! Et, en effet, composition des engrais, fermentation des liquides, analyses des gaz et influence des miasmes, qu'est-ce que tout cela, je vous le demande, si ce n'est de la chimie pure et simple?

[Of course I understand it, since I am a pharmacist, that is, a chemist! And chemistry, dear madame Lefrançois, having as its object the knowledge of the reciprocal and molecular action of all the bodies in nature, it follows that agriculture is included in its domain. And, after all, consider the composition of fertilizers, the fermentation of liquids, the analysis of gases, and the influence of miasmas, what is all that if not pure and simple chemistry?] (165)

Homais's pretense at mastering the encyclopedia of "all the bodies in nature," and hence total reality, is perforce fraudulent. But his belief in the totality of discourses called science is not insincere, even if no single mind short of God, Hegel, or Laplace's absolute mind could encompass them all. The Laplacian hypothesis about a mind that could, in principle, grasp all connections seems to be reflected in Homais's foolishness. Homais presents a buffoon's version of the ideal of a mind that would be a mirror of the absolute. The total mind is part of the fiction of the Flaubertian Ideal, the Ideal by which we judge the fall of real science into the so-called real world, Flaubert's world of agricultural fairs in which pigs win prizes and pretty wives let themselves be seduced by handsome bounders.

Science exists as discourse, as language, and it is only in language that one can invent such strange notions as a total grasp of some total reality. The belief in totality shows that language can infect the world with strange practices and even stranger beliefs. Interestingly, if Flaubert seems parodistic of the idea of a totalization, he does not question the language he gives to his narrator, the observer whose language is presupposed entirely adequate to his purposes. The narrator never challenges his own capacity for adequate expression. Language falls and fails only when it exists *in* the world of the characters—to wit, multiple times with Emma, but also with Charles. For example, the language of science aborts when it induces Charles into attempting to practice medicine in some significant way. The telling example of this failure occurs when Homais reads about a surgical procedure that might cure a clubfoot. The cure exists, described in a book, as a textual feat in that ideal realm where cause and effect are united seamlessly by language. Beguiled by Homais and seduced by the promise of fame, Charles starts to read medical texts in a vain attempt to learn how this procedure is done. This reading in turn prompts the equally vain attempt to learn how to diagnose the malformation in the first place. Caught up in medical texts, he is led to believe that he can accomplish the cures set forth in the books as so many exploits derived from proper analysis. Like a medical Don Quixote, Charles enters the world of texts not only at his peril, but at that of his patients.

Medical history weighs upon this central episode in which Charles nearly causes his hapless patient to die of gangrene, since history is also a measure of the fall into the misery that afflicts all things. Flaubert's narrator ironically insists on Charles's place in this history as Charles attempts to make history in his village. Historical objectivity and irony contend for the dominant rhetorical mode as the narrator describes, with due historical references, that, as a surgeon, Charles has little hope of making an incision on the right spot on his patient's body:

> Ni Ambroise Paré, appliquant pour la première fois depuis Celse, après quinze siècles d'intervalle, la ligature immédiate d'une artère; ni Dupuytren allant ouvrir un abcès à travers une couche épaisse d'encéphale; ni Gensoul, quand il fit la première ablation de maxillaire supérieure, n'avaient certes le coeur si palpitant, la main si frémissante, l'intellect aussi tendu que M. Bovary quand il approcha d'Hippolyte, son *ténotome* entre les doigts.

> [Neither Ambroise Paré, applying for the first time since Celsus, after a period of fifteen centuries, an immediate ligature to an artery; nor Dupuytren going to cut open an abscess through the thick layer of encephalon [the brain]; nor Gensoul, when he did the first ablation of a maxillary; none certainly had such a palpitating heart, such a quivering hand, or such a strained intellect as did M. Bovary when he approached Hippolyte, with his *tenotome* [tendon-cutter] in hand.] (205)

A quick gloss of this paragraph shows that Flaubert's narrator can double as a medical historian. Though Paré was famous as a surgeon in the Renaissance—he was the first important surgeon since Roman times—only in the eighteenth century did surgery detach itself from the barber's bloody knife and become a medical specialty. The medical necessities of the Napoleonic wars had endowed France with eminent and well-practiced surgeons, and Paris was the European center for the development of surgical knowledge. Best known perhaps for the contracture that bears his name, the surgeon Guillaume Dupuytren (1777–1835) could become rich and famous, as one sees in a painting in the Carnavalet in which Dupuytren shows, to Charles X on a visit to the Hôtel-Dieu, a woman whose cataracts have just been removed. Paired with Dupuytren, the most famous surgeon of the early nineteenth century, is the far lesser-known Joseph Gensoul (1797–1858), the chief surgeon at the hospital in Lyons from 1826, the year during which he did, indeed, excise a maxilla, or upper jaw, in its entirety. Moreover, as Flaubert knew, orthopedic surgery was becoming a specialty so that William Little could open in London in 1838 his "Infirmary for the Cure of Club Foot [sic]."[17] Applied science, combining pathological anatomy and technical skill, seemingly meant science could have repercussions in the world of practical affairs—though not in the world in which the history of surgery eventuates in a Charles Bovary. History, as it unfolds in his village, documents the fall into misery.

Charles knows nothing, but, as the above passage shows, the narrator ideally knows all. So the novel is split by the tension between the ideal knowledge of the narrator—scientist and historian—and the dismal results Charles obtains from his lack of understanding. When gangrene sets in after Charles's experiment, it is a doctor narrator who, with professional expertise, observes Hippolyte as the suffering lad is tortured by Charles and Homais. The *stréphopode* (or "taloped," in Steegmuller's translation, though "talopes" is the more usual nineteenth-century English term) is suffering atrocious convulsions: the foot disappears into a horrible swelling, and the reader "sees" that the skin is covered with ecchymoses. Removed from Bovary's curing contraption, the edema disappears, though once the curing machine is placed back on the limb, tumefaction spreads through the leg, with numerous phlyctaena appearing and through which oozes a black fluid. (In paraphrasing the narrator's description of Hippolyte's torture, I use the same Greco-Latin medical terminology the narrator uses; since the narrator clearly is meant to embody a medical observer, translators make a mistake when

17. Cf. Dieter Jeter, *Geschichte der Medizin*, 338.

they translate this vocabulary into ordinary language.) Only a scientific medical observer can see phlyctaena—small cutaneous blisters—on
a patient's skin. The narrator possesses the ideal medical knowledge
that Charles lacks and which he direly needs to keep the "invincible rot-
ting" from reaching his patient's stomach. Only the rapid surgical in-
tervention performed by Doctor Canivet, a doctor skilled with a scalpel,
can save the boy by cutting off his once quite useful, if deformed, leg.

In résumé, the narrator, with his power as an observing presence, affirms the power of medical and scientific discourse, while the events of
the narration show the mismatch between ideal epistemic discourse and
practices in the fallen world. After this demonstration has been made,
after the disastrous operation on Hippolyte, confirming Charles's inca-
pacity and showing how little purchase science has on the fallen world,
the novel's third part gives relatively little direct attention to science until the work's conclusion. In the novel's last scenes, Flaubert calls again
upon medical discourse, this time to describe Emma's death from poi-
soning. A rather morbid propensity in Flaubert's work—his detailed
description of death and decomposition—has often been ascribed to the
fact that, as a child, he witnessed autopsies performed in the hospital in
which his father worked. Another perspective is useful in this regard.
However much direct information about the biological processes involved in death Flaubert may have gleaned from the hospital, it is also
clear that there is an intrinsic meaning to the novel's finale drawing
upon a medical vision. The narrator, as a medical observer, comments
upon the final outcome of Emma's pursuit of the ideal in her own life.
What unfolds is less an obsessive diagnosis than the drama involved in
medical prognosis, which is to say, the description of the necessary
course of a pathology. This distinction between diagnosis and prognosis goes back to the Hippocratic corpus, and Flaubert's mastery of the
medical tradition is clear in the way he traces out, with prognostic mastery, the course of Emma's death as it runs through its various necessary
manifestations. The narrator's stance is rather like that of a medical professor pointing out the relentless development that characterizes the fatal causality that Emma has embraced with her mouthful of arsenic.

The structural significance of this juxtaposition of the narrator's ideal medical knowledge and the reality of Emma's death is again that,
within the novel, scientific knowledge is useless, at least when applied
by Homais, Charles, and even the doctor Canivet, who arrives quickly

on the scene. Charles tries finally to open his *Dictionnaire des sciences médicales* that, blinded by his distress, he cannot see. Homais's sententious knowledge is as useless as Charles's ignorance, for all he knows is that, in such cases, one must "do an analysis." Canivet administers an emetic that causes Emma great suffering, and then prepares a theriac, or a concoction to serve as an antidote, when the last representative of science in the novel arrives, the celebrated doctor Larivière.

Some critics have seen a portrait of Flaubert's father in doctor Larivière, and medical historians have quoted Flaubert's passage on Larivière for a historical description of what French medicine was, ideally at least, in the early nineteenth century:

> Il [Larivière] appartenait à la grande école chirurgicale sortie du tablier de Bichat, à cette génération, maintenant disparue, de practiciens philosophes qui, chérissant leur art d'un amour fanatique, l'exerçaient avec exaltation et sagacité! Tout tremblait dans son hôpital quand il se mettait en colère, et ses élèves le vénéraient si bien, qu'ils s'efforçaient, à peine établis, de l'imiter le plus possible.

> [He [Larivière] belonged to the great surgical school that had unfolded from Bichat's medical apron, to that now departed generation of philosopher-practitioners who, cherishing their art with a fanatical love, exercised it with exaltation and sagacity! All trembled in his hospital when he got angry; and his students venerated him so much that they tried, as soon as they were established, to imitate him as much as possible.] (339)

Larivière is the last doctor to appear within the world of the novel, and he is also the last representative of a medical tradition that, after Magendie, positivism replaced. The reference to Bichat, often named the inventor of histology, recalls that vitalist tradition. One of the last important vitalists and perhaps the last major worker in medical research to refuse the microscope, Bichat was also one of the last major scientists to believe in the power of direct or unmediated vision to reveal truth without experimentation. (And, like many a romantic poet, he died very young.) One might suspect that the medical historian in Flaubert saw in him the last romantic scientist, a believer in the power of unmediated vision, who contrasts totally with the saint-turned-positivist Anthony, who exults before the microscope some years later.

Strictly speaking, however, the final reference to a "scientist" in

Madame Bovary is of course the final reference to Homais. From the novel's last line, the reader learns that the pharmacist has received the cross of the Legion of Honor. The deadpan irony, created by this final reference to the misery of events in the world, justifies the title of "stoic comedian" with which Hugh Kenner described Flaubert in his study *Flaubert, Joyce, and Beckett: The Stoic Comedians*. Homais has triumphed, a triumph that marks the ultimate defeat of the epistemic ideal that the narrator implicitly embodies. The universal "chemist" has been recognized by society and awarded for his charlatanry. Complementary to Homais's victory is the fact that Madame Bovary's unwanted daughter has been sent to work in the spinning-mill that had entranced Homais earlier in the novel. The nineteenth-century spinning-mill is, metonymically, an image of all the applications of chemistry to the growth of the cancerous industrial development that, using crude chemical processes to bleach fabric, was spewing hydrochloric acid over the French countryside. (Acid rain is not a recent invention.) Industrial degradation and fraudulent, but victorious, medical practice are the final images of the scientific enterprise that the reader sees in the world of the novel, this coming after Emma's death has marked the degradation and demise of that ideal that reflects Flaubert's own longing-filled aesthetic Ideal.

Emma is the novel's central character in that most of the episodic experience is centered on her and on the aesthetic ideal she wants to pursue, and does pursue, albeit in an altogether dysfunctional way. The aesthetic ideal, that absolute of feeling, like the epistemic ideal of scientific knowledge, is embodied in texts, though with a difference. Science, and specifically medicine, can be contained ideally in one encyclopedia, whereas the aesthetic ideal is diffused throughout a vast realm of poems and paintings, sonatas and novels, magazines and illustrations. However, like science, these multiple aesthetic texts can be reduced to theories that the would-be seeker of the ideal can apply. But instead of applying the theories to a patient, a seeker of the ideal like Emma applies them to a husband in order to make him into a lover: "D'après les théories qu'elle croyait bonnes, elle voulut se donner de l'amour. Au clair de lune, dans le jardin, elle récitait tout ce qu'elle savait par coeur de rimes passionnées et lui chantait en soupirant adagios mélancholiques; mais elle se trouvait ensuite aussi calme qu'auparavant, et Charles n'en paraissait ni plus amoureux, ni plus remué" [According to the theories that she believed valid, she tried to give herself love. By the light of the moon, she recited all the passionate rimes that she knew by heart and sang to him while sighing melancholy adagios; but she found herself afterwards as calm as she'd been before, and Charles seemed not to be made more loving by them, nor even more moved] (78). For her pretensions, Emma can be compared with Homais as much as with Charles. Homais is a caricature, to be sure, since he believes without discrimination in the possibility of applying all the "theories" of Enlightenment science and philosophy. Emma comes close to caricature when she wants to apply the romantic theories of ideal passion that she has largely garnered from fictions and poems of the eighteenth and early nineteenth centuries, from works such as *Paul et Virginie,* the novels of Walter Scott, and a good many other historical romances. No matter how trivial the "text" may be, replete with "little angels with golden wings, Madonnas, lagoons, gondoliers" or English keepsakes, Emma has had the gift for discovering in all the disparate artistic hokum of her youth an aesthetic ideal that reveals itself in a fleeting glimpse, like some Platonic idea (72). Flaubert underscores that, for Emma, this ideal has nothing religious about it, since she is not at all interested in the theological side of her convent education. She is a resolute materialist, with a mind characterized as positive, for whom the ideal must be found in a material embodiment that can work upon her senses.

Emma has two lovers, Rodolphe and then Leon, and to each she applies her theoretical ideal in an attempt to make some conformity exist between the ideal world she had perceived in texts and the affairs she carries on in the fallen world of Yonville and Rouen. She first meets Rodolphe when he brings the servant who wants to be bled. Charles's ineptitude sets Rodolphe's aristocratic ease in relief, and, as I suggested, the encounter of the future lovers seems guaranteed by the contrast between Charles's image as an inept blood-spiller and Emma's capacity to project onto Rodolphe an image making of him the embodiment of her aesthetic ideal. Flaubert passes discreetly over the pleasures of physical love in Emma's first tryst, if not the second. In her first affair the physical contact of the lovers is secondary to the way Emma integrates her affair into the aesthetic realm of ideal lovers. Through the play of her imagination she must convert her rather banal experience into some reflection of the ideal. After making love on the ground with Rodolphe, she repeats, like some mantra, that at last, "I have a lover! a lover!" This refrain aims at convincing her that she can project herself into the imaginary realm of ideal lovers drawn from all the texts that had ever fed her dreams: she imagines that she is going to enter into something marvelous where she will know only passion, ecstasy, delirium—"tout serait passion, extase, délire"—and where she will be surrounded by "a bluish immensity" wherein "pinacles of feeling" will sparkle "beneath her thought" (191). Once projected onto these "heights," into these Platonic heavens of the ideal passion, Emma can then link her fate with the literary sisters, that "lyrical legion of adulterous women" who have preceded her into this realm where feeling is an essence. Emma will participate in an *eidos* accessible only to those who have been initiated into the emotional geometry of sentimental forms (191). She believes she has become a type, one that she only previously knew abstractly in books. There is an epistemic side to this attempt to live a romantic Platonism: Emma *knows* in advance what her life can be if she can force it to be the embodiment of the books' ideal type. Knowledge of the ideal is a program for life.

When Emma first meets Leon, her second lover, they indulge in an exchange of textual clichés that make them sound like bad actors in a second-rate play as they clumsily quote for each other the received notions of the aesthetic ideal. In his correspondence, Flaubert said that he wanted to render Emma and Leon grotesque, in what Flaubert took to be the first example of a writer mocking his young leading actors.[18] Flaubert's theatrical terminology points up that the imitation of the aesthetic ideal is much like imitating a role, another one existing in the romantic Platonic heaven dictated by the multifarious texts that dictate our sentimental lives. The theatricality of her affair with Leon, beginning in the novel's third section, is also underscored by the way it begins when Emma meets Leon at the opera in Rouen. At this moment, after her sickness caused by Rodolphe's jilting her, Emma is swept up again into the realm of passion by the opera—which, typically, Charles cannot understand. As long as she is caught up in the affair with Leon, Emma again plays in order to incarnate a type, or, indeed, a host of types that should confer meaning and plenitude onto her existence. She wants simply to be "the beloved of all the novels, the heroine of all the plays,

---

18. Flaubert disliked not just these characters, but claimed to dislike his entire novel and its subject matter. See his blanket terms in the *Correspondance*, ed. Jean Bruneau, vol. 2, 416.

the vaguely-defined *her* of all the volumes of poetry," as well as the *Pale Woman of Barcelona* and, "above all else she was the Angel" (289). The narrator here emerges as a connoisseur of romantic texts, if not a literary historian, in his listing of types that underscore the fall of the ideal into pointless hyperbole. The symmetry of Emma's situation with Charles's is not total, however, for Emma must possess some of the knowledge that the narrator has, even if she possesses this knowledge in order to misuse it. She is more knowledgeable than Charles, but to no purpose, except to fail even more miserably.

For Emma, the fall is not long in coming, since Leon soon joins the pale figures of Emma's past who once seemed to promise the ideal, but who inevitably disappoint her. An indirect quotation describing Emma's despair shows that she, for a moment at least, is aware of the nature of the fall: "D'où venait donc cette insuffisance de la vie, cette pourriture instantanée des choses où elle s'appuyait?" [Whence this in-sufficiency of life, this instant rottenness of things whenever she sought support from them?] (306). The principle of life's insufficiency is the ro-mantic principle in its most concise form, for the bedrock of the roman-tic worldview is that self-realization is impossible in this world. In Flaubert's work, the romantic principle of insufficiency is analogous to the principle of the fall, because the principle of the fall, with its theo-logical origins, also declares the doomed insufficiency of all human undertakings. Neither science nor art can compensate for the world's ontological deficiency. There is a romantic overdetermination then to Emma's failure in her attempts to live the ideal, for neither the world nor her own capacities could ever allow her to succeed. Suicide is almost like a corollary entailed by these principles that Emma lives out in her own death, if such a contradictory expression can be allowed.

The contrast between the clinician-narrator's all-knowing perception and the fallen world he sees is again underscored in several ways at the novel's end. The narrator reports with unflagging clarity as he describes the stages of Emma's death. Moreover, he notes that her last sight is the blind man who has appeared several times in the novel. She looks at the unseeing man (whom Homais will have incarcerated when he cannot cure him) and sees only the unseeing. Emma's last sight on earth is blindness, an ironic situation suggesting that she has not seen what the narrator has led the reader to see: her fall was inscribed in an ideal that neither she, nor probably anybody, could realize. The narrator has de-

scribed a causal chain of events leading to predictable catastrophic results. Predictably, Emma's body is restored in death to the world of
things. As the narrator's description makes clear, her death affirms a
world of deterministic laws, occurring as the result of a series of causally related events the novel has described with the fatality of a well-
known laboratory experiment.

The question of determinism brings us back to the fundamental question about the relation between the Flaubertian novel and the dominant
epistemic discourses of the nineteenth century, deterministic discourses
such physics and chemistry, physiology, and pathological anatomy. After watching Emma die, the reader may feel that, for all Flaubert's wistful desire to be a mystic and to plumb the ideal, Flaubert really accepts
the dominance of these scientific discourses in their positivist and materialist interpretations. Emma's death is pathology in action. There is
no vitalism in Flaubert, and no metaphysical underpinnings that suggest there might be some transcendence of the world described by scientific discourse, and by Flaubert's narrator. Flaubert accepted the consensus that, if scientific knowledge was always subject to doubt, there
was nonetheless one absolute a priori principle that enabled one to engage in the epistemic quest: the principle of determinism as derived
from the principle of causality—the nineteenth-century version of the
principle of sufficient reason.

This belief in determinism as a methodological axiom is central to
Claude Bernard's thought. He described the principle of determinism
as a logical necessity. Without deterministic causality knowledge would
not exist:

> If a phenomenon, in an experiment, had such a contradictory ap-
> pearance that it did not necessarily connect itself with determinant
> causes, then reason should reject the fact as non-scientific. We
> should wait or by direct experiments seek the source of error which
> may have slipped into the observation. Indeed, there must be error
> or insufficiency in the observation; for to accept a fact without a
> cause, that is, indeterminate in its necessary conditions, is neither
> more nor less than the negation of science.[19]

Rejecting skepticism as inimical to the nonetheless dubitive attitude of
the scientist, Bernard may seem unnecessarily restrictive to readers who

19. Bernard, *An Introduction to the Study of Experimental Medicine,* 54.

live in the era of quantum mechanics (though Einstein also accepted Bernard's axiom). But the consensus about determinism sets the stage for any discussion of the way the mid-nineteenth century conceived knowledge. In brief, before a novel could make epistemic claims, it was obligatory for a novel to respect this principle in some way or another. This was the case with Flaubert, and for those later realists and naturalists, like Zola, who directly developed the axioms for fiction Flaubert had outlined in theory and practice.

The reader may well ask how a contrived fiction demonstrates the determinism that is the working axiom for the chemist or physiologist in their interpretation of an experiment. There are at least two answers to this question. Determinism is a mimetic principle in *Madame Bovary*, prescribing the way in which events and effects are linked. It is also a principle of exclusion, demanding the elimination from the narration of all events and effects that are not caused by potentially knowable principles. The principle of determinism eliminates from the narration any final causality that might endow the novel with some metaphysical dimension. Madame Bovary does not die to illustrate her moral dilemma; her death comes about because she is beset with a moral dilemma. And this dilemma derives causally from a set of antecedent conditions.

Let me adduce one example to stand for the kind of mimesis relying upon determinism that is found throughout the novel. Struggling with her first erotic desires for Leon, with her "fantaisies luxueuses" that cause her to suffer great turmoil, one day Emma hears the sound of church bells. This physical sensation acts causally to activate memory and, with memory, associations that cause her to have both psychological and physiological reactions:

> A ce tintement répété, la pensée de la jeune femme s'égarait dans ses vieux souvenirs de jeunesse et de pension. Elle se rappela les grands chandeliers, qui dépassaient sur l'autel les vases pleins de fleurs et le tabernacle à colonnettes. Elle aurait voulu, comme autrefois, être confondue dans la longue ligne des voiles blancs, que marquaient de noir çà et là les capuchons raides des bonnes soeurs inclinées sur leur prie-Dieu. . . . Alors un attendrissement la saisit: elle se sentit molle et tout abandonnée comme un duvet d'oiseau qui tournoie dans la tempête; et ce fut sans en avoir conscience qu'elle s'achemina vers l'église, disposée à n'importe quelle dévotion, pourvu qu'elle y courbât son âme et que l'existence entière y disparût.

[As the ringing continued, the young woman's thoughts began to stray among old memories of youth and the convent. She recalled the tall candlesticks that rose above on the altar the vases full of flowers and the columned tabernacle. She would have liked again, as in those days, to be one with the long line of white veils that were marked here and there by the black of the nuns' stiff cowls as they bent over their *prie-dieu.* . . . Then a moment of emotion seized her: she felt soft and completely abandoned like some bird's down swirling in a storm; and then without being conscious of it she started going toward the church, ready for any kind of devotional practice, so long as she could make her soul pliant and completely lose her existence in it.] (143–44)

Emma responds at first unconsciously to physical sensation. This is a causal relation that, through the associations, is at once physical and cultural in nature. Bells are sensorial causes that set off, deterministically, a series of associations that have behavioral effects. In this case, unconscious reactions are mediated by sensations that are common to the past and the present. The sensations come from the exterior environment and determine a physiological reaction in the inner environment—to use terms Claude Bernard used only slightly later in *La Medécine expérimentale.* Almost mechanically, Emma is drawn toward the church to seek a solace, the nature of which she is barely aware.

In conclusion, it does not seem hyperbole that to say that Flaubert's modernism, if that is the word for the deliberate act by which he expiated his romanticism in *Madame Bovary,* consists in having endowed the novel with a form that imitates epistemic discourse. In this regard he has shifted the emphasis one finds in Balzac, a writer in whose work science is at once theme and topic, or, if one prefers, science is demonstrated. In Flaubert's case, his attenuated and ambiguous rivalry with science resulted in the invention of the rhetoric of modern realism, deriving directly from scientific epistemology. To use again Claude Bernard's epistemological distinctions, I conclude that Flaubert made of the novel a form that imitates what Bernard called a science of observation. Bernard divided the sciences into the sciences of observation—such as astronomy—and the experimental sciences, such as chemistry and physiology, in which the scientist can intervene experimentally to force epistemic relations to reveal themselves. Bernard's point of view reflects what was a growing consensus about the nature of knowledge, and there can be little question that Flaubert was consciously influenced by this development—as when he declared that art would aspire to the condition of science. To this end, Flaubert inscribed the epistemic observer into the novel to observe the workings of the world and show "how" but not "why" the world worked as it does. The positivistic refusal of "why" is, again according to a scientist like Claude Bernard, the mark of the scientific observer: "How" is all the scientist can demonstrate. "Why" is Emma Bovary determined by her contact with the aesthetic ideal to become the tawdry rebel who finally seeks an escape in suicide? Within the limits imposed by nineteenth-century epistemology, this is not a question that can be answered. Accordingly, Flaubert permits the reader only to see "how" it happens: in conformity with a deterministic series of causes and effects that, with the inexorable linking of a fatality, correspond to the determinism that had become the axiomatic starting point for all nineteenth-century science. After Flaubert, and perhaps to Flaubert's own distaste, this determinism had become a basis for narrative structure and, hence, a basis for literature to make its claim to knowledge in its rivalry with science.

FOUR

Zola's Collaborative Rivalry with Science

Je vais tâcher de prouver à mon tour que, si la
méthode expérimentale conduit à la connaissance
de la vie physique, elle doit conduire aussi à la
connaissance de la vie passionnelle et intellectuelle.

*[I am going to try to prove in my turn that, if the
experimental method leads to knowledge of physical life, it
must also lead to knowledge of passional and intellectual
life.]*

—Zola, *Le Roman expérimental*

HISTORICAL OVERVIEW

1835: Quételet uses, in *Sur l'Homme*, theory of probabilities to describe the average man.

1838: Pinel's student Esquirol publishes *Des Maladies mentales* in the same year in which France undertakes reform of care of the insane and mandates that an asylum be opened in every *département*.

1840: Zola is born. Agassiz publishes *Etudes sur les glaciers*, part of his work defending the catastrophism of Cuvier against Lyell's uniformitarinism.

1859: After Joule's work on the principle of the conservation of energy, Clausius publishes a paper showing the energy of a system remains constant while its entropy strives toward a maximum.

1865: Claude Bernard publishes *Introduction à l'étude de la médecine expérimentale.*

1869: Mendeleyev works out his first version of the periodic table tabulating the elements in terms of atomic weight.

1871: In *The Descent of Man,* Darwin explores paths of human evolution from other animal species, having avoided the topic in *The Origin of the Species* (1859).

1871: Zola begins publication of *Les Rougon-Macquart.*

1873: Maxwell's *Treatise on Electricity and Magnetism* gives mathematical treatment to Faraday's theory of electricity and magnetism.

1877: Boltzmann publishes his equation relating thermodynamic entropy and the statistical distribution of molecular configurations.

1881: Pasteur demonstrates effectiveness of his vaccine against anthrax.

1892: Zola begins work on *Le Docteur Pascal,* reading a translation of Weismann's work on heredity, *Das Keimplasma—eine Theorie der Vererbung,* also published that year.

1901: De Vries, having discovered Mendelian work on genetics in 1900, publishes *Die Mutationstheorie.*

1909: Bateson, having produced the first English translation of Mendel, introduces the term *genetics* one year after he became the first Cambridge professor of the subject.

Flaubert maintained a friendly relation with his younger contemporary, Emile Zola, though in temperament and ideology they were dissimilar. Wanting to join the march of triumphant science, Zola openly vaunted that his literary ambitions were scientific in nature. Quite simply, he wanted to join science and literature in a common epistemic achievement. Zola took much from Flaubert for the novelistic side of this enterprise. He was quite aware of the epistemic nature of Flaubert's work, and even declared *Madame Bovary* to be the first naturalist novel. However, he hardly shared Flaubert's pessimism about the possibility of applying science to the world. In the series of novels called *Les Rougon-Macquart,* Zola wanted to create the scientific novel, and, by scientific, he meant the term in a strong sense: he believed that the novel could be an epistemic discourse participating in common research with sciences such as medicine or biology. By scientific, Zola understood that in these novels literature itself could become a discourse epistemologically commensurate with the scientific theories that, by 1870, had transformed our understanding of the cosmos and our place therein. With a self-confidence that seems improbable today, Zola intended to rival science by making literature its equal, and hence to contribute to science. He intended to do so while accepting science's own self-estimation that it was the arbiter of all epistemic discourse. But literature, in the form of the novel, could, according to Zola, participate in this decision-making process.

In this chapter I want to show that Zola is not necessarily benighted in his judgment about himself, as many critics imply, for he did indeed transform the novel into an instrument using scientific theory. It may not be true that he transformed the novel into a lab report, as sometimes seemed to be Zola's intent, nor do his novels always embody what we take to be scientific truth. However, where Zola is wrong, the science of his time was largely wrong, at least from today's perspective. And where Zola is right, from the perspective of today's science, Zola transformed the novel as a scientific recorder of social reality in innovative ways. With Zola's work, fiction realized epistemic ambitions that mark a heretofore unparalleled accomplishment with regard to its desire to be an epistemic discourse. From the perspective of the history of science, the science Zola incorporates in his novels is a mixture of now antiquated speculation and fruitful theories. From the perspective of the history of literature, his work seems almost too epistemically ambitious for us to understand it fully today. We shall make that attempt here.

Zola's desire to rival science is well known from his oft-quoted manifestos, but the desire is also clearly inscribed in *Les Rougon-Macquart*. Most appositely, for example, in Zola's novel of 1886, *L'Oeuvre (The Masterpiece)*, the fictional novelist Pierre Sandoz echoes Zola's ambitions when Sandoz says he wants to construct a series of novels that would parallel science. Only science can be the source for the epistemic inspiration that the would-be novelist seeks:

> Ah! que ce serait beau, si l'on donnait son existence entière à une oeuvre, où l'on tacherait de mettre les choses, les êtres, les hommes, l'arche immense! Et pas dans l'ordre imbécile dont notre orgueil se berce, mais en pleine coulée de la vie universelle, un monde où nous ne serions qu'un accident, où le chien qui passe, et jusqu'à la pierre des chemins, nous compléteraient, nous expliqueraient; enfin le grand tout, sans haut ni bas, ni sale ni propre, tel qu'il fonc-

tionne. . . . Bien sûr, c'est à la science que doivent s'adresser les ro-
manciers et les poètes, elle est aujourd'hui l'unique source possible.
Mais, voilà! que lui prendre, comment marcher avec elle? Tout de
suite, je sens que je patauge. . . . Ah! si je savais, si je savais, quelle
serie de bouquins je lancerais à la tête de la foule!

[Ah, it would be so fine if you were to give yourself over to a work
in which you'd put everything, beings, men, the whole immense
ark [*arche*]. And not in the idiotic order in which our pride deludes
itself, but in the full flow of universal life, a world in which we
would appear simply as an accident, in which a passing dog and
even a rock in the road would be our complement and would explain us. You know, the great totality, without anything high or low,
or dirty or clean, just as it functions. . . . Of course novelists and poets have to turn to science, today it is the only possible source. But,
voilà, what can you take from it, how can you keep astride with it?
Right away, I feel as if I'm floundering. . . . Ah, if I only knew, if I
knew how, what a bunch of books I'd throw at the crowd.][1]

Sandoz does not know how to handle his desire to do science, though
he knows he wants to participate in the elaboration of that totalizing discourse that nineteenth-century epistemology had theorized as possible.
Sandoz differs from his creator insofar as Zola certainly thought, at least
in his more sanguine moments, that he had found the intellectual means
by which to meet the challenge of keeping astride with science. And to
this end he did indeed throw a good many novels at the crowd, novels
incorporating Claude Bernard's refusal to judge normal and abnormal,
the high and the low, and incorporating a Darwinian perspective in
which the accident called life is elucidated as the product of micro- and
macroforces that no novelist had ever presented in quite the same way
before.

Before turning to this Darwinian perspective, I want first to examine
the general epistemological issues Zola engaged in his work. These considerations can set the stage for understanding Zola's epistemic originality. Since I mean here to take seriously Zola's belief that he could do
science with the novel, I must also attend to the science, or rather sciences, that he relied upon. The issue is not always clear. Zola sometimes
proposes literature as the epistemic equivalent of a biology text or a

1. Zola, *Les Rougon-Macquart*, vol. 4, 46.

work in practical physiology. At other times he seems to think that a novel can be the equivalent of a statistical study of a social macrocosm whose state at any given moment is produced by the random movements of the microscopic elements composing the system. All of these issues clearly reflect various developments in the science of the second half of the nineteenth century.

These issues, in science as in Zola's novels, are embodied in a fully secularized discourse that refuses any transcendental dimension to the world. Zola's distance from Balzac in this respect is very great, but Zola is also more in harmony with positive science than the Flaubert in whose work a nostalgia for transcendence is detected in the depiction of its emphatic absence. For Zola, as for any working scientist, the world is the world, and that is all. In the naturalist novel the world represented is the physiological and physical world in which suffering animals known as human beings are driven by passions, genetically determined madness, the desire for justice, and the need for a redemption that most likely will occur because of fortunate mutations—to use concepts such as genetics and mutation that Zola as well as then contemporary biologists were groping for. Critics often describe Zola as an allegorical and mythic writer. However, he is a writer in whose work allegory and myth are largely naturalized as ways of knowing our being in the world, for transcendence is not suggested by mythic images in Zola. And, equally important, an epistemic intent dominates Zola's novels even when his ideology or temperament drive him to look for an adequate mythic image to express them.

Zola's model of science and its practices is by and large not our model today, or at least this model is no longer a well-received model. However, it is well to have this model in mind to understand the optimism with which Zola could envisage his success in developing a new type of novel. His model of science makes of science an always future discourse, by which I mean that for Zola, science is a discourse whose essential dimension belongs to the future. In the future one will know ever more and, by knowing that one will know more, one can transform the present by looking at it in light of the promise of future revelation. A myth of progress is certainly behind this belief in a necessary future dimension to science. The effect of this myth is that it allows the seeker of knowledge to posit a future state in order to transform the present. The present, with its contingent knowledge, is illuminated by a hypothetical future in which knowledge will be greater in scope and more certain in its claims. With what is really the a priori definition of knowledge as an ever greater future state, our presently contingent knowledge can be converted into the basis for a future necessity. This hypothetical necessity for future knowledge allows one to take as an axiom that one is certain one is going to know ever more about the world. The future of knowledge can only be a future in which present uncertainty is progressively eliminated and the present is enlarged—for what can be the basis for future knowledge except what we already know today? There is an enabling circularity in this process of extrapolation that allows the seeker of knowledge to find certainty in the future, a future about which there should only be a probable presumption. This extrapolation of certainty from the uncertainty of the present moment is partly mathematical, and partly ideological, and, in spite of the probabilistic nature of the extrapolation, it still often underlies an unwavering faith in science's ever-increasing capacity to know.

This model is found in Zola's programmatic essay on the "experimental novel," the once widely read *Le Roman expérimental*. Drawing upon Claude Bernard, Zola accepts as fact, or certainty, the hypothesis according to which all living bodies will be explained by the "general mechanism of matter": "La science prouve que les conditions d'existence de tout phenomène sont les mêmes dans les corps vivants que dans les corps bruts; et, dès lors, la physiologie prend peu à peu les certitudes de la chimie et de la physique" [Science proves that the conditions of existence for every phenomenon are the same for living bodies as for inanimate bodies; and, from that moment, physiology acquires gradually the certainties of chemistry and physics].[2] Physiology emerges as a form of certain future knowledge extrapolated from the reasonable probabilities that chemistry could offer. This model of science further presupposes the future necessity of a unified scientific discourse that will unite the novel with other sciences in the great epistemic project of explaining life:

> Quand on aura prouvé que le corps de l'homme est une machine, dont on pourra un jour démonter et remonter les rouages au gré de l'expérimentateur, il faudra bien passer aux actes passionnels et intellectuels de l'homme. Des lors, nous entrerons dans le domaine

2. Zola, *Le Roman expérimental*, 15.

qui, jusqu'à présent appartenait à la philosophie et à la littérature; ce sera la conquête décisive par la science des hypothèses des philosophes et des écrivains. On a la chimie et la physique expéri-mentales; on aura la physiologie expérimentale; plus tard encore, on aura le roman expérimental.

[When it has been proved that the human body is a machine whose cogs one will be able some day to take apart and put back together as one pleases, it will then be necessary to go on to consider the emo-tional and intellectual acts of human beings. After that we will en-ter into a domain that, until the present, belonged to philosophy and literature. Then we will see science's conquest of hypotheses advanced by philosophers and writers. We have experimental chemistry and physics. We will have experimental physiology. And later on we will have the experimental novel.] (15)

The novel will cease being a source of hypotheses, which is its current role, according to Zola, even in *Les Rougon-Marquart*. The novel will en-ter into the great unified discourse of future epistemic certainty that all sciences will know. The same certain determinism that rules over the movement of rocks and stars will be found ruling the movements of the human brain, for a unified determinism will characterize all discourses that are truly knowledge.

What is most impressive in Zola's manifesto is not simply his en-dorsement of the positivist credo—though there is certainly a great deal of that in Zola's model for the future development of science. Rather, it is his admittedly weak use of probability theory as a springboard to put together a credo proclaiming the unity of all epistemic discourse. One might also see in his credo a renovation of the doctrine of totalization that, by the mid-nineteenth century, had lost scientific credibility. But there is a difference: Zola has faith in the probability of an a priori mod-el prescribing the future unity of all knowledge united in terms of in-terlinking discourses. And he knew that there was, at the time he wrote, no basis for a present totalization; there was relatively little experimen-tal evidence that could count for or against the possibility of unifying all epistemic discourses ranging from physics to medicine. With suffi-cient prescience, however, one could have pointed out that the demise of the hegemony of classical mechanics, unfolding as Zola began writ-ing, was really a sign of the end of epistemic unity, though the demise of classical dynamics was not yet truly evident until the first decade of the twentieth century. In fact, then as today, the model of epistemic unity was alluring by its promise of logical completeness. Zola's totalizing science, like today's, was not based on the power of mind, as in Hegel, but on the belief in a final theory that, under the aegis of physical theory, would unite all sciences into one unified discourse—including the novel as Zola saw it.

To create this unity of epistemic discourses one postulates, then and now, that at each level of epistemic analysis is an appropriate discourse that can describe the organization of that level, going from the most general discourse of physics to the more particular science of chemistry, then from chemistry to discourses like biology and physiology that deal with increasingly complicated systems. Each level is constrained by the laws describing the preceding level so that physical theory is the bedrock discipline constraining all others. Zola saw that this hierarchy culminates in the humanistic discourses with their concern for absolute particulars organized in systems having the greatest complexity. When looking at the overall shape of this hierarchy, it is difficult not to think of some Neoplatonic vision in which being, like a great fountain gushing over with ontological outpourings from a central spring, overflows from level to level as knowledge unfolds to describe ever more complex systems. Probability theory aside, however, it has required something of an act of faith to argue, from Zola's time to the present, that the emerging relationships of physics, chemistry, and biology point to the possibility that more complex levels of organization might emerge from the simpler levels of analysis. Contemporary complexity theory has, in fact, argued just the opposite, to wit, each "higher" level is incommensurate with the "lower" level, or, as Nobel laureate biologist Gerard Edelman argues in works such as *Bright Air, Brilliant Fire: On the Matter of Mind,* quantum mechanics will never explain genetics. (Quotation marks here indicate the rather arbitrary nature of the spacial metaphors, going up and down or vice versa, as one goes from discipline to discipline.)

In *Le Roman expérimental* of 1879, Zola held up experimental physiology as a model for scientific discourse that pointed to interlinking connections, going from physics to literature. Zola's comparison of medical physiology with literature was not entirely inapt. Medicine could be looked upon, well into the nineteenth century, as something of an empirical "art." Medicine's uncertain status between art and science might appear to justify Zola's claim that the novel was analogous to medicine.

Both were about to cease being mere art in order to become "scientific." Work in experimental physiology had pointed toward a transformation of medicine, and, presumably, Zola's fiction was to do the same for literature. However, Zola's epistemic interest was larger than medicine, and his "literary science" is richer than what some critics have seen as an outdated medical theory of heredity and a summary view of human conduct as simply instinctual in nature. Zola's *Rougon-Macquart* is a compendium of much of the science of the second half of the nineteenth century.

Cultural historian Michel Serres has pointed out the scope of Zola's epistemic ambitions in *Les Rougon-Macquart,* and I turn to his dithyrambic analysis of Zola's science for a suggestion about the broad approach necessary to grasp Zola's epistemic project. Writing about the last novel of the series, *Le Docteur Pascal,* Serres outlines Zola's epistemic goals in terms of three centers of scientific interest that emerge from the novel's mythological "bric-a-brac." These centers are a mathematical theory of heredity, "synoptically condensed in the genealogical tree"; a physics of "fire and heat," based on a global cosmology, with quantification of energy; and a "dynamics of exchange and displacements, directed toward integral equilibria by differentiated systems, local transfers, permutations, replacements, and returns." These three sciences, Serres goes on to say, are juxtaposed with already existing cultural formations, constellations of myth, religious symbols, rules of social organization in a well-defined locus in which all models relate to each other as an ensemble.[3] In brief, in his analysis Serres emphasizes that Zola's work is something like a cosmography, with several dominant epistemic focal points serving as the basis for a worldview.

These epistemic focal points draw upon the science of the time for their content. Building upon Serres's ideas, with perhaps more critical analysis, I am going to argue that, in addition to being concerned with a theory of heredity, Zola used concepts parallel to those that were emerging in physics in the decades from 1850 to 1880. These were the decades during which Maxwell, Clausius, and Boltzmann were developing thermodynamics and interpreting it in terms of statistical kinetics. What Serres calls a "physics of fire and heat" describes the fact that Zola's portrayal of the energetics of a social system parallels the ther-

3. Serres, *Feux et signaux de Brume: Zola,* 114.

modynamic explanations of the behavior of macrosystems that are created by the activities of individual agents, and for which a statistical description can provide general laws. Moreover, Zola's literary dynamics reflects the development of probability theory that, in the second half of the nineteenth century, was used to explain the nature of the laws of kinetics. In this sense, his grasp of probability theory was in harmony with developments in the physical sciences. In physics, probabilistic explanations had, in fact, become necessary to explain thermodynamics and its puzzling first and second laws—laws that were not totally in harmony with Newtonian dynamics. I shall return to this latter point presently.

This new sense of probability underlies Doctor Pascal's genealogical tree that provides the schematic model for the overall structure of *Les Rougon-Macquart*. It is in this sense that we can understand Serres's claim that mathematics are involved in this tree outlining the development of the clan. It is not in the sense that Zola had any inkling of Mendel's quantification of inheritance. He didn't. Rather, a genealogical tree is also a probability schema: it is a tree diagram that shows a sequence of events whose conditional probabilities can be calculated by multiplying the probabilities along any sequence of events. And according to the tree, the probability seems very great that Pascal may go mad. Even without any formalization, we intuitively understand Pascal's anguish about the high probability that his own heredity is defective—he comes at the end of the line of degenerates whose heredity determines his fate. Like Zola, Pascal believes at once in an a priori materialist model that should undergird a new physiology and in the farmer and breeder's very old empirical techniques that allow the rough calculation of possible hereditary combinations.

In short, one can argue that, if part of Zola's science is outmoded, a period piece as it were, part of it is quite modern. The two sides of his science—his outmoded heredity and his sense of probabilities and energetics—are interlinked. In this regard, Zola's situation is not unlike Darwin's. Darwin had no inkling about the mechanism of heredity, and yet he formulated a way of understanding how species emerge in time. Darwin's outmoded views of inheritance did not prevent him from accounting for the group dynamics of living populations and finding a nearly mechanistic explanation for the evolution of species. Much the same thing can be said about Zola's formulation of scientific explanations and the embodiment of models in his works, specifically with regard to heredity and population dynamics.

Heredity is often invoked in the novels to explain characters' actions. It is this side of Zola's science that seems most outmoded, and one wonders if it is for this reason, rather perversely, that his views on heredity have been well documented by critics eager to show Zola's deficiencies. It is easy to demonstrate that Zola used various medical works of the mid-nineteenth century to concoct part of his theory of heredity. Some of Zola's ideas are taken from the work of Prosper Lucas, a medical theorist rarely mentioned in modern histories of biology, medicine, or heredity. Zola also recycled medical myths about heredity that were part of a historical tradition that disappeared with the elaboration of modern genetics, roughly beginning after 1900. Needless to say, the history of modern genetics is usually written as the history of a success story, not of unsuccessful theories, nor of folk myths. To be sure, little in Zola's work, or in medical science of the mid-nineteenth century for that matter, has much to do with the success story of modern genetics, a story usually taken to begin with the rediscovery of Mendel's work and the understanding of chromosomes in the early twentieth century.

The mythic side of Zola's descriptions of heredity and its effects is especially clear when we realize that they owe as much to the Renaissance doctrine of signatures as to a theory of physiological determinism that seems proto-modern. Zola's characters are described, for instance, as being genetically formed by impressions or mental images that imprint a signature on the child in the womb. The conditions for this signature exist even before the child is conceived. Biologist François Jacob has described the way in which the Renaissance belief in the role of signatures in heredity also included a role for the imagination:

> Thus in the confection of perfect beings who engender their own kind, the network of similitudes ends up dividing in two. On the one hand, the reproduction of form and of temperament is assured by the resemblance that heredity brings about. On the other hand, by the intermediary of sensations perceived by the parents, or under the influence of their imagination, the product of generation is accessible to influences from the exterior world that can print upon the child the signature of all possible analogies.[4]

4. Jacob, *La Logique du vivant: Une histoire de l'hérédité*, 35.

The microcosm and macrocosm, and the analogies they maintain, reflect each other in this circular causality in which the child is a prism for the universe, and the universe can imprint a pattern on the child. In Zola's work, this universe is also the deterministic universe in which a character's development is overdetermined by physiological decadence and environmental decay, by what we shall see is Zola's version of entropy.

Zola was hardly alone among nineteenth-century writers in accepting these nearly magical traditional views of heredity. Michelet, whose book on love, *L'Amour*, was undoubtedly an influence on Zola, also quoted Lucas to buttress his claim that a woman could be imprinted by exterior influences. The magical view of inheritance was in Michelet's case, though not in Zola's, part of the ideology that made a woman into a permanent male possession, or as a nineteenth-century translation of Michelet reads:

> But there is yet something of greater importance. Facts, coming from another source (*v. Lucas*, vol. ii, p. 60), commence to prove that the union of love, whither the man betakes himself so lightly, is for the woman more profound and definitive than has ever been believed. She gives herself up, entirely and irrevocably. The phenomenon observed in the inferior female animals is found, less regularly indeed, but still is found in woman. Fecundation transforms her in a lasting manner. The widow frequently bears to her second husband children which resemble her first.[5]

The magical view is embedded in what appears to the discourse of natural history, for the comparison of women with female animals seems to naturalize what is (today) errant nonsense concerning genetic inheritance. Yet, this embedding points up an important fact. Traditional or magical views can be mixed with emerging scientific views. The fusion of the two may only be clear in retrospect, from the perspective of a later observer who can sort out science and magic. In short, the acceptance of traditional (and now) mythic views of inheritance did not preclude Michelet and Zola's acceptance of what are (now) modern views of systemic relations.

Zola's reliance upon the hereditary doctrine of signatures illustrates an important point about the history of science and its role in culture.

5. Michelet, *Love*, trans. J. W. Palmer, M.D., 18.

His example shows that in the course of the history of Western medicine, from the Greeks through the latter part of the nineteenth century, every medical theory or doctrine had been subject to reprise. Well into the nineteenth century it had been possible to recycle every theory from those founding doctrines of Hippocrates through the successful quackery of the Broussais whom Balzac satirizes (Broussais's early nineteenth-century theory of hyper-irritation described almost all disease as a manifestation of gastroenteritis that could be cured with leeches). No medical theory was ever really dead, at least not until modern modes of inquiry marked the irreversibility of medical history. For medicine, as with practically all sciences except mathematics, modernity for a given science only begins to exist when its history becomes largely irrelevant for the practice of that science. After Newton, Aristotelian physics were reduced to a matter of antiquarian interest. After Lavoisier, the same can be said about the phlogistic chemistry of the seventeenth and eighteenth centuries, or the alchemy of earlier times. In medicine, Claude Bernard's remarks in his *Introduction to the Study of Experimental Medicine* signal a turning point, and his strictures *against* history mark the beginning of the irreversibility of history for experimental physiology, if not for diagnostics:

> Literary and artistic productions never grow old, in this sense, that they are expressions of feeling, changeless as human nature. . . . But science, which stands for what man has learned, is essentially mobile in expression; it varies and perfects itself in proportion to the increase of acquired knowledge. Present day science is therefore necessarily higher than the science of the past; and there is no reason for going in search of any addition to modern science through knowledge of the ancients.[6]

Bernard's dictum is not a late restatement of the quarrel of the ancients and moderns, but a description of the irreversibility of history that characterizes the modernity of what we call modern science.

For all the use Zola made of Bernard, Zola did not like Bernard's attitude toward art and literature. As a writer, Zola wanted to offer knowledge of societal and cultural conditions, and this knowledge is perforce inscribed in historical becoming. So Zola confronted opposing impulses

---

6. Bernard, *An Introduction to the Study of Experimental Medicine*, 142.

in himself. On the one hand, in his desire to contribute to science, Zola believed he needed to annex literature to science as part of the irreversible process of epistemic development that had rendered history meaningless for the practice of natural science. In a sense, this meant the novel itself should be an ahistorical form. On the other hand, Zola could hardly assign the history of culture and especially literature to the dustbin of history—to underscore the paradox of historicity—since it is clear that the very form of the novel partakes of this history. Nor could he ignore that the science he wanted to undertake was historical insofar as historical becoming is a dimension of the social system of which the novel should offer knowledge. He could not readily accept Bernard's harsh dictum on the meaning of history for science.

Zola's discomfiture about history is, from our perspective, inscribed then in a history of science that allows us to read where Zola stood between modernity and premodernity as far as medicine and heredity are concerned. He is on the other side of that moment, before Mendel's work on genetic distribution was rediscovered, and after which no earlier model of heredity could be recycled. But Mendel's quantification of the distribution of inherited traits could not be read with understanding until the beginning of the twentieth century. After Mendel's paper was rediscovery by at least three biologists in 1900, genetics became a science, especially after De Vries enriched evolutionary theory with the concept of mutation. In terms of the history of heredity, then, Zola was writing *Les Rougon-Macquart* at a premodern moment when the recycling of nearly all earlier models explaining inheritance was still possible. Or as Y. Malinas succinctly says in the conclusion of his excellent discussion of Zola and the doctrines of inheritance Zola drew upon, Zola's fictional Doctor Pascal knew as much about inheritance as any of Zola's real contemporaries. Zola was badly advised about the science of heredity by a doctor friend, Maurice de Fleury, though he was probably predisposed to believe any "scientific" explanation in his great desire to find a great general explanation of heredity. In any case, using Lucas's classification, Zola was able to construct a genetic theory that was "neither more nor less valuable" that Galton's or Darwin's.[7]

The comparison of Darwin and Zola is fruitful in several regards. Darwin's thinking about populations as the basic unit for evolutionary

7. Y. Malinas, *Zola et les hérédités imaginaires*, 90.

theory finds parallels in Zola's attempt to organize fiction in terms of populations as well as individual characters. With no viable theory for inheritance, Darwin formulated the basic theory of population development on the basis of changes undergone by individuals. Theories of evolution and of heredity are complementary, but quite different theories. Darwin could only speculate about the "black box" of heredity, but he could describe its effect in terms of population dynamics and the production of species.

Analogously, Zola's very conception of *Les Rougon-Macquart* series is designed to provide a literary illustration of how population dynamics works through the permutations that are generated by the initial three characters of the series' first novel, *La Fortune des Rougon* (1871), beginning the "fortune" of the Rougon family. In this novel, the founder of the clan, Adélaïde Fouque, first marries a Rougon, has one son, then takes a Macquart as a lover, and has a son and daughter. Whence *Les Rougon-Macquart* and its hereditary stock, and whence Zola's population of characters. Whatever be the mechanism for transmitting traits— and Zola strains our imagination on this issue—his first novel does set out a "population" as the basic unit of discourse in terms that are modern. In conceiving the development of the population of characters that spring from this initial stock, Zola tried to think of characters no longer in terms of fixed types, as in earlier biology and fiction. Rather, he increasingly thought in terms of individuals who constitute a population subject to evolutionary development. This is one of Zola's remarkable achievements, and it parallels nineteenth-century biology in its conceptual transformation.

After Darwin, the very basis for conceptualizing biology changed— and this is an essential point for understanding how our contemporary basis for theorization is fundamentally different from that of the early nineteenth century. The radical nature of the conceptual change that led to thinking in terms of populations is characterized by the evolutionary theorist Ernst Mayr as the passage from earlier "essentialist" thinking about types to post-Darwinian thought about individuals:

> Population thinkers stress the uniqueness of everything in the organic world. What is important for them is the individual, not the type. They emphasize that every individual in sexually reproducing species is uniquely different from all others, with much indi-

viduality even existing in uniparentally reproducing ones. There is no "typical" individual, and mean values are abstractions. Much of what in the past has been designated in biology as "classes" are populations consisting of unique individuals.[8]

Darwin's new theory entailed in effect a transformation of science's conceptual tools. One can maintain that this change marks the beginning of modern scientific thought, not only in biology, but in physics, physical chemistry, and all sciences that rely upon these disciplines: thinking about group dynamics as statistical ensembles is the hallmark of a modernity that was emerging as Zola advanced in his career.

This nineteenth-century modernity can be described by a web of homologies that characterize the emergence of modern physical theories and biology. Contemporary thinkers such as François Jacob and Ilya Prirogine depict a number of analogies between the theory of evolution and statistical mechanics that are relevant for our purposes, especially for understanding group dynamics. Not only does the irreversibility of time and entropy characterize both evolutionary time and the time of physical systems, but evolution and physical systems are defined precisely by the dynamics of a population or a group. A common understanding of time unfolding as a group process unites Darwin and Boltzmann, so that in their book *La nouvelle alliance,* Ilya Prigogine and Isabelle Stengers interpret Boltzmann's work in statistical mechanics as part of the same transformation of scientific rationality that led to Darwin's formulation of evolution in terms of population dynamics:

> For Boltzmann, to frame the question of the evolution of a physical system, not in terms of individual trajectories, but in terms of the *population of molecules,* described by a function of an average distribution, was in a sense to accomplish Darwin's tactics for physics: neither can the motor of biological evolution, natural selection, be defined on the scale of the individual, but only for a large population; this is a statistical concept.[9]

Darwin was the leader of the shift that led to what was essentially a new way of conceptualizing knowledge and, eventually, a new world-

8. Mayr, *The Growth of Biological Thought: Diversity, Evolution, and Inheritance,* 46.
9. Ilya Prigogine and Isabelle Stengers, *La nouvelle alliance,* 272.

view. And if the axiom about the group behavior of particles that statistical mechanics uses is not unlike the attitude a biologist has toward population groups, it does not strain the imagination to see that the novelist may also draw upon this model involving group dynamics. In fact, analogies relating literature and the sciences are suggested by the shift in thinking in biology, emphasizing populations and individuals, and by the shift that led to the new conceptualization of kinetics in physics and physical chemistry. For the novelist also viewed the individual as the basic unit of group reality, but recognized that knowledge can only be formulated about statistical aggregates that derive from the behavior of innumerable individuals. Specifically with regard to Zola, then, this conceptual framework applies to the representation of characters in several of his naturalist novels. In Zola's novels we see individual characters as the basic unit of social reality, but we are aware that knowledge can be had only concerning the statistical ensembles to which they belong, such as clans, groups, societies, or nations. In Zola's work, as in post-Darwinian biology, the type is no longer considered as the basic unit of knowledge. In fine, the novelist, like a scientist, recognizes that only populations, though composed of individuals, are the object of scientific thought.

With these issues in mind the reader can turn to the beginning of *Les Rougon-Macquart*. In the preface, Zola says in effect that he wants to create a novel that studies a "group," or the family of the Rougon-Macquart. He claims that the work incorporates at once a theory of heredity, and that by studying individual "wills" he will show the "dynamic thrust" of the ensemble. Or we might say that he wants to explore history conceived as the probable energetics describing group dynamics. The preface to the series can thus be read as an introduction to a study of heredity and to an exploration of social dynamics, or as the very first lines of the preface read: "Je veux expliquer comment une famille, un petit groupe d'êtres, se comporte dans une société, en s'épanouissant pour donner naissance à dix, à vingt individus, qui paraissent, au premier coup d'oeil, profondément dissemblables, mais que l'analyse montre intimement liés les uns aux autres. L'hérédité a ses lois, comme la pesanteur" [I want to explain how a family, a small group of beings, behaves in a society, expanding to give birth to ten or twenty individuals, who appear at first sight to be profoundly different, but whom analysis shows to be intimately related to each other. Heredity has its laws, like gravity].[10] Zola refers to a delimited population made up of unique individuals who are characterized by family resemblance. This resemblance is brought to light by the observer—the natural historian or the novelist as natural historian—so that the population can be said to contain the same "species," even if no individual is identical with any other: all are *dissemblables.*

Moreover, if hereditary science has its putative laws, in this context it appears that Zola's belief in laws is an expression of his a priori faith in the unity of science, an argument propped up by a comparison with the Newtonian explanation of gravity. What is really interesting, if somewhat confused, in Zola's formulation is that he proposes a new sense of the relation between individuals and society. Though he invokes heredity here, in the novels it is clear that he wants to study the relation between what I have called, making an analogy with evolutionary biology and statistical mechanics, the dynamics of the individual and the ensemble or group. Each character or "particle" is an individual, yet when all are taken together, they are "intimately bound together" as aggregates obeying general statistical laws—laws that are essentially formulations based upon statistical probability.

In the preface to *La Fortune des Rougon,* Zola says that the work's scientific name should be "The Origins." With this homage to Darwin, Zola begins the series by presenting the woman who is at the origin of the population to be studied. Adélaïde might be likened, in today's terminology, to a mitochondrial Eve from whom the clan descends. In more familiar terminology, she is rumored to be "crackbrained like her father," which gives her a genetic endowment that will ensure the probability of recurrent deviance and insanity among her progeny and a statistically high probability of dissolute behavior. French doctors from Moreau to Morel, and, more generally, nineteenth-century psychiatrists used rough statistical correlations to decide in favor of the probability that hereditary factors are a causal agent in madness. Zola was unduly impressed by these mediocre doctors. His source of deviant heredity in the novels, Adélaïde, has one legitimate child, Pierre, the male progeny who is the source of the Rougon inheritance in the novel. She also has two bastards, the Macquart boy and girl who bring another line of in-

10. Herbert S. Gershman and Kernan B. Whitworth, eds., *Anthologie des préfaces de romans français,* 253.

heritance into the population that Zola will study in the next nineteen novels constituting the entire *Rougon-Macquart*. Curiously, little is said in the novels about either the legitimate father, a peasant who suddenly married Adaléïde, or about the father of her bastards, a poacher who became her lover after her husband's death. To describe the legitimate son's heredity, Zola simply decrees that there is in Pierre an equilibrium, an "average" that unites the maternal and paternal inheritance in a "fusion," fusion being one of the categories of hereditary combinations used by the medical biology of 1870: "Jamais enfant ne fut à pareil point la moyenne équilibrée des deux créatures qui l'avaient engendré. Il était un juste milieu entre le paysan Rougon et la fille nerveuse Adélaïde. Sa mere avait en lui dégrossi son père. Ce sourd travail des tempéraments qui détermine à la longue l'amélioration ou la déchéance d'une race, paraissait obtenir chez Pierre un premier résultat."[11] [Never was a child to such an extent the balanced average of the two creatures that had engendered it. He was an exact middle-point between the peasant Rougon and the nervous girl Adélaïde. In the child the mother had polished up the father. This secret work of the temperaments, which determines in the long run, the improvement or the decadence of a race, seemed to have obtained in Pierre a first result.] This use of hereditary determinants shows that Zola had in mind from the beginning the categories he would use loosely throughout the series. These categories are more or less borrowed from the doctor and theorist Lucas.

Zola specialist Eliot Grant says that Zola pilfered Lucas's *Traité de l'hérédité naturelle* in which he found that

> sometimes a child will inherit his physical or moral traits exclusively from his father, sometimes from his mother. Lucas' term for this type of heredity is *election*. Again, there may be *mixture* (*mélange*), achieved by *fusion, dissemination,* or *soldering* (*soudure*). But now and then, through *combination* (*combinaison*), a new type is formed. When that happens we are in the presence of *innateness* (*innéité*). The phenomenon of *innéité* is in a class by itself; but the others may logically occur either in the direct line or collaterally, and sometimes they may skip a generation.[12]

11. Zola, *Les Rougon-Macquart*, vol. 1, 57.
12. Eliot Grant, *Zola*, 47.

In brief, Lucas offered Zola a series of a priori categories to describe much of what one already knows empirically to be the case. Lucas had no theory to explain the transmission of traits and their combinations, nor a theory of mutation (or *innéité*, in his system). Zola had no theory either and, by the time he was finishing *Les Rougon-Macquart*, was sufficiently skeptical to make his doctor Pascal into a very distanced believer in contemporary theories. Wanting to compete with medicine, Zola borrowed, but hardly endorsed, its categories that explain, in the form of vague laws of inheritance, the individuals who make up his total population.

What is important are not the outmoded categories, but the sense that probable combinations give rise to individual characters. Characterization is not determined by a type given in advance. In *Les Rougon-Macquart*, it is a roll of the dice that unfolds as the generations succeed each other. Legitimate Pierre and bastard Antoine and Ursule are each a product of chance combinatory factors that are due to the moment's hazard. For example, in the daughter Ursule, fantasy and science are allied to explain the probability of her character: "Seulement la pauvre petite, née la seconde, à l'heure où les tendresses d'Adélaïde dominaient l'amour déjà plus calme de Macquart, semblait avoir reçu avec son sexe l'empreinte plus profonde du tempérament de sa mère. D'ailleurs, il n'y avait plus ici une fusion des deux natures, mais plutôt une juxtaposition, une soudure singulièrement étroite" [Only the poor little thing, born second, at a time when the tenderness of Adélaïde was dominating the already calmer passion of Macquart, seemed to have received with her the deeper imprint of her mother's temperament. Moreover, there was no longer in her the fusion of two natures, but rather a juxtaposition, a singularly tight soldering] (57). Zola is in the thrall of Lucas for the various categories he uses—"fusion," "juxtaposition," and "soudure"—but these are imaginary descriptive components that generate the probability that presides over chance encounters. These rolls of hereditary dice will continue for another nineteen volumes so that, with various degrees of plausibility, the narrator and, in the final novel, the fictional doctor Pascal can study the probable evolution of individual types that exemplify some putative general laws—laws that exist only because it is difficult to imagine that they don't.

More interesting than imaginary heredities, however, is Zola's insertion of his characters in a social whole. Unlike Flaubert, his characterization is not based on atomistic determinism, since each character can be likened to a particle participating in the social aggregate. In Zola's novels, the laws of development hold as much for the group as for the individual. Moreover, the laws presiding over society are experienced and known in the form of history, since the development of a social system is presented in terms of its nonreversible movement in time. Dealing with social groups or populations, his novels' epistemic projects are historical in the same sense that evolutionary biology is. To offer a concrete example, the laws of the social aggregate, as Zola describes them, dictate that historical development entails the formation of ever larger units of capital organization that necessarily eliminate smaller economic units. This development is seen, for example, in the creation of department stores in the novel bearing the name of an imaginary emporium, *Au Bonheur des dames* (translated variously as *The Ladies' Paradise* or *Ladies' Delight*). This department store is a creature spawned by social development, though the development comes admittedly to an entropic conclusion. The entire system undergoes the disorder accompanying the destruction of the Second Empire portrayed in *La Débâcle*—this destruction having been foreshadowed by the dissolution developing in Zola's description of social pathology in *Nana.* Showing the creation and dissolution of social aggregates, Zola creates a sense of the indeterminacy that envelops the individual characters struggling in a social context in which aggregate determinisms are at work. To be sure, characters must struggle with their hereditary penchants as well as the forces that create aggregate historical dramas. But few of Zola's characters can be reduced to a type; rather, they are products of combinatory factors in which inner propensities combine with social determinants to give rise to a literary phenotype or unique individual.

Consider the unique nature of one of Zola's best known characters, Etienne Lantier, the strike organizer and hero of *Germinal.* Etienne's birth to Gervaise is recorded in the first novel, *La Fortune des Rougon,* which means that his heredity goes back to Gervaise's father, the Antoine mentioned above. Later, Gervaise, the unfortunate heroine of *L'Assommoir* (*The Dram-Shop*), falls from proletarian prosperity because she suffers from alcoholism. Given the probability that alcoholism is inherited, the odds that Etienne might be something other than a degenerate are slight. His brother Jacques of *La Bête humaine* (*The Beast in Man*) becomes "the human beast" or a homicidal maniac when he drinks. However, the roll of the dice allows for the less as well as the most probable. Etienne is a potential homicidal maniac because of the influence alcohol can have upon him. Yet, he emerges as a possible leader of the masses who, in a different historical context, might have worked to create a society in which working families are not forced to live on starvation wages. However, Etienne is out of phase with the processes of societal macro-organization that determines defeat for the workers, and for himself, in their attempts to stymie the organizing forces of capital. And so Etienne (French for Stephen, the first Christian martyr) becomes a saint, as it were, lapidated at one point like his namesake, Saint Stephen, when he is assaulted by the workers who cannot understand why Etienne's message of justice has resulted in their slaughter at the hands of soldiers defending capitalist investment. Remarkably, Etienne is not a type, not a "good worker," or some "product of his genes"—as popular sources say today in the usual misrepresentation of hereditary science (and which the educated also repeat in spite of the fact that we know that we don't know how genotypes relate, in human developmental terms, to phenotypes).

Etienne is an individual immersed in his "milieu"—to use the name for Taine's determinant that Zola liked to use in reference to social determinism. He is an active individual in this milieu made up of innumerable participants engaging in innumerable micro-events. Only once does he seem to give in to his hereditary destiny. In almost justifiable circumstances, when trapped in the mine, Etienne gives vent to his homicidal impulses by killing his enemy, the remarkably obnoxious Chaval. Yet, this moment of murderous frenzy really points up, by contrast, how other, individualizing determinants have been at work in producing Etienne, this revolutionary individual who has been buffeted about in the storm of macrosocial forces unleashed upon Europe by developing capitalism. Not the least of those social forces are the cultural developments that emerge from societal organization, or what we may simply call the forces of human culture. Culture and the development of scientific thought have produced in Etienne a nascent thinker who self-reflectively wonders, at the novel's end, if Darwin's struggle for survival offers, for understanding the workers' condition, a more appropriate theory than the Marxism of the now enfeebled International. Culture induces self-reflexivity, and self-reflexivity is part of the group behavior that induces new developments known as culture. With this portrayal of the self-reflexive loop, in this novel and others, Zola points toward a larger understanding of how the individual emerges against the great backdrop of cultural forces.

Zola's characters are at once physiological beings and receptors of the forces of culture, and it is an inaccurate simplification to claim that Zola's characters are motivated strictly by instinct. Culturally, the characters' trajectories are motivated by struggle in the milieu determined by the historical coordinates of the Second Empire, the historical time Zola has chosen for his study. Physiologically, it is true that the characters confront probable determinants provided by lines of what we today call genetic factors for which there was (and is) no adequate description—theoretically or empirically. But Zola is our contemporary in wanting to show that cultural and physiological forces combine differently for individual characters. For example, Etienne struggles at times with his own genetic determinism, but cultural determinants are dominant in determining his acts. By contrast, his brother Jacques, the railroad worker of *La Bête humaine*, gives in to a largely physiologically determined deviance, as does, in a sense, the third brother, Claude, the painter who is finally driven to suicide by melancholia in *L'Oeuvre*. Jacques Lantier's deviance takes the form of homicidal rage against women, especially in moments of desire, and it is also compounded by alcohol. Zola adds a strange twist to individualize this compulsion, for Lantier can successfully make love to Severine, perhaps because she is a woman who participated in a murder that Lantier witnessed. Up to that point in the novel, Jacques had avoided women by burying himself in work—for his self-awareness is also part of his character. And well he should have done so, for, in rage, he finally murders Severine Roubaud when she wants him to murder her husband.

Scientific explanation provides a self-referential dimension that enters into the motivation of at least some characters. For example, some characters use scientific theories to analyze their own desire. Not just culture, or science as part of culture, but the perception of culture is part of the motivation leading to the realization of acts. Jacques Lantier is a Lamarckian insofar as he attributes his own homicidal rage to hereditary determinants. He imagines himself to be paying for generations of alcoholic fathers and grandfathers whose acts have caused the "acquired trait" of deviance to be passed on from one generation to the next. In his meditation on himself Jacques relies on a theory that Zola himself considered plausible. Thus the character himself uses a product of culture to understand himself, and in this sense, scientific culture is interiorized to become a determinant of character. I shall presently return to this question of self-reflexivity in the exemplary case of Doctor Pascal, Zola's scientist, who is the main character in the last novel of the series. For the moment, I want to emphasize that Zola integrates self-reflexivity into the way that some characters understand themselves and hence modify their conduct. A knowledge of how the individual relates to the aggregate forces of culture is part of Zola's epistemic project: one might even argue that, given the unique nature of this self-reflexive project, only literature is really in a position to study imagined possibilities of the self-reflexive loop of self-understanding.

Not all, and not even the majority, of the characters are self-reflexive. Perhaps the majority can be compared to "particles" of a kinetic system, driven probabilistically by instinctual forces. These particles, composing the larger macrosystem that makes up France and French culture during the Second Empire, are nonetheless each unique. Gervaise's daughter by Coupeau, Nana, provides a complementary example to her three half-brothers. Nana is an individual in her unique capacities, for she clearly contrasts with her brothers in that she has no theories about culture. Rather, she is endowed with the capacity to attract every male she meets and has no qualms about using her sexuality for the most capricious and egotistical purposes. In so doing, she degrades or destroys all those who associate with her. She drives men, young and old, to suicide or financial ruin, until, finally tired of men, she begins a lesbian relationship. She is, as the penultimate chapter thirteen says, an unconscious animal that unwittingly has sought vengeance on the rich for all the miseries of her social caste.

In *Nana*, Zola desires to rival medicine in his portrayal of pathology, and this portrayal undoubtedly accounts for the lack of self-reflexivity in characters like Nana. Individual microbes act without feedback. It is their aggregate presence that produces a collective syndrome that the social doctor's task is to describe. In this novel, as in several others, Zola uses a medical metaphor as the central leitmotif for describing how Nana produces decomposition in society as she ruins numerous wealthy and prominent men. If she is a Pasteurian agent for pathology, she is so without being so named—for she is never a type, nor is she an allegorical figure. She is a unique pathological agent who, at the end of the novel, dies of smallpox just as masses of Parisians are marching in the street, crying "A Berlin." Pathology, individual and collective, runs rampant.

The masses will never make it to Berlin, but their behavior manifests the collective pathology behind the war, which takes the form of an aggregate behavior. As a form of pathology, it infects a population of individuals. At the same time, Nana's once desirable flesh is exhibited in its decomposition. Zola underscores that she has been a deviant particle that has upset the system's equilibrium, like the one rotten fruit that causes an entire basket of apples to rot. Or so she is described in *L'Assommoir* as the individual who brings about the demise of the collectivity. Each individual gives in to a pathology that manifests itself as the law of historical development—in the form of a collective disease. For purposes of historical verisimilitude, or so it appears, Zola keeps his metaphors pre-Pasteurian.

However, Zola's metaphors turn as much on mechanical and statistical models as on medical images. The crowd at the end of *Nana* represents a state of high excitement in which energy is being expending by the masses as they obey the law of collective motion. Of course, this state will find its lowest level of energy in the debacle portrayed by the novel of that name—*La Débâcle*—which portrays the defeat of the French army that brought the Second Empire to an end. In other words, in his encounter with science, Zola's reliance upon physics and energetics is as important as the explicit use of medicine and physiology.

To pursue an analysis of Zola's literary physics, and thus science beyond medicine and heredity, I will elaborate now further upon some points that I adumbrated above. Parallels between literature and kinetics are perhaps not obvious, but the full scope of Zola's originality, and rivalry, is measured by these parallels. What is perhaps readily apparent is that in these novels presenting whores or strikers, such as *Nana* and *Germinal*, or department stores or warfare, such as *Au Bonheur des Dames* and *La Débâcle*, Zola wants to describe social forces and the movement of masses as well as individuals. The science of forces, and energy, is physics. So it is not surprising that Zola would have recourse to physics, if only for metaphors. Science has in store a number of ways of describing forces: The physics of Zola's time had especially made great advances in describing the laws of energy systems. Physicists such as Boltzmann and Gibbs—two of the most important thinkers for linking thermodynamics with statistical mechanics—theorized that "it is not on individuals that the laws of nature act, but on large populations," and that "statistical analysis and the calculus of probabilities give the rules of the logic of our world."[13] The locus for studying force is therefore the population, and the language for that study is given by probability. This can apply to many types of systems.

For example, heat is a form of energy characterizing a system, and an adequate description of heat requires recourse to a statistical theory. Kinetic theory interprets the pressure, temperature, and other macroscopic properties of a gas as functions of the average values of the momentum and energy of its constituent particles—but one must keep in mind that each particle is an individual with its own unique behavior. The same kind of statistical description also found application in the development of social theory and provides a link between physics and novels. Before Zola, in fact, the statistical explanation for social phenomena had been suggested by the work of the Belgian astronomer Adolphe Lambert Quételet. Using the probabilities of large numbers, Quételet had theorized that social laws applied to "l'homme moyen," an abstract human being who is not the same as the real individual. Probability theory could describe societal regularities on the basis of observed recurrences, with varying degrees of probability, and with no recourse to subjective interpretation.[14] In the same way, the interpretation of the second law of thermodynamics said that macrobehavior or group dynamics can be described as the function of individuals, having their own individual reality, that are nonetheless contributory to statistical regularities. From a statistical point of view, gases and mobs are not without commonality, a point that brings the reader back to the mobs Zola dramatized in many novels.

The physics of thermodynamics, as developed by Clausius, Boltzmann, and Maxwell, showed that the heat energy of a system—a gas, for example—was found in the motions of its individual molecules or particles. In 1857 Clausius proposed again that gases consist of molecules in motion. In developing this theory, Maxwell showed in 1866 that the chance collision of the molecules in a gas give a few molecules more

13. Jacob, *La Logique du vivant*, 215.
14. I draw here upon Robert A. Horvath, "Les idées de Quételet sur la formation d'une discipline statistique moderne sur le rôle de la théorie des probabilités," in *Quételet et la Statistique de son époque*, ed. Robert A. Horvath, 13–20.

energy than average, and they leave others with less energy. This demonstration occurred a year after Clausius had worked out the second law of thermodynamics and invented the concept of entropy. Clausius's mathematics for thermodynamics were obscure, and in 1866 Boltzmann interpreted this law about the distribution of energy to mean that the most probable distribution was the most random or disordered, while the more orderly distribution was less probable. The combined work of Carnot, Clausius, and Boltzmann resulted in the mathematical law of entropy. It received its capstone formulation in 1877 when Boltzmann showed that the entropy of a system was proportional to the logarithm of the probability. In brief, entropy was, as Cecil Schneer has observed, the first example in physical science of a purely mathematical idea for which the mind has no immediate intuitive feeling.[15]

By the time Zola was elaborating his social history of France, the two basic laws of thermodynamics offered a new way of understanding group dynamics. The problem was to interpret them, without contradiction, for reality. As a law of classical mechanics, the principle of the conservation of energy is reversible, but the principle is also supposed to apply to gas particles organized in a system characterized by the irreversible process of entropy. As Nobel laureate physicist Emilio Segrè has pointed out, this was the central contradiction that occupied physics and physical chemistry in the mid-nineteenth century.[16] Probability theory takes on its full importance in this context. The upshot of what Boltzmann, as well as Maxwell, proposed as a solution for the contradiction is that the second law of thermodynamics is not absolute: It is a statement of relative probabilities, a law for the probable behavior of individual particles making up the behavior of a group or a population. And since Balzac we have seen that probabilities are used to construct fictions, those realist fictions that attempt to describe how individuals are the probable locus wherein are found those manifestations of probability sometimes called the forces of history.

This transformation of how one can conceptualize living organisms and physical systems is reflected in Zola's presentation of groups and

15. Cf. Stephen F. Mason, *A History of the Sciences,* 495–96. See also Kenneth Laidler, *The World of Physical Chemistry,* 105, and Cecil J. Schneer, *The Evolution of Physical Science,* 201.

16. Emilio Segrè, *Die grossen Physiker und ihre Entdeckungen,* trans. into German by Hainer Kober, 373.

populations, for Zola's naturalism, if it has any meaning, is based on representing group probabilities. Zola's novels make of the population the largest unit of meaning while they trace out the trajectory of the individual particle—the hapless character—through historical change. In theory and in practice, Zola orients the modern novel toward translating into historical plots the dynamics of population models.

Usually opportunistic, though often idealistic, driven by their viscera and by the cultural forces of the Second Empire, Zola's characters fit into various subsets of individuals who make up, in their total random collisions, what can be likened to a historical macrosystem, to wit, the society of the Second Empire. As I have suggested, the usefulness of framing Zola's characterization in this way is that it shows that, in his encounter with science, Zola is thinking of individuals and populations in much the same terms as nascent biology and statistical mechanics. That is, Zola thinks in terms of post-Darwinian concepts characterizing the relation between individuals and a hypothetical social context. In this context, individuals form populations that are subject to evolution, disequilibrium, or probable forms of diachronic change. Through this representation of populations, the metaphysical distinction of type and ideal is abolished in favor of a pragmatic attempt to arrive at averages about total populations, whatever be the deviance of some individuals in that population. Yet, the deviance points up the average, as is found in perhaps no better example than Nana's return from Russia with smallpox. She dies of bodily illness, contracted because of her erratic life. In the immediate context her death is a foil to the militant masses clamoring to go east, to Berlin. Nana's individual deviance points up that deviance en masse will lead to the general destruction of the system. And one may conclude that the masses that want to go on a homicidal crusade against Prussia are an ensemble of particles that will encounter the same laws of physical reality that killed Nana. Indeed, the entire novel, *La Débâcle*, details at length the massacre in the east: the war is the outgrowth of an entropic system in which men are literally particles whose "average movement" results in catastrophic loss of energy, in death and mutilation.

La Débâcle, the penultimate novel of *Les Rougon-Macquart*, published in 1892, is one of the greatest war novels ever written precisely because it convincingly sets forth individuals—the Parisian Maurice Levasseur and the peasant Jean Macquart—as individuals who, in war, illustrate the laws that govern great populations. Jean is part of the Rougon-Macquart clan and had already been a main figure in *La Terre* (*The Earth*), Zola's harsh depiction of the peasant society of La Beauce region in France. An outsider to that region, Jean had been driven from it by the murderous scheming of the local peasants who deprived him of his wife and land. In *La Terre*, the relation of a deviant individual—deviant because he is different—to the macroforces of the society is sketched out as a relation of antagonism over which hostile laws hold sway. The novel effects a ferocious demolition of the sentimental image of the "virtuous peasant," created by painters like Millet and others, not to mention the genre literature created by writers as distinguished as George Sand. Thus, the novel also serves as a prelude to Zola's historical account of the disintegration of the French army in 1870—under the inept leadership of the kind of men whom Nana had victimized during her career as a whore. Jean is a Macquart, but he has no special vices. He is not a typical farmer; nor, as a soldier, is he inclined to any special deviance, unless one were to maintain that his is the deviant situation in which all soldiers find themselves during war. He is a decent soldier who finds himself victim of the greater forces that emerge from the social group that, in its entropic disequilibrium, is plunged into homicidal disorganization and humiliating defeat.

The other major character in *La Débâcle* is the soldier Maurice. Maurice is an individual who responds to cultural forces centered on Paris, especially to the radical political organizing that resulted in the Commune's attempt at a socialist revolution. He joins the Parisian Commune, another aggregate of individuals subject to a catastrophic historical evolution that ends in disintegration and destruction. At the end of the novel, Jean, an obedient soldier sent to put down the Paris insurrection, unknowingly kills Maurice, in the night, with a random bayonet thrust against a *communard*. In effect, Jean kills the man who had twice saved his life. The collision of these two companion soldiers—once two individuals obeying the same commands—shows that the dissolution of the social system brings about increasingly unpredictable acts of destruction due to random collisions that characterize the entropic evolution of the system.

Zola is, I have argued, the first novelist to define so sharply the distinction between the social collective, conceived as a population, and the individual's participation in that collective population. *Germinal*, Zola's best-known novel, offers perhaps the best example of this portrayal of social forces that are generated by individual trajectories. This novel portraying the industrial organization of coal mines culminates in the strike of the miners who want a living wage. As the organizing forces run down, as the energy level of the miners sinks, more and more random acts of violence occur, which is practically a textbook example of entropic dissolution and its effects as seen in the random deviation of individuals composing the "system." The anarchist Souvarine sabotages the mine. Etienne Lantier then finds himself trapped in the mine with his rival, Chanval, and finally gives in to hereditary impulse and kills him. Improbable events seemingly become more probable as the dissolution proceeds, as the system's energy is depleted and random destruction becomes the rule—so that, as in *La Débâcle*, a decent man can end up killing another in the random violence of the night. Etienne had resisted the impulse to kill Chanval up to this point, but, when multiplied, the random moves of individual violence give rise finally to social pathology.

Zola's portrayal of the existence of macrosystems in which individuals pursue, so to speak, individual paths within the context of the collective is a fundamental aspect of his creation of plot structure. Of course, not all individuals are at cross purposes with collective forces, and the successful individual finds that his or her relation to the macrosystem can be characterized by its resonance with the average. This motif is given extended development, for example, in Zola's novel about the growth of the department store, *Au Bonheur des dames*. The department store represents an economic unit that is at once locally visible and concentrates within itself all the systematic changes in the larger economic macrosystem that were, and are, organizing social systems as global units. In Zola's example, the reorganization of social units is also placed under the sign of Darwin, since capitalist competition is likened in this novel to the struggle for existence that many thinkers in the nineteenth century highlighted as the dominant feature of evolutionary theory. According to the capitalist Octave Mouret, he must relentlessly increase the size of his merchandising empire, since the imperative of economic systems is to vanquish or die. It may appear, then, that he is allied with an anti-entropic development in that the department store represents a higher form of organization. The question of the evolution of units of greater organization was a vexing question for biology and physics, for it appeared to contradict entropy. Of course, the fact that the growth of the department store is predicated on the destruction of smaller organizations suggests that entropy is being respected by its development. This is a question to which I will return at the end of this chapter, for Zola himself was never quite sure how to resolve it.

Zola's capitalist is an individual, in this case, Mouret, a member of the Macquart side of the clan, who has married well in Paris and used his wife's money to begin the department store that soon dominates Parisian retail merchandising. Mouret is a resonant participant in the most probable organization of the economic system once market forces have begun to function. These forces inevitably ensure that the organization produced by greater quantities of capital destroys smaller economic units. And so the petit bourgeois *commerçants*—each an individual in his or her own right—are eliminated from business by the capacity of the larger units of capital to undersell them. The "law" of this macrosystem, as its organization becomes more complex, is to eliminate all deviant individuals, and this with a probability approaching certainty. This law is spelled out in the novel by the young heroine, Denise. Though a child of the threatened petite bourgeoisie, she understands the "logic" of the system and throws her lot in with the giant department store that will, in effect, eliminate her relatives—small entrepreneurs who cannot compete. The fact that she also marries the magnate Mouret at the end of the novel is somewhat incidental to the novel's portrayal of the ongoing organization of the aggregate economic system, though the reader tired of the struggle for survival may appreciate a touch of capitalist romance. The novel's epistemic power lies in the depiction of the ineluctable destruction of those who cannot adapt to the new mode of organization promoted by society's population of individual merchants and purveyors of goods. The majority of the small merchants will, the novel suggests, be eliminated as the new "species" of merchants supplants them.

One could well argue that Zola is successful in his rivalry with science: The study of the individual and the portrayal of the group are interrelated in Zola through a kind of statistical causality analogous to what emerged as the new mode of explanation of science during the second half of the nineteenth century. Characters remain individuals in spite of a collective vision of explanation. As an individual, Denise rises to the top. In so doing, she may seem like some improbable particle that deviates from the average, but most characters, like most particles in a system, move in accord with the law of averages. At the beginning of the series of *Les Rougon-Macquart,* some characters can ally themselves with the forces that are creating the Second Empire and survive— Pierre Macquart or his son Eugene, or the aforementioned magnate, Octave Mouret. But equally as probable, especially as overdetermined by the Darwinian point of view, when the macrosystem known as the Second Empire begins to disintegrate, characters are destroyed by the general entropic development in which the random grows more frequent, and disorder augments. Gervaise and Coupeau, the painter Claude Lantier, the railway men of *La Bête Humaine,* the miners in *Germinal,* the masses in *Nana,* or the armies in *La Débâcle* are all subject to the entropic development of a social system, and this portrayal of social entropy is, I would suggest, one of the fundamental epistemic demonstrations Zola's fiction sets out to illustrate. Of course, Zola was lucky, if that is not too perverse a term, that a war came along, since he needed the war of 1870 for his epistemic demonstration, which he recognized when, in the introduction to *La Fortune des Rougon,* he expressed his gratitude to history. Experimenters are rarely so well served.

Le Docteur Pascal (1893) was written after the development of statistical thinking in physics had taken place. This novel explicitly addresses the problem of reconciling the growth and increasing organization of systems, such as knowledge itself, with the second law of thermodynamics. This law calls for the ultimate dissolution of all systems, for entropy is the basic law of all forms of organization, and this includes art, communication, and knowledge. In this regard, the novel also reflects the potential conflict between biology and thermodynamics that arose in the second half of the nineteenth century because of competing interpretations of the history of the universe. On the one hand, scientists felt obliged to accept the second law of thermodynamics and its prediction of entropy; but, on the other hand, they also accepted the theory of the progressive evolution of more complex life forms that had seemingly culminated in humanity. How did one reconcile entropy with the evolution of complexity? There was hardly any consensus about an answer, and scientists in the nineteenth century had varying answers to the question. Physiologist and physicist Helmholtz argued that living organisms had to obey the law of the conservation of energy, since they would be perpetual motion machines if they could derive energy from some vital force that was not subject to thermodynamics. This particular argument against vitalism, and in favor of the conservation of energy, specifically focused the debate on the question as to whether the second law held sway for living organisms. Lord Kelvin thought they might get around entropy, though Maxwell—who in a thought experiment invented a demon who might produce order for nothing—thought living beings were no different from inorganic matter when it came to obeying the laws of thermodynamics.[17] These are questions that offer a fruitful context for reading *Le Docteur Pascal*, since Zola's Doctor Pascal ponders the meaning of the organization of the system that has produced him as its end product. He is perplexed because, as something as highly organized as a scientist doing research on the Rougon-Marquart, it appears to him that he has escaped from the random doings of entropic dissolution.

Le Docteur Pascal is the final novel of *Les Rougon-Marquart*, though, as the doyen of Zola studies, Henri Mitterand, has observed on several occasions, the series really has two conclusions. The historical conclusion is the apocalypse at the end of *La Débâcle*, in which the Second Empire disintegrates in a final series of random explosions that are a massive illustration of social entropy. The conclusion of Zola's narrative discourse, however, is *Le Docteur Pascal*, in which Zola's scientist reflects back upon his family, its heredity, and the theory or model that might make sense of the clan's development. Pascal, the son of Pierre and Felicité of *La Fortune des Rougon*, is of course a member of the clan, a specified subpopulation that provides for his genetic makeup. In reflecting upon this population, he reflects upon the forces or laws that have determined him to reflect upon the forces or laws that have resulted in his scientific vocation. Paradoxical self-reference hovers over the horizon of this novel that theorizes its own genesis, as well as that of the nineteen preceding novels in the series. Pascal seeks a theory that can explain how a theory has produced itself through him, and thus a theory that, in reflecting on the family's genealogical line, explains itself. A century later, in his best-selling *A Brief History of Time*, Stephen Hawking seems to have had much the same thing in mind when he made the claim that this self-explanation would be the ultimate result of any total theory that

17. Mason, *A History of the Sciences*, 492–96.

physics might come up with. Pascal is the virtual scientist of the future that Hawking seems to posit with a gesture toward some future total knowledge.

As a scientist, Zola's Pascal is an exception to the general determinants that have manifested themselves in the struggles of the other members of the Rougon-Macquart clan. Neither a homicidal maniac nor a struggling member of the proletariat, he has become a disinterested doctor. He was once concerned with curing the sick, but, in the present moment of narration, he is preoccupied with the research that might explain the meaning of life forms and their manifest operations. He has sought no academic or professional glory. Living in semiretirement in Plassans, Zola's fictional version of Aix-en-Provence, he pursues his research while rearing a young niece who has been entrusted to his care, the beautiful Clothide. The love affair that ensues between the aging doctor and the young girl lends itself to both a Biblical allegorical interpretation, as well as a bit of scandal (though Biblical allegories rarely avoid scandal). It also provides a scaffolding for the narrative that gives the novel an existential dimension: The desiring doctor is a man of flesh as well as an epistemic saint questing for knowledge.

Published in 1893, the novel is set in 1872, shortly after the defeat and fall of the Second Empire—and so its action unfolds somewhat before the revolution in microbiology that made much of Pascal's theorizing outmoded. However, much of the debate in the novel also reflects the polemics of the late nineteenth century when the triumphant positivism of a scientist like Claude Bernard was now on the defensive. Various irrationalisms as well as an internal critique of science had begun to attack the often excessive claims of science to be the universal arbiter of knowledge. Pascal himself is guilty of such claims, which characterized a good many nineteenth-century theories. For example, he thinks at one point that he has found a panacea, and the good doctor's unfounded belief to have found the universal cure is clearly a reflection of nineteenth-century hyperbolic hopes for science and medicine. The failure of Pascal's panacea reflects the demise of the inflated hopes of science to triumph over all that might render men and women unhappy. Consequently, he becomes a more modest scientist. He still wants to determine the laws of heredity, but he is quite conscious of the probable limits of any success.

He also wants to inculcate a respect of science in his charming ward.

In *Le Docteur Pascal,* Zola has written an anticlerical version of *Pygmalion,* in which the doctor's charge, Clothide, is at first a religious fanatic. She wants to destroy the dossiers in which, through the years, Pascal has patiently collected his research about each member of the Rougon-Marquart family. From the antiscientific point of view Clothide first embraces, Pascal's research is the devil's work because his science undermines religious belief. Clothide is also a fairly adroit epistemologist who attacks Pascal's "faith" in the scientific method as the only rational approach to human problems. Declaring that, as a child, she thought Pascal was speaking of God when he spoke of science, she rejects science for its lack of completion. Her attack on Pascal presents a résumé of the late nineteenth-century trend to reject science: "Avec la science, on allait pénétrer le secret du monde et réaliser le parfait bonheur de l'humanité. . . . Selon toi, c'était à pas de géant qu'on marchait. Chaque jour amenait sa découverte, sa certitude. Encore dix ans, encore cinquante ans, encore cent ans peut-être, et le ciel serait ouvert, nous verrions face à face la vérité. . . . Eh bien! les années marchent, rien ne s'ouvre, et la vérité recule" [With science you were going to grasp the secret of the world and achieve humanity's total happiness. . . . According to you, we were headed that way with giant steps. Every day was bringing its discovery, its certainty. Just ten more years, just fifty more years, perhaps just a hundred years, and heaven would be revealed, we would see truth face to face. . . . Well, the years are going by, nothing has been revealed, and truth keeps receding in the distance].[18] Pascal tries to counter this accusation, the accusation against science made by many members of that historical generation of the fin de siècle that was ready to throw itself into mysticism, pseudoscience, theosophy, and other irrationalisms, including nationalist political beliefs that were becoming overtly racist (a racism often buttressed by the dubious science of heredity and eugenics). To Clothide's accusation, Pascal replies that science never promised happiness. Science is simply the unending pursuit of reality—though he goes beyond this methodological modesty and shows his idealist background when he also declares that science is the only source of health and beauty (139). After Clothide tries to destroy the research dossiers that, from her point of view, threaten Pascal's salvation, Pascal decides that only by revealing to her the entire truth of his re-

18. Zola, *Le Docteur Pascal,* 143.

search can Clothide be cured of her need for illusion, the need for illusion being Pascal's concept of religious faith.

Therefore, Pascal shows her the genealogical tree and reads to her all
the dossiers he has put together about the Rougon-Macquart clan. In
this way, Zola inserts an imaginary *mise en abyme*—or inner mirror—
within the final novel, for the dossiers reflect the entire work dealing with
the Rougon-Macquart. The dossiers coincide, virtually as it were, with
the preceding nineteen volumes of "research" Zola had written on the
family and its evolution. Beginning with "Tante Dide" and her offspring,
Pascal has compiled all this information about the Rougon-Macquart
family in the hopes of finding a hypothesis that can explain the data.
Though he makes some use of Lucas's categories to organize his find-
ings, the doctor admits that he has found little in the way of a theory to
explain heredity: "Ah! ces sciences commmençantes, ces sciences où
l'hypothèse balbutie et où l'imagination reste maîtresse, elles sont le domaine des poètes autant que des savants! Les poètes vont en pionniers,
à l'avant-garde, souvent ils découvrent les pays vierges, indiquent les so-
lutions prochaines" [Oh! these beginning sciences, sciences in which
one's hypothesis stammers and over which the imagination remains the
master, they are as much the realm of poets as scientists! Poets go forth
as pioneers, in the avant-garde, often they discover virgin territory, they
point out future solutions] (166). So, in a self-reflexive homage to the
novel itself, the fictional doctor recognizes that the poet—his own creator—is in the avant-garde in the discovery of heredity. From Zola's totalizing viewpoint, this discovery would explain nothing less that the
genesis of families, societies, and the aggregate system of culture.

In this self-reflexive position, Pascal finds himself in the position of
the writer who writes about his writing, or the researcher who seeks to
know himself. The discovery of the laws determining the evolution of
the clan would reveal the laws that have allowed Pascal to be in the position in which he has been determined to discover the laws. This self-
reflexive cognition would represent a superior level of organization that
has emerged in spite of the entropic tendency toward dissolution that
characterizes heredity. An interesting argument is involved in this question, since every scientist is, to one degree or another, implicated by the
knowledge that will provide knowledge about how we get knowledge.
Thus it seems that Zola is arguing that every researcher seeking knowledge is undertaking an anti-entropic activity. (Against this viewpoint, I

point out that contemporary scientists argue that the expense of energy involved in acquiring knowledge is always greater than the organization finally achieved: knowledge is work in a physical sense.) The self-reflectiveness of epistemological activity reveals the conditions of possibility for generating the novel and, through this work, a state of higher organization. From Zola's epistemic perspective, the novel emerges as a full-fledged, organized body of knowledge. With this recognition, *Le Docteur Pascal* declares itself a triumphant novel, modest as it is, demonstrating literature's successful rivalry with science in the common enterprise of gathering knowledge.

Zola's provocative formulations in his earlier essay, *Le Roman expérimental,* had offered an analogous formulation with regard to the novel and its relation to science. In a sense, Zola was working there toward a concept of literary knowledge that is finally embodied in *Le Docteur Pascal.* Zola early saw the novel to function, in producing knowledge, as a self-reflective discourse. Zola's model of knowledge as a future state means that a novel should have a self-reflective relation to the future knowledge science will offer. Or perhaps one should say that science of the future will loop back to explain the present hypotheses that a novel, say *Le Docteur Pascal,* embodies:

> Et c'est là ce qui constitue le roman expérimental: posseder le mécanisme des phenomènes chez l'homme, montrer les rouages des manifestations intellectuelles et sensuelles telles que la physiologie nous les expliquera, sous les influences de l'hérédité et des circonstances ambiantes, puis montrer l'homme vivant dans le milieu social qu'il a produit lui-même, qu'il modifie tous les jours, et au sein duquel il éprouve à son tour une transformation continue.

> [And that is what constitutes the experimental novel: possessing the mechanism of human phenomena, showing the wheels and cogs of sensual and intellectual manifestations such as physiology will explain them to us one day, under the influence of heredity and surrounding circumstances, then showing a living human being in the social milieu that humanity itself has produced, that it modifies every day, and in the heart of which humanity undergoes continual transformation.][19]

19. Zola, *Le Roman expérimental,* 19.

Presuming a future state of knowledge, Zola is also arguing for a science in which the observer is part of what is observed. This is, admittedly, not part of the classical deterministic science that Zola also endorses at times, but, by the time he had arrived at the end of *Les Rougon-Macquart*, Zola was aware of the limits of classical determinism. His view here anticipates a type of discourse that is based on a feedback loop in which the production of knowledge modifies the process of knowing oneself and for which the novel could be a form of representation.

This question of the knowing subject's participation in the known surfaces when one turns to the structure of *Les Rougon-Macquart*, especially in considering the final involution narrated in *Le Docteur Pascal*. In investigating the meaning of the genealogical series—the series of the novels themselves—that has culminated in his own research, the doctor wants to establish a scientific discourse that gets around the separation of subject and object, since he is at once the investigator and the investigated. Pascal needs a science in which the knowing subjectivity is transformed by the experience of knowing. With the portrayal of his doctor, Zola makes, I think, new claims for literature, especially in the representation of fiction as the active knowing process in which participants in the process are transformed by the act of knowing. This is an epistemological stance underlying Zola's belief in the ethical power of knowledge, for, quite simply, knowledge can change the knowing subject.

In Pascal's case, research involves more than a case of the researcher being implicated in the known. It is also a question of destiny, for the laws of heredity he seeks are also the laws of his own being, and hence of his possible destiny. When he reads the dossiers to Clothide, he wants to skip over hers and his own. This hesitancy is not simply due to modesty, for his own dossier presents the crucial problem of a self-referential information loop: the dossier should account for its own genesis. Pascal can only grope for an explanation of how he came to be what he is by suggesting some break in the causal chain of which he is the end product: "Oh! moi, à quoi bon parler de moi? Je n'en suis pas, de la famille! . . . Tu vois bien ce qui est écrit là: 'Pascal, né en 1813. Innéité. Combinaison, où se confondent les caractères physiques et moraux des parents, sans que rien d'eux semble se retrouver dans le nouvel être. . . .' Ma mere me l'a répété assez souvent, que je n'en étais pas, qu'elle ne savait pas d'où je pouvais bien venir!" [Oh, as for me, what use is there to talk about me? I don't belong to the family! . . . You see what's written there: "Pascal, born in 1813. Inneity. A combination in which are mixed the moral and physical characteristics of the parents without it appearing that anything from them is found in the new being. . . ." My mother repeated it to me often enough, that I wasn't part of it, that she hadn't any idea where I could come from!] (182). The need Pascal feels to break the deterministic chain is understandable, though the concept of *innéité* is simply a folk wisdom that had anticipated a theory of mutation. In this case, Pascal's need for a theory of mutation is also the need to escape a tragic destiny, for nineteenth-century medicine made up for its lack of theory with the severity of the destiny it promised those with defective inheritance. As many doctors presented it, and as Zola seemed sometimes to believe, God's damnation was no more severe than defective inheritance.

Pascal's own interpretation of himself is also that his singularity may really be a hereditary form of madness. If the family chain isn't broken, then Pascal's inheritance destines him to the mad search for the laws that determine his madness—or the singularity that his mother, Félicité, like a moralizing psychiatrist, is happy to interpret for him in medical terms: "On ne se laisse pas envahir par l'idée fixe, surtout quand on est d'une famille pareille à la nôtre" [You don't let yourself be taken over by a fixed idea, especially when you come from a family like ours] (196). Pascal is the only scientist in the family, but he is tortured by the idea that this may simply be the form that his madness, or *folie des grandeurs*, has taken: "Et . . . dans son besoin de guetter les ennemies qu'il sentait acharnés à sa perte il reconnaissait aisément les symptomes du délire de la persécution. Tous les accidents de la race aboutissaient à ce cas terrible: la folie à brève échéance, puis la paralysie générale, et la mort" [And . . . in his need to watch out for the enemies that he felt were determined to destroy him, he easily recognized the symptoms of a persecution delirium. All the accidents of his race were coming down to this terrible case: madness in the short run, then general paralysis, and finally death] (197). Tortured by the idea that his heredity does not represent a break with his family (or "un cas remarquable d'innéité") but simply a return of hereditary traits that have reappeared after three or four generations, Pascal finds that his entire career and the meaning of his life are threatened by the laws that he has dedicated his life to discovering: the laws of the madness that would explain his desire to discover these same laws.

Pascal's cure comes from Clothide. She accepts science, she accepts the endless quest, and she accepts finally Pascal and his desire. Pascal cannot decide if hereditary causality has been broken or not, though in the end he accepts that it is a probably hereditary determination that kills him with heart disease. And in accepting this death, he accepts whatever natural laws have made him what he has been. This is a movement of tragic reconciliation, and with it, I think that Zola wants to overcome the entropic vision of disorder and violence with which his work came to an end in *La Débâcle*. Pascal knows that whatever theory he may hold about heredity will soon be outmoded, and he knows that his hypotheses only have value for having contributed to the future progress of science toward new theories (375). But even as he dies, Pascal is sketching out a new theory of health—one based upon the necessity of work.

At this point I wish to return to the fact that most critics of Zola have seen his concern with disorder and chaos as deriving from his concern with fatal heredity. There is, however, some overlap between kinetics and hereditary theory, especially as elaborated by thinkers fascinated with decadence, for they often emphasized motifs resembling the dismal conclusion, drawn from the second law of thermodynamics, predicting that the worst of all possible worlds is also the most probable. For example, Roger Ripoll points out in his thesis on myth in Zola that something like the concept of entropy seems to be incorporated in Lucas's theory of heredity, which Ripoll also sees as a question of energy. Degeneration is the fate of every family since, as Lucas said, every family gives in to a process in which energy is drained and the family loses its capacity for renewal. Life, according to this interpretation of hereditary theory, is always threatened from within, and every family's fate is a loss of vitality, impotence, and finally death.[20] However, by the time Zola is writing *Le Docteur Pascal*, he is clearly as much concerned with energy, entropy, and organization as the fatality of heredity.

Actually, throughout much of *Les Rougon-Marquart*, Zola traces out the entropic disorder characterizing the development of the clan. This development of disorder finds an outcome, striking an aggregate social organization, in the destruction of France in *La Débâcle*. In the final novel, *Le Doctor Pascal*, Zola brings up the basic question as to how the sys-

20. Roger Ripoll, *Réalité et mythe chez Zola*, tome 1, 168.

temic organization of energy known as life continues in spite of entropy. Dissolution brought about by loss of energy thus stands challenged by a sense that the future—as exemplified by the ongoing development of science—holds the promise of greater organization. This is the epistemological dilemma of a generation for which science as evolution promised emergent forms, and science as thermodynamics promised the slow extinction of the universe.

Confronting the entropic dissolution that thermodynamics and, from one perspective, his own hereditary science describe, Pascal defends his belief in the integrity of life by framing a homeostatic vision of health. Health is equilibrium maintained in the face of disequilibrium. It is antientropic. The body's health is an equilibrium between the sensations received from the exterior world and the work rendered by the organism in its response to its milieu. Having meditated upon the basic law of thermodynamics in the form of work, Pascal knows that work is the great law of the universe (376), and any therapy of the body must aim at restoring the equilibrium of energy exchanges: "il voyait de nouveau le monde sauvé dans cet équilibre parfait, autant de travail rendu que de sensation reçue, le branle du monde rétabli dans son labeur éternel" [He saw again the world saved in this perfect equilibrium, with as much work rendered as sensation received, and the movement of the world restored to its eternal labor] (377). By work one must understand both its normal sense of accomplishment and its scientific meaning describing the transformation and conservation of energy.

Pascal's final theory about work springs from a poet's attempt to suggest where science must go. From Pascal's perspective, science must reconcile the principle of entropy with the evidence that life is an emerging form of higher organization that does not seem to be disappearing. However, Pascal's own theory disappears at the end of the novel: fearing the scandal for the family that might result from Pascal's research, Pascal's mother destroys his dossiers. All that remains of his work is the genealogical tree, or that marker of probabilities that is Pascal's most succinct résumé of *Les Rougon-Macquart*. Entropy seems to be confirmed at the novel's end, for all that remains of Pascal's dossiers are burned fragments, not one of which is entire. This is a desolate image of the dissolution produced by the loss of energy that went into this work.

Yet, the genealogical tree remains intact, and it points not only backwards, but also forwards, toward the continuation of the family, the population, and the ongoing process of life. As represented by the genealogical tree, and hence by all the novels for which it is a schema, Zola's final image is an affirmation of life. It is also a clear call for more knowledge to understand and to explain that life does indeed exist over and beyond the dissolution that threatens every system in the universe, including the universe itself. Life exists as the baby that Clothide suckles at the end, and in all the other children that are to be added to the tree. In speculating on why the genealogical tree is not necessarily an unrelenting schema of decline, Pascal notes that the daily renewal of the race's blood brought about by marriage stops the "mathematical and progressive degeneration" that threatens humanity (178). And this is the case. So the final meaning of Pascal's having a child, posthumously, by Clothide is to ensure what Pascal would see as the anti-entropic continuance of the species.

Today one can argue that DNA has a capacity for self-repair that stops the entropic loss of information that affects other organized systems. The felicitous mutation can also overcome the tendency for disorder. But I am not sure that this argument answers the fundamental question as to how life as a system evolved in a universe subject to entropy (which leads to a contemporary argument that entropy does not apply to all systems). In any case, for Zola, and for a generation with no theory of information transmission, it was a mystery that the second law of thermodynamics had not entailed, in the course of the ages, the total deterioration of the system we know as human life. And so, with its double ending in *La Débâcle* and in *Le Docteur Pascal*, the series of works called *Les Rougon-Macquart* narrates, on the one hand, entropic decline of a culture and, on the other hand, an affirmation of life as the great organizing force of the universe. Materialist that he was, Zola ends his work with the affirmation of the mysterious renewal that inheritance brings about by overcoming entropy. In 1893, that affirmation was the work of a poet, not a scientist, as Zola conceived the task of the writer in his collaborative competition with science, the task of pointing the way to future knowledge that, he believed, could only augment human happiness as it increased human understanding.

Proust and the End of Epistemic Competition

Chaque jour j'attache moins de prix à l'intelligence.

[Each day I value intelligence less.]

—Proust, *Contre Sainte-Beuve.*

HISTORICAL OVERVIEW

1826: Lobachevsky lectures on a non-Euclidian geometry in which more than one parallel to a given line goes through a given point.

1854: Riemann's essay *Uber die Hypothesen, welche der Geometrie zu Grunde liegen* develops non-Euclidian geometry with treatment of how distance and curvature can be defined generally in n-dimensional space.

1871: Proust born. Flemming uses dyes to study cellular division.

1874: Boutroux publishes his critique of determinism in *De la Contingence des lois de la nature.*

1887: Michelson and Morley report failure to measure relative velocity of earth and aether, finding that the velocity of light is constant in all directions.

1889: Poincaré initiates the study of modern dynamic systems with publication of his paper on the three-body problem.

1889: The leading anti-Kantian in France, Bergson, publishes *Matière et mémoire,* a study of two types of memory. With Bergson in mind, Renan publishes next year *L'Avenir de la science.*

1900: Planck publishes paper on black box radiation in which he postulates the discontinuous emission of discrete packets of energy called quanta.

1904:   Lorentz develops mathematics to interpret Michelson and Morley experiment by showing that contraction of length and dilation of time could occur to instruments in the direction of the movement.

1905:   Einstein publishes paper containing special theory of relativity, which, in abolishing absolute notions of space, time, and mass, explains the results of the Michelson and Morley experiment.

1907:   Minkowski describes the space-time of Einstein's relativity theory with four-dimensional "Minkowski space."

1909:   Poincaré publishes *Science et méthode,* one of several works for a general public in which he epouses conventionalist epistemology and rejects the axiomatic approach to mathematics.

1913:   Proust publishes *Du Côté de chez Swann,* first volume of *A la Recherche du temps perdu.*

1916:   Einstein finishes his general theory of relativity.

1919:   Eddington verifies a prediction of general relativity by measuring the deflection of starlight at the edge of the sun during an eclipse.

After Zola, naturalism remained a dominant influence on fiction, in France and throughout the Western world, for decades. It remains, in fact, a model for fiction that aims at a seizure of the world refusing any form of transcendence. But even as Zola was writing, modernist forms of fiction began to appear, often created in the attempt to get around what seemed to be naturalism's submission to science. Literary history often presents the development of modernism as an overcoming of naturalism. In its rejection of naturalism, modernism promoted fictional works that, using myth and symbol, attempted to find realms of essential revelation that somehow transcend the historical world, often conceived as the world of fallen experience. This world, bereft of any transcendental workings, was, after Flaubert and Zola, rather much the exclusive domain of naturalist fiction. It was also the world in which took place science's cognitive endeavors, and for which science could claim to be the final arbiter. And so, seemingly wishing to avoid rivalry with science, modernism often sought to lay bare another realm in which literature could claim to have priority in its search for truth and knowledge.

The development of modernism in France is undoubtedly best illustrated by Marcel Proust's novel *A la Recherche du temps perdu,* which can be translated "in [re]search of time lost." (Montcrief's borrowing from Shakespeare's *Remembrance of Things Past* is evocative, but inaccurate.) Proust's title implies that his novel is research into a realm not usually open to science—unless one finds an oblique reference to paleontology in the title, which is not inapposite. Science, as we will see, is hardly absent from the novel, for Proust set out to reconcile science and art by granting them separate but equal domains. From this perspective, Proust's novel is, on the one hand, a key work of the early twentieth century for understanding the modernist reaction to the imperial claims of science, and, on the other hand, the key work for understanding how this rivalry came to an end. To effect this reconciliation that ends competition, Proust's novel offers an extraordinary counterpoint of literary realism and modernist transcendence. Reconciling realism and the modernist thirst for transcendence, it relocates literature's epistemic quest so as to dispense with literature's rivalry with science and grant literature its own object of knowledge.

Proust did not achieve this transition by ignoring his novelistic predecessors. On the contrary, he self-consciously built upon their work. His critical reflections on Balzac and Flaubert, for example, view them in clearly epistemic terms. In commentary on Balzac found in *Contre Sainte-Beuve,* Proust assesses the writer's capacity to confound the real and the imaginary in such a way that fictional and real scientists exist on the same plane. By implication, research in fiction and research in reality have the same ontological status for Balzac, which Proust takes to be a positive contribution to the development of fiction. In evaluating Flaubert's rhetoric in *Madame Bovary* in his "A propos du style de Flaubert"—one of the most important pieces of Flaubert criticism—Proust saw in Flaubert's rhetoric nothing less than an epistemological revolution in fiction nearly equivalent to what Kant did with his theory of knowledge. This is not a point of view that I have disputed in the preceding pages. I add that what Proust learned from Balzac and Flaubert, as well as from Zola, was precisely an epistemological lesson about drawing upon science for models describing social dynamics in time, and a capital lesson about transforming the narrator into an epistemological agent. We will discuss these issues in some detail presently.

From a slightly different perspective, *A la Recherche* is a far-reaching attempt to reconcile the scientific worldview with the artistic possibility of vouchsafing poetic value to the individual life. In his novel, Proust wants to find a space in which poetic salvation can be achieved in spite of the relentless reduction of the world, by science and by naturalism, to a world that can be described, if not explained, by deterministic laws. Proust does this by redefining the epistemic function of literature by drawing directly upon scientific epistemology to justify his demonstration that literature can have access to realms that science cannot describe. With this demonstration using science's own epistemology, Proust's novel presents a way of ending the sense of rivalry literature had felt with science. Considerations of literary history buttress this conclusion, since it is accurate to say that, after Proust, the European novel has rarely sought to rival science on its own terms. In part, this conclusion came about because the development of science, especially of sciences like molecular biology and quantum mechanics, meant that it was no longer useful or credible for literature to claim to rival science. But this historical development also came about because Proust, more systematically than any other writer I can name, developed an epistemic viewpoint that ended literature's desire for rivalry by declaring this rivalry untrue to the nature of literary knowledge. Proust was hardly alone, or even the first, to make this point, but he made it in a kind of summation whose scope no other writer approaches.

As critics have often noted, Proust drew upon developments in modern poetry as a springboard for the creation of his novel. Proust's accomplishment can be best grasped if we understand that his work is, in many respects, the culmination of the search for a unique form of experience that characterized the quest undertaken by symbolist poetry— a quest for experience conceived as a unique form of knowledge. In Proust's novel we can find reflections of both the antagonistic rivalry with science that symbolist poets felt and their attempt to render this rivalry nugatory by achieving transcendence through poetry. Modernism inherited from symbolist poetry, in France and elsewhere, the forms designed to get around science's imperial claims to regiment knowledge. One response to these claims was that poetry proclaimed itself to be an autonomous realm in which the individual could find transcendental revelation through poetic form. Thus understood, poetry can be seen as making a counter-claim in that it proposed to offer access to superior epistemic spaces not accessible to science. Proust took up the task of finding a transcendental form, but not simply, as was the case of some poets, with the idea of simply rejecting science. Proust was interested in science and, by the time he began writing, had assimilated virtually all the major questions that science was addressing at the beginning of the twentieth century—and this with a sense of the epistemological stakes that few writers, or scientists for that matter, have ever shown. Proust wanted to deal with science on its ground and in its own terms so as not to limit the epistemic issues a novel can embody. His novel demonstrates that fiction offers knowledge that at once uses what science offers and then goes beyond science to offer its own knowledge of a realm inaccessible to science.

A corrective reexamination of the historical context is a good starting point for delineating Proust's understanding of epistemic issues as well as what he took from other writers. Therefore, I am going to deal at some length with the literary and then the scientific context in which Proust's novel takes on its full meaning as the culmination of a century of developments. To this end, it is relevant first to sketch out scientists' attitude toward science, since Proust's encounter with science takes on full meaning only when viewed against the backdrop of science's self-understanding. Then we may turn to poets' attitudes toward science and knowledge.

Toward the end of the nineteenth century, many scientists viewed science as a soon-to-be-completed task, especially as far as the basic laws of nature—or the laws of physics—were concerned. There was a widespread belief that, with Maxwell's work on electromagnetism, physics had practically arrived at, to use a more recent expression, the final theory. (Physicists enjoy telling the anecdote according to which the young Max Planck was supposedly told to give up physics since there would soon be no problems left to solve.) This smugness, if that is the right expression, was coupled in many quarters with a positivistic belief that epistemological questions had largely been resolved. Parallel to this belief in the final theory, there developed at the same time a revolt against the self-satisfied imperial attitude of positivistic philosophy, such as we have already seen when Zola's Doctor Pascal finds himself on the defensive as he undertakes to save humanity through science. Finally, there was also, among the more thoughtful scientists of the latter part of the nineteenth century, a feeling of disquiet that there were really too many problems in the details of the worldview proposed by Newtonian celestial mechanics and dynamics, thermodynamics, and electro-magnetism. For example, for these scientists it was not at all clear that Maxwell's new theory unifying electromagnetic phenomena was con-sonant with Newtonian mechanics. In France, as he worked on unre-solved problems of celestial mechanics, Henri Poincaré was among those scientists who hardly saw the end in sight. In Germany, young Max Planck was another, and the solution he found in 1900 for quanti-fying black box radiation would lead to nothing less than quantum me-chanics. But during the final decades of the nineteenth century, the rad-ical changes to come in physics after 1900 were hardly apparent.

The nineteenth-century revolt against science was not entirely the work of poets, nor does it begin, as some assume, entirely with roman-tic writers. For our purposes, several French poets concerned with sci-ence and writing in the wake of romanticism are most relevant for un-derstanding what Proust was about when he set out to develop an epistemology for literature. One should read back through three gen-erations of postromantic poets—Valéry, Mallarmé, and Baudelaire—to understand the literary epistemology that impressed Proust as he sought to enlarge the epistemic sphere that he had found in Balzac, Flaubert, and Zola. And one should undertake this reading without as-suming that all poets were hostile toward science. In his *Literature and Technology,* Wylie Sypher has argued quite pertinently that in fact most poets throughout the nineteenth century were actually favorably dis-posed (or indifferent) toward science. Blake notwithstanding, the En-glish romantics were largely empirically inclined and took great inter-est in the physics and chemistry of their time. It is only after Poe, and largely in France among the next generation of poets—or among the symbolists in general—that poets like Baudelaire, Mallarmé, and Valéry elaborated on Poe's ideas and attacked openly the claims of scientists to be the final arbiters of knowledge. A literary epistemologist, Poe was something of an amateur scientist himself, not only for his conception of poetry as a mathematics of feeling, but, I note with some amusement, also in his plagiarizing treatise on conchology that brought Cuvier's work to a popular public. Poe was not a simple figure: he wanted to be a scientist of verse, and his French followers were duly impressed by the scope of his ambitions.

The symbolists took up Poe's view of poetry as the science of emo-tion, and so Sypher argues ingeniously that the symbolist poets, from

Poe through Mallarmé and Valéry, relied upon technique in a way that suggests that they believed in the same methodological axioms as the scientists. For these poets, method was all—it was the key to elevating literature and making of it a form of epistemic exploration. In short, through the proper method, literature could offer superior knowledge. This belief in methodology, in the wake of Poe, is exemplified by Proust's contemporary, Valéry, born in 1871, the same year as Proust. Notably, the young Valéry's *Introduction à la méthode de Léonard da Vinci* (1894 in its first version) defines "rigor" for poetry as essentially the same as scientific rigor.[1] The idea of rigor is derived from Valéry's definition of intelligence. He calls intelligence the "discovery of relations" in places where we did not previously see "the law of continuity." This definition echoes the definition of science as the knowledge of relations, not of substances, that the physicist Poincaré often formulated (1160). In his *Introduction à la méthode,* Valéry explicitly refers to Poincaré's work, stating that he has found in Poincaré's description of the scientific mind an analogy for the autonomous workings of the artistic mind. In science as in poetry, as Valéry sees it, the creative mind engaged in epistemic inquiry must attempt to seize itself in its own workings. Analogous to a scientist, Valéry sees the poet as enacting a drama of epistemic bootstrapping. Wanting to emulate scientific rigor—and in no way hostile to the values of science—Valéry tries to formalize the idea that the mind itself, in seizing itself, is the privileged locus of knowledge that the poet can explore. Valéry calls this self-reflexive seizure the "double mental life." In this movement of self-seizure, thought develops as a series that can be "brought to the limit" so that all possibilities of intellection can be seen. With this comparison of self-reflexive thought with the limit procedure taken from calculus, Valéry aims at showing that intellection is a method that produces meaning, leading the "mind to foresee itself, to image the ensemble of what was going to be imagined in detail, and, with the effect of the succession thus resumed" one arrives at the "condition of every generalization" (1162–63).

Valéry claims that this procedure is "an operation that, known by the name of recursive reasoning" gives to "analyses their extension." Valéry alludes to Poincaré's concept of mathematical induction, and this allu-

---

1. Paul Valéry, *Oeuvres*, ed. Jean Hytier, vol. 1, 1157. In this edition, *Introduction à la méthode de Léonard de Vinci* is part of *Variété*.

sion points up the way Valéry would like to incorporate the very idea of a mechanism—here the rule given by a recursive procedure—to show that artistic creation can be defined as a method given by pure intellection. What is important here is that the intellect is defined in scientific terms: intellection is a question of procedure and method. Proust, undoubtedly another reader of Poincaré, also accepts this definition, and yet he draws somewhat different conclusions from those that Valéry accepts. For Proust, the intellect is an epistemic tool that nonetheless is separate from the epistemic realm to which literature aspires. As we shall presently see, this belief figures prominently in the way Proust constructs his novel so as to separate the work of the autonomous intellect from the work of imaginative recall. For Valéry, Poincaré's concept of recursive reasoning shows the autonomy of mind. This is essential: Poincaré's example allows one to argue the autonomy of mind on the basis of what mind does, not on the basis of what it is, as in the case of Kant. No a priori categories are involved. The autonomy of the mind is then used to argue for the mind's founding role in grounding knowledge. For Proust, this view of the autonomy of mind is a key for the very structure of his novel as well as the rhetoric of narration: his narrator quite literally demonstrates this autonomy in demonstrating the operations of his mind.

To move back a generation from Proust and Valéry, we see that comparable concerns with the mind's autonomy were found earlier in Mallarmé's attempt to expel the irrational, the contingent, and the aleatory from literature. Mallarmé, the most tortured symbolist of all, was driven by a desire to render revelation mathematically certain in the sense that poetic revelation would exclude anything contingent from the oracular knowledge poetry should offer. The quest for certainty is a late nineteenth-century leitmotif, brought about in part by the triumph of empiricism and its doctrine that all knowledge of the world is contingent. And the quest for certainty was also brought about in part by epistemological difficulties in mathematics, for the arrival of non-Euclidian geometries placed the very foundations of mathematics and epistemological certainty in doubt. In literature, Mallarmé's anguish about the contingent nature of knowledge produced a dismay analogous to the consternation many felt about the elaboration of non-Euclidian geometries. If anything is certain, it is that Mallarmé lived uncertainty as a kind of prolonged anguish, and much of his work is a self-referential exploration of the impossibility of grounding poetic revelation in an autonomous affirmation of itself. Mallarmé's quest for certainty was to find final formulation in *Le Livre,* or Mallarmé's "Book," a projected work that would offer an embodiment of logos—with which the Book would found being. In this never-finished oracle, Mallarmé wanted to present the revelation of universal relations as a book of poetry, which is to say, epistemic revelation conceived as the Orphic explanation of the earth.

Mallarmé's notes published under the title of *Le Livre* are cryptic, to say the least, and function more like a thought experiment than a work in any ordinary sense. In a suggestive interpretation, Steven Cassedy sees in them Mallarmé's vision of dance, conceived as the incarnation of mathematics: "It is the genius of algebra having been geometrized, the final expression of how the idea, the Logos, passes from the mathematics of pure number and pure relation to the mathematics of concrete form to assume the status of an aesthetic, but entirely phenomenal, object."[2] From this perspective, Mallarmé's idea of an absolute book was the dream of "a pure network of numerical relations between a limited number of suggestive and emblematic terms ("Drame," "Mystère," "Idée," etc.)" (1072). In this interpretation, it is striking that we again find Poincaré's concept of knowledge as a series of relations, a description of forms through mathematical symbolism, that the poet would reveal. This revelation should act as a kind of privileged knowledge that abolishes the contingent and the hated groundless nature of being that nearly drove Mallarmé to suicide.

For programmatic purposes, Mallarmé's book did not really need to exist. Like Plato's ideas or like some fictional book dreamed of in a novel, the very idea of the Book as the embodiment of all relations was enough to suggest that certain knowledge might exist somewhere—at least in the fictional realm in which certainty could be postulated as (fictionally) existing. Like a resumé of Borges's library of Babylon, Mallarmé's Book was to embody an ideal, autonomous nature. As such it would be a realm of transcendental revelation that must exist somewhere if it can be imagined to exist at all—if only in another work of fiction. From a Proustian perspective, then, we can say that the Book suggests the existence of a book of revelation, or a certain form of knowl-

2. Cassedy, "Mallarmé and Andrej Belyj: Mathematics and the Phenomenality of the Literary Object," 1070.

edge, that is only found in a fictional realm because only fiction has the autonomy to vouchsafe existence to certainty. Literature appears then as a discourse that might supplant mathematics as the guarantor of certainty in a world where the philosophy of science and especially mathematics was losing its belief that there could be certain knowledge at all. Mathematicians were asking, sometimes with anguish equal to Mallarmé's, "What could be certain if Euclid no longer was?" The answer might be in the Book, in which certainty is certain because it cannot be imagined otherwise. Proust's idea of certain knowledge lies in germ here as the work of the imagination on impressions that are certain because one cannot have any other impressions than the ones that the imagination entertains—more on this conceptual conundrum presently.

The mathematically inclined rationalist Valéry and mystical nihilist Mallarmé offered Proust their models and metaphors for a poeticized mathematics (or vice versa) grounded in a thirst for transcendence and certainty—but no real belief in any transcendental realm characterized either poet. However, if we go back to an even earlier generation, it seems Baudelaire was willing to entertain the hypothesis that there might be a transcendental realm, one needing fiction to exist—and a fair amount of hashish. Baudelaire is a singularly important spokesman for literature in its confrontation with science's epistemic imperialism because he was one of the most important rhetoricians for developing strategies of revelation. These strategies aim at revelations that science cannot rival, and these were strategies Proust was to make his own. Baudelaire's opposition to science, in defense of poetry, led him to rhetorical ploys that foreshadow directly the way Proust sought to elude the limits on knowledge imposed by science. Baudelaire's defense of poetry is based on the belief that poetic language can reveal the essence of particular moments and that these moments, in their absolute specificity, effect a disclosure of a truth that science cannot encompass. As we will see, the Proustian doctrine of essence is a rather direct borrowing from Baudelaire's celebration of the divine particular.

Baudelaire's refusal to allow science to usurp the role of arbitrator of knowledge turns on his rejection of the idea that there are a limited number of worlds literature can entertain. In addition to the world Newton described, the world sometimes taken to be the real one, Baudelaire maintained that there are many worlds to be revealed and known. An indefinite number of epistemic realms exist that poetry can explore.

And Baudelaire concluded that, if there is a plurality of possible epistemic realms, these realms of revelation lie outside the generalizing framework imposed by classical physics to define reality. Opposing the limits of Kantian rationalism, Baudelaire claims that any individual world is as worthy of epistemic exploration as that Newtonian-Kantian world defined by the parameters of public space, time, and motion. This claim derives from his belief that there is particular knowledge limited to the individual subject. Baudelaire's reasoning here opens the way for Proust's exploration of the knowledge of the particular stored in human memory, because individual memory, for both Baudelaire and Proust, is one of those worlds lying outside the confines of Kantian epistemology.

Baudelaire's poetical works propose to explore these individual worlds, although typically his poems also portray the impossibility of dwelling in any realm of transcendental revelation longer than the moment of intoxication that offers access to that realm. If one turns from his poems to his critical writing, one finds that Baudelaire spells out, with clarity and with less irony than in his poems, his refusal to allow science to claim all epistemic space. In his critical writing, Baudelaire elucidates, with great self-consciousness, the self-defensive position of the nineteenth-century poet who wants to carve out a realm outside of science. Baudelaire believed that, if he were not successful in finding a specific object for poetic activity, he would be reduced to the role of a simple versifier who, were he to make truth claims, could only repeat the truths science has discovered. Rejecting in effect the Keatsian claim that truth is beauty, Baudelaire separated out the realms of truth, beauty, and duty, declaring each to be the object of a different type of inquiry. Truth is found by science, beauty by poetry, though Baudelaire says the novel may represent a mixed discourse in which both truth and beauty are present. This view foreshadows Proust's conception of the novel, since in his novel the truths of scientific determinism exist as the framework in which the revelation of the unique truth of subjectivity takes place.

Finally, in Baudelaire's economy of discourse, beauty is conceived as separate from ethics and truth. As Baudelaire puts it in an essay on Gautier, beauty is the product of a discourse that takes itself as its own object: "La poésie ne peut pas, sous peine de mort ou de déchéance, s'assimiler à la science ou à la morale; elle n'a pas la Vérité pour objet, elle n'a qu'Elle-même" [Poetry cannot, under pain of death or degradation, assimilate itself to science or ethics; it does not have the Truth as its object, it has only Itself].[3] Whatever be the ultimate origins of the doctrine of the autonomy of art, in Baudelaire's theory this doctrine is part of a defensive posture directed against the encroachment of imperial science as well as the imperialism of moralizing discourses that would reduce poetry to a repetition of the ethical truths of triumphant bourgeois ideology.

Baudelaire's doctrine of the autonomy of poetry does not preclude its having an epistemic function, though poetry's task does not consist simply in the enunciation of Truth. In writing on his contemporary Victor Hugo, Baudelaire celebrates those thinkers like a Fourier or a Swedenborg who revealed that the world is made up of analogies. Perhaps it is not inapposite to suggest that these thinkers undertook something like the disclosure of the relations that, as Poincaré later said, it is science's task to reveal. Baudelaire drew the conclusion that poets, like other thinkers, can reveal analogies: "Chez les excellents pöetes, il n'y a pas de métaphore, de comparaison ou d'épithète qui ne soit d'une adaptation mathématiquement exacte dans la circonstance actuelle, parce que ces comparaisons, ces métaphores et ces épithètes sont puisées dans l'inépuisable fonds de l'*universelle analogie,* et qu'elles ne peuvent être puisées ailleurs" [One inevitably recalls Poe in translating Baudelaire into Poe's language, or back into Poe's language: In the work of excellent poets, there is no metaphor, no simile or epithet that is not the equivalent, within the present circumstance, of a mathematically exact adaptation, because these similes, metaphors, and epithets are extracted from the inexhaustible stock of *universal analogy* and they can be extracted from nowhere else] (705). One wonders how a rhetorical figure can be mathematically precise. The answer is that Baudelaire has used a figure here, one comparing figures to equations, to suggest that poetic rhetoric can serve a function analogous to that of scientific language couched in mathematical formalism. In defining an epistemic realm for poetry, Baudelaire says that this realm is accessible, metaphorically, through the same analogical precision through which the world of classical dynamics is accessible: through metaphorical language that can be as exact in its translation of reality as mathematical equations. In a sense, Baudelaire conceives of the task of literature to be a parallel research program to physics, a program whose conjectures supplement or complement

3. Baudelaire, *Oeuvres complètes,* ed. Y.-G. Le Dantec, 685.

the realm of truths that empirical science offers. There is a historical difference between Proust and Baudelaire in this regard. Proust's search begins two generations later when Newtonian dynamics, though still accepted, had lost its claim to be the universal paradigm for knowledge. Baudelaire may have surmised that this was the case, but, by 1890, it was clear to all who were scientifically literate that Newtonian dynamics did not offer the only way to describe the world.

Baudelaire did not need the end of the Newtonian consensus to find concrete examples of what he meant by the exploration of multiple worlds. For example, in Victor Hugo's work in *La légende des siècles,* Baudelaire finds a concrete example of poetic conjecture that properly fulfills the mission of poetry. Baudelaire finds in the Hugo who wrote "La pente de la rêverie" a demonstration of the limits of mathematical reasoning: In Hugo, much as in Balzac, the reader sees that the paradoxes involved in unity and infinity cannot be resolved (709). Baudelaire finds in Hugo that literature and science have separate domains, separate realms, for which each is best suited—even if it seems that science proposes a model that literature is tempted to emulate and not the contrary. Baudelaire's is a somewhat contradictory position: Poetry *should* owe nothing to science, though science is nonetheless a model for truth or knowledge that poetry is obliged to recognize. The tension created by this contradictory mixing of prescriptive and descriptive aesthetics runs throughout the rest of the nineteenth century. It is a tension that finds its most ambitious expression in Proust's novel, in Proust's demonstration that literature has no ethical role per se, for his novel is an epistemic project that can incorporate both the truth of science and knowledge of subjective worlds.

Baudelaire's own resolution of this tension comes in some of the major poems of *Les Fleurs du mal,* these "flowers of evil" that enact and celebrate the attempt to escape from the world of tedium or ennui, or in short, the world of time. The rhetoric in these poems points the way to Proust's use of images for garnering nonintellectual knowledge of the individual who lives in a world of universal laws obeying temporality. For Baudelaire, the world known by intellection is the mechanical world of classical physics over which clocks rule as absolutes. Newton's belief in absolute time is the starting point for Baudelaire's poems that want to overthrow the intellectual tyranny of physics by destroying the emotional tyranny of clocks. Escape from this world of absolute temporality begins nonetheless with the recognition of the primacy of the mate-rial world, a primacy recognized as much by Proust as by Baudelaire, though Proust no longer recognizes the primacy of absolute time. In Baudelaire, this recognition underwrites the possibility of mechanical-ly manipulating matter so as to change states of consciousness, or what we might call the creation of knowledge through pharmacology (349). Realms outside of science's purlieu can be found with stimulants—like poetry or hashish, eros or wine—that propel the mind outside of itself into a new world:

> Cette acuité de la pensée, cet enthousiasme des sens et de l'esprit, ont dû, en tout temps, apparaitre à l'homme comme le premier des biens; c'est pourquoi, ne considérant que la volupté immédiate, il a, sans s'inquiéter de violer les lois de sa constitution, cherché dans la science physique, dans la pharmaceutique, dans les plus grossières liqueurs, dans les parfums les plus subtils, sous tous les climats dans tous les temps, les moyens de fuire, ne fût-ce que pour quelques heures, son habitacle de fange.

> [This sharpness of thought, this enthusiasm of the mind and the senses, must have, in every era, appeared to humanity as the great-est of goods; that is why, considering only immediate voluptuous rapture, and without worrying about violating the laws of our con-stitution, humanity has sought in physical and pharmaceutical sci-ence, in the strongest liquors, and in the most subtle perfumes, in every climate and every era, the means to flee, be it only for a few hours, its little abode of filth.] ("Le Poëme du haschisch," 348)

The experience of flight is the goal of art, or art as intoxication, which is to say, art affords a nonintellectual experience that is a revelation of worlds that do not belong to science and the intellect. Experience is not reducible to some intellectual proposition, though it is an epistemic state involving knowledge of a unique realm. Using a rhetoric based on metaphor and analogy, Baudelaire says that poetic experience is direct knowledge of a superior realm beyond the intellectual realm of classi-cal physics, which redeems existence, at least momentarily. And because poetic experience redeems a moment that is unique to the individual, it is a more valuable state of knowledge than knowledge provided by uni-versal scientific laws. Or so argues Baudelaire in defense of nonintellec-tual knowledge.

After Baudelaire, the goal of poetry is often proclaimed to be the communication of this unique revelation, if communication is the right word to describe the perception of unmediated knowledge. Proust was especially sensitive to the potential contradiction found in the desire to communicate a unique, individual experience through the language composed of general concepts that poetry is obliged to use. From this perspective, it may appear that Baudelaire makes of the very notion of poetic experience a contradiction: a poem as language is a verbal communication, but a poem as poetic experience is unmediated knowledge. The very idea of communication presupposes mediation by a structure of communication—be it linguistic, iconic, or whatever. Baudelaire's rhetoric is motivated by his attempt to get around the difficulty of seizing unique experience through the mediation of universal concepts.

Baudelaire's poetic use of language points directly to Proust's attempt to find, in the language of his fictional discourse, a way of communicating a privileged experience that only literature can know: in brief, a nonintellectual knowledge that science cannot duplicate. In the exactitude of figurative language—mathematical or not—Baudelaire saw the key to the communication of experience uncontaminated by the intellect. The revelation of unsuspected relations, afforded by tropes, is in fact constitutive of this experience of unique knowledge. These relations can be revealed, for example, by poetical analogies, as in Baudelaire's famous poem "Correspondances." In this sonnet, an entire world of analogies springs from the relations perceived in correspondences among the senses. The relations are abstract, but they are given only in the figures created by the language of immediate sensation.

Or, equally apt for Proust, other relations are discovered in analogies between past and present when the poetic text evokes perfumes that call up the past, as in a sonnet like "Le Parfum." A brief excursus on "Le Parfum" can serve as an introduction to Proust's rhetoric and lead us from Baudelaire's epistemic dreams into Proust's novel. The first quatrain of the sonnet, "Le Parfum," evokes, with a question, a world found in a moment of sensuality. With ironic directness, Baudelaire asks if the reader has ever been intoxicated by odors:

> Lecteur, as-tu quelquefois respiré
> Avec ivresse et lente gourmandise
> Ce grain d'encens qui remplit une église,
> Ou d'un sachet le musc invétéré?

[Reader, have you sometimes breathed in
With intoxication and slow delight
This grain of incense which fills a church
Or the deep-seated musk of some sachet?]

This question is followed in the next stanza by an indirect answer. Baudelaire presents an analogy that defines the poetic experience as knowledge of the past re-created sensually in the present. One inevitably thinks of Proust's description of the pastry called a *madeleine* and the cup of linden tea that generate his narrator's discovery of time past in the opening section of *A la Recherche:*

Charme profond, magique, dont nous grise
Dans le présent le passé restauré.
Ainsi l'amant sur un corp adoré
Du souvenir cueille la fleur exquise.

[Profound and magic spell in which we are made drunk
By the past restored in the present.
So a lover, bent over an adored body,
Gathers the exquisite flower of memory.]

As Baudelaire's lover caresses the beloved, the full intoxication occurs when the past is fully restored in the present. The odors of the present moment find an analogy with odors in the past and, through the sensual relation thus revealed, allow the past to invade the present.

The sonnet's tercets draw the conclusion that this privileged sensual experience is analogous to the experience of a religious plenitude produced by the odors in a church full of incense:

De ses cheveux élastiques et lourds,
Vivant sachet, encensoir de l'alcôve,
Une senteur montait, sauvage et fauve.

[From her elastic and heavy hair,
A living sachet, a censer for the boudoir,
Was arising an odor, one wild and animal-like.]

The sachet and the censer are likened to the mistress's heavy hair in the web of analogies linking the altar, the boudoir, and the poem itself, at

once present in the past, and present as the fullness of an experience lying beyond whatever we can know through mere intellection. The final
tercet stresses that it is a uniquely sensual realm that is (or was) the
source of our experiential elevation:

> Et des habits, mousseline ou velours,
> Tout imprégnés de sa jeunesse pure,
> Se dégageait un parfum de fourrure.

> [And from her clothes, be they muslin or velvet,
> Quite saturated with her pure youthfulness
> Was emanating a perfume of fur.]

Baudelaire's sensualism proposes a triumph for poetry over the world,
though this victory is fleeting and hence ironic in its evanescence, since
the reader inevitably feels that the tedium of the physical world is ready
to assert itself as the bedrock of existence. Baudelaire's ironic poses, and
the contradictory affirmations of his mystical materialism, seem to cry
out for the creation of an artwork that at once affirms the knowledge of
the material world, described in all its deterministic grimness by science, while it offers permanent knowledge of a realm that might escape
from reductionist materialism.

   In other words, Baudelaire's paradoxes seem to call out for the creation of a literary work that is at once a novel incorporating the knowledge of the laws of physical necessity, and a poem offering unique
knowledge of an individual realm that transcends the world of intellection. Later symbolists seemed to point out by example that the pursuit
of pure transcendence could only result in empty gestures or celebrations of failure. Mallarmé showed that poetry, pursued as a celebration
of its impossible transcendence, could result only in a cryptic knowledge of its own impossibility. Attempting to circumvent the failure that
is the glory of Mallarmé's poetry, Valéry's work showed that poetry can
also offer knowledge of its own conditions of possibility. However,
Valéry knew well that this self-reflective knowledge would fail to satis-
fy the writer or reader wanting knowledge beyond the text's knowledge of itself. Valéry dramatized this desire in his poem "Le Cimetière
marin," with its portrayal of the life forces that inevitably blow open the
sheets of paper that seek to enclose the text upon itself. In fine, the work
of these major symbolist poets suggested the possibility of a literary cre-

ation consonant with the truths of the scientific intellect, but which went beyond these truths. In the wake of the symbolists, Proust understands that such a work would offer knowledge of a transcendental realm of unique experience and would also account for its own operation through a self-reflexive epistemic justification of its existence. This, in essence, is what we find in Proust's *A la Recherche du temps perdu*—this and a vision of an objective world ruled over by scientific law.

Proust, like Baudelaire, desired to find for literature a field of inquiry that is at least as valuable as the one defined by science. Like Valéry, he was respectful of science, of the science that included by the time Proust was writing such new theories, ideas, and disciplines as Darwinian biology, the medical revolution based on microbiology, the nearly completed systematic classification of modern chemistry, Maxwell's field equations, Poincaré's early formulations of relativity, and, after the reception of non-Euclidian geometries, the now-generalized recognition that mathematical creation had no a priori limits. By the early twentieth century, the epistemic space carved out by science had become far larger, in a relatively short time, than the world described by Newton and Laplace, those emblematic mechanical thinkers whom Baudelaire mentions with distanced respect. Proust's science includes of course Newton and Laplace, but as rethought by epistemologists like the Parisian philosopher Boutroux or, more importantly, Poincaré. For by the early twentieth century, any consideration of the world of science in France, or Europe, had to take account of the work of the most influential modern French mathematician and theoretical physicist, Henri Poincaré. After considering the French symbolists and some ideas about Proust's relation to them, we can gain much by considering Proust's work in the light of the thought of an emblematic scientist like Poincaré. Poincaré is not well known among literary historians, though he dominates the physics and mathematics of the time, and no history of epistemology is complete without considering Poincaré along with Mach, Duhem, and Boltzmann. In the French context, his thought offers the most influential scientific epistemology Proust contemplated as he began working on *A la Recherche du temps perdu*.

Poincaré's work is quite diverse. Anticipating Einstein, Poincaré proposed an early version of a theory of relativity shortly before Einstein published his 1905 paper on the special theory of relativity. In working on the difficulty of calculating the mutual attraction of three centers of gravitation—the three body problem—Poincaré developed some of the early work upon which chaos theory is based. The fact that Valéry borrows his procedure for defining mind from Poincaré underscores that Poincaré had become in France the public model of the scientist as thinker, especially for his role in debates concerning the foundation of mathematics. For example, Poincaré's writings were at the center of debates in which questions about the foundations of mathematics inevitably led to concern about the nature of knowledge and certainty. Poincaré's role was especially visible in the debate set off at the time by the dissemination of ideas in France about non-Euclidean geometry. The debate, argued in widely read journals, was between, on one side, Kantians who defended the a priori necessity of Euclidean geometry and, on the other side, positivists and empiricists who rejected the metaphysical idealism Kant's position implied. In her important study of the role of non-Euclidian geometry in art, Linda Henderson stresses Poincaré's role in bringing this debate to a wide public:

> The importance of the French debate was twofold. It gave non-Euclidean geometry currency in Paris among intellectuals, and out of this debate emerged the definitive statements on this subject by Henri Poincaré, the mathematician-scientist and writer who, more than any other individual, was responsible for the popularization of non-Euclidean geometry in Paris. . . .
>
> In 1887 Poincaré first published his theory that the axioms of geometry are neither synthetic a priori nor empirical, but are conventions, a view now generally accepted as the solution to the controversy.[4]

Poincaré's conventionalism rejected the experimental nature of geometry, as well as its a priori nature, since the belief in the a priori nature of mathematics argued against the possibility of establishing new geometric systems. And it was now obviously the case that the mind is capable of new geometries.

Poincaré's conventionalism seemed to entail that one was free to chose the geometry one found most convenient, for neither Euclidean nor Lobachevsky's geometry were true or false. Poincaré made this conventionalism into a coherent epistemological doctrine that Proust, as

4. Henderson, *The Fourth Dimension and Non-Euclidean Geometry in Modern Art*, 15.

well as Valéry, took to heart, for the doctrine made mathematics seem more like art: Mathematical formalisms were viewed as a product of the human mind that one could use according to one's needs. Yet there was a loss to the viewpoint. Certain truth no longer belonged to the ontology of mathematics and, by implication, to physical systems constructed as mathematical deductions. The "conventional" nature of mathematics entailed the conclusion that truth was a matter of use, not of ontology, and with this conclusion one could no longer point to mathematics as a body of certain truths about the world. Certainty no longer seemed to belong to a world that science could describe in any number of different ways.

Poincaré himself pushed the point about what we today call the underdetermined nature of reality when he argued that conventionalism in mathematics carries over to physics and other sciences:

> If a phenomenon carries with it a complete mechanical explanation, it will carry with it an infinity of other explanations that will equally as well account for all the particularities revealed by experiment.
>
> And that is confirmed by the history of every part of physics; in optics, for example, Fresnel believed in vibration that was perpendicular to the plane of polarization. Newmann thought it was parallel to this plane. Scientists looked for a long time for a "experimentum crucis" that would allow a decision between these two theories and one could not be found.[5]

The choice of a theory is guided, as Poincaré puts it, by considerations where "the personal contribution" is very great, though considerations like elegance and simplicity are also usual. Conventionalism, describing the epistemological underdetermination of reality, undermines the belief in certainty as a form of a priori necessity. Kant's epistemology founders here, as do the Newtonian underpinnings of the realism of a preceding century of realist writers, and Zola's future-oriented epistemology suddenly seems rather naive: The theory of progress is largely emptied of theoretical content when any conceivable number of theories may work, now or later. (From Poincaré and Mach through Popper and Quine, there is in this regard a continuity.)

5. Poincaré, *The Foundations of Science*, trans. George Bruce Halsted, 181. Halsted's translation includes three works by Poincaré: *Science and Hypothesis, The Value of Science*, and *Science and Method*. Translation slightly changed.

The conventionalist epistemology elaborated by Poincaré finds strong resonance in the aesthetic modernism of a writer like Proust, for whom certain truth cannot be given by science, because science's generalized laws, in their contingency, have probability, but no certainty. Certainty would have to be granted by some necessity that science does not deal with and that not even mathematics can vouchsafe. Recognizing that epistemic necessity is not found in the objective world of science, Proust, in resonance with Poincaré, allows his narrator to develop the idea that certainty may be found in the subjective world of unique experience. Actually, it is hardly necessary that Poincaré be Proust's direct source, for one could just as well argue that Poincaré and Proust share a common epistemology that developed in reaction to the loss of certainty at the end of the nineteenth century. And going beyond Poincaré as it were, Proust affirms that certainty and necessity can characterize knowledge if that knowledge is granted by unique experience, because of the nature of what is unique: It can only be what it is. In this move, Proust seems to have taken a cue from Mallarmé, for his narrator argues, implicitly, that fiction, by its autonomy, can create a realm in which certainty can exist because it can be imagined to exist. Poincaré leads to Mallarmé (and to Borges), and from this perspective Proust's novel appears to be a quest that stakes out an epistemic space outside of those realms carved out by science: Proust's narrator can find certain knowledge if he can gain access to that subjective realm that is *not* subject to the underdeterminism Poincaré ascribes to the objective world known by the various sciences.

It cannot be said that Proust or his narrator flaunts any relation to Poincaré. In fact, Proust makes only one reference to Poincaré in the course of *A la Recherche du temps perdu*. This reference occurs when a character, the aristocratic Saint-Loup, says in conversation that Poincaré has shown that mathematics isn't all "that certain." One may wonder whether Saint-Loup has been a diligent reader of Poincaré, but his comment mirrors public reaction to the debates on scientific epistemology that had been widespread in France and in Europe in general. Saint-Loup's comment on Poincaré points up that certainty and uncertainty were public issues in France, and that something as esoteric as concern about the foundations of mathematics, brought about by non-Euclidian geometry, could occupy the aristocracy of Faubourg Saint-Germain. Saint-Loup's reference to certainty shows that epistemological and scientific questions were being asked, at the beginning of the twentieth century, in works by scientists and, as we see, by novelists.

As Proust's novel itself centrally demonstrates about literature, novelists as well as mathematicians can be concerned with apodictic structures or procedures that grant certain knowledge. The criteria by which certainty is granted or recognized may vary from one discourse to another, as may what exactly certainty even means. Proust, as much as any thinker or writer, was well aware that the difficulty of defining certainty exists in direct proportion to the anguish one may feel upon needing some certainty in a world in which one finds merely probable truth, or uncertainties. With an intellectual rigor perhaps unparalleled in literary history, Proust framed the question of the certainty of artistic truth in direct response to the uncertainties of the intellect that scientific conventionalism portrays. At this juncture, we find again a potential rivalry between literature and science, for the claims to certain knowledge could lead to claims of superiority. In Proust, this rivalry is actually defused by Proust's concept of artistic truth, for artistic truth, as we shall see presently, is really complementary or symmetrical to scientific truth. The essential point to grasp here, the starting point for understanding Proust's intellectual context, is the way in which Proust frames the question of certainty in terms that mirror the emerging epistemological consensus for which Poincaré, mathematician and epistemologist, set out the basic terms in a series of his nonmathematical works, the most popular of which was *La Science et l'hypothèse* (*Science and Hypothesis*) of 1902.

To allay the doubts some readers may now be entertaining, I will concede that Poincaré is not a thinker whose name is usually coupled with Proust's. My point is of course that it should be (and indeed has been in the very most recent book I have read on Proust, Nicola Luckhurst's *Science and Structure in Proust's "A la recherche"*). Bergson and Einstein are more usual names bandied about when it comes to intellectual analogies, though a little scrutiny shows that these names are not especially relevant. Proust knew Bergson's work, but Bergson's concepts about time are not Proust's. I do not believe that Proust really made much use of Bergson, or that Proust even knew much about Einstein before late in his life. Einstein did not become a media star before Eddington's 1919 expedition affirmed that gravity could bend light and thus offered an important and widely acclaimed confirmation of Einstein's general relativity theory. If a meaningful comparison can be made between Proust

and Einstein—and an argument can be made for analogies—this overlap is a question of coincidence, not influence, for Einstein and Proust
were subject to the same intellectual developments.

The reference made by Proust's narrator in "Combray" (1913) to time
as the "fourth dimension" of spacial reality is a reflection not of Einstein's relativity theory, but of Poincaré's claim that, if we were to re-
ceive a different education, we could localize phenomena of the exterior
world in non-Euclidian space or even in a space with four dimensions.
Consider the chapter on "Space and Geometry" in *Science and Hypothesis:*

> Beings with minds like ours, and having the same senses as we, but
> without previous education, would receive from a suitably chosen
> external world impressions such that they would be led to construct
> a geometry other than that of Euclid and to localize the phenome-
> na of that external world in a non-Euclidian space, or even in a space
> with four dimensions.
>
> As for us, whose education has been accomplished by our actu-
> al world, if we were suddenly transported into this new world, we
> should have no difficulty in referring its phenomena to our Euclid-
> ean space. Conversely, if these beings were transported into our en-
> vironment, they would be led to relate our phenomena to non-
> Euclidean space. (66)

Not only does Poincaré grant us the power to perceive four dimensions,
but he even imagines that we could visualize Lorentz transformations,
that is, we could perceive that objects get smaller as they approach the
speed of light. Poincaré was a scientist with an imagination that a novelist might well envy. In any case, perceiving a fourth dimension seems
to have been an idea that Proust found quite congenial.

With such ideas as these, Poincaré was close to formulating a theory
like Einstein's relativity theory, but only close. As Martin Gardner points
out, neither Lorentz nor Poincaré imagined that time was relative to an
inertial framework. This was the great conceptual step that Einstein
took, in which he rejected Newton's premise that one time permeated
the entire cosmos.[6] If it does not seem that Einstein's ideas influenced
Proust, it does seem plausible to say that Proust's relativizing his nar-

6. Gardner, *The Relativity Explosion*, 48.

rator's position in time parallels what Einstein developed in building on Poincaré, Lorentz, and others in framing the theory of special relativity in 1905. What seems most probable is that Proust drew directly upon Poincaré for an image of space that allowed the affirmation of the non-Euclidian image that time is a dimension of space. And with this, Proust was empowered to set free his narrator's inner space, making all in the novel relative to it, and inventing, as it were, his own special theory of relativity.

Equally fundamental is the way Proust interpreted Poincaré's type of epistemology in his search for ideas that might vouchsafe certainty to art as a form of knowledge. In a very real sense, Proust used the loss of certainty in mathematics and science that he found in Poincaré or in the wake of Poincaré. The loss of absolute certainty in science is the springboard that offered Proust grounds for arguing for the certain knowledge that he seeks in art.

Proust's narrator knows of course that the physical sciences do offer a type of truth; and, in dealing with knowledge, Proust's narrator alludes frequently to scientific paradigms that dictate truth about reality. As part of its epistemic premises, the novel accepts that medicine and physiology, as well as classical mechanics and thermodynamics, describe an objective world—by definition, that is their realm. The narrator explicitly accepts science's role in allowing us to know contingent reality. All contingent reality should be amenable to description by laws, and in fact Proust's narrator actually extends the range of phenomena described by laws beyond what science had really accomplished in the early twentieth century (or today). He constantly evokes, for example, the "laws" that putatively dictate the development of individuals and culture in time. Proust's narrator accepts for contingent, objective reality, moreover, the descriptive power of the positivist hierarchy of discourses. This hierarchy proposes that every level of epistemic analysis is subject to a superior determination by the laws of the next, more general level of discourse. On one level, for instance, Proust's narrator declares that there are specific social laws, and that these are then subject to the higher and more general laws of temporality, by which we might think of thermodynamics and entropy. There are the specific laws of the body and the mind, which are then subject to determination by the more general laws of physiology and, above all, the laws of the heredity invented by nineteenth-century medicine. Like an unending research project, Proust's novel needs its three thousand pages to document how these putative laws dictate the way society and characters develop—for the laws of physics and physiology are so many examples of the most general "laws of time" at work. Time is the space these laws need— much time—for their realization.

This aspect of Proust's narration may seem at times to present something of a caricature of determinism, and it is at this point that we see that Zola's influence is very strong, in spite of Proust's critical remarks about naturalism. Consider, for example, when, after hundreds of pages, the narrator begins to discover that he himself offers one more example of the way hereditary laws determine character development. Zola would certainly have approved of the development that leads to the discovery by Proust's aging narrator that he has come to resemble, not only his father, but above all, his Aunt Léonie, the old maniac who refused to leave her room in Combray—the room that was the center of the child's paradise recalled and re-created in "Combray" at the novel's beginning. As a young man, the narrator thought that he was, in every important respect, the opposite of the aunt who found reading to be a waste of time. As a mature man, he discovers that his aunt's character has come to rivet him, too, to his bed, where he endlessly meditates in jealousy upon his lover, Albertine: "Or, bien que chaque jour j'en trouvasse la cause dans un malaise particulier, ce qui me faisait si souvent rester couché, c'était un être, non pas Albertine, non pas un être que j'aimais, mais un être plus puissant sur moi qu'un être aimé, c'était transmigrée en moi, despotique au point de faire taire parfois mes soupçons jaloux, ou du moins de m'empêcher d'aller vérifier, s'ils étaient fondés ou non, c'était ma tante Léonie" [Now, even though each day I found a cause for it in a particular discomfort, what made me remain so often in bed was a being—not Albertine, not a being that I loved—but a being having more power over me than a loved being, one who had transmigrated into me and was despotic enough to quiet my jealous suspicions, or at least to stop me from going to see if they were grounded or not, and that being was my Aunt Leonie].[7] Transmigration is Proust's mythic equivalent of inheritance; it is his translation of the laws of the transmission of character traits that dominates the development of all characters in *A la Recherche* with a mechanical rigor in which only late nineteenth-

7. Proust, *A la Recherche du temps perdu*, vol. 3, 78–79.

century medicine could believe. From Saint-Loup to the Baron de Char-
lus, every Proustian character is ruled mechanically by laws that model
one's flesh and pick one's sexual preferences, that color the eyes and determine posture and gait, and that cause tics and manias.

If the narrator constantly consults a barometer because his father
did so maniacally, this suggests that Proust also had in mind a neo-
Lamarckian theory of the acquisition of traits. But this is only one of
many theories that can be evoked with regard to what the narrator frequently calls the laws of time, as well as the laws of the soul, the laws of
the body and its development. These are all so many laws or paradigms
that are interlinked to create a deterministic tapestry portraying decline,
hereditary transformations, and death as the inevitable pattern of human existence. When at the novel's outset, the older narrator looks back
upon his childhood to ask if his entire past is dead, he is implicitly making appeal to a number of frameworks that make sense of such a question. He knows that thermodynamics, physiology, and hereditary science all spell out death as the end product of human development. But
these truths granted by science are contingent in that any number of scientific models could be used to explain them. There is no necessary or
certain truth in science, only the indifferently used laws that could be
replaced by other laws to explain what one perceives, for these laws are
the product of our intelligence. And these products of intellect are un-
able to reach the truth of our subjective world, because, as the narrator
says, this world is locked up in nonintellectual sensations: "Il en est ainsi de notre passé. C'est peine perdue que nous cherchions à l'évoquer,
tous les efforts de notre intelligence sont inutiles. Il est caché hors de son
domaine et de sa portée, en quelque objet matériel (en la sensation que
nous donnerait cet objet matériel) que nous ne soupçonnons pas" [And
so it is with our past. We waste our effort when we attempt to evoke it;
all our intellect's efforts are useless. It is hidden outside of the realm of
the intellect and its reach, in some material object (in the sensation that
this material object would offer us) whose existence we do not suspect]
(1:44). As Baudelaire's work demonstrated—and which the narrator
seemingly fully accepts—only sensation can get around the limits of intellect and provide the substantive plenitude that restores knowledge of
our subjective world. Knowledge is, in this regard, conceived as a fullness of things in their sensorial richness. Here we should recall Baudelaire's practice with regard to the contradictions of immediacy: in a lit-

erary work, sensation must be captured by linguistic means, by images and metaphors, and by the rhetorical structure in which these images are embedded. The writer's task is, as Mallarmé's nonexistent Book suggested, to find the images and the rhetorical structure that can offer access, in a fiction, to a world of certainty that exists therein because of the autonomy of fictional discourse: fiction itself guarantees certainty, because there is no alternative to certainty's existence if it is declared to exist. (Or, more prosaically, it is not a contingent statement to say, "Madame Bovary's eyes are blue." Nor can I imagine that she does not exist once the novel declares that she does.)

One of the goals of Proust's novel is to describe the necessity and hence certainty that Proust's narrator finds in the fullness of his own subjective truth. So the novel must show, convincingly, that subjectivity has a certainty that contingent truth does not have. An understanding of the novel's rhetorical structure is the key to understanding how one can meaningfully speak of the necessity of a unique experience or revelation. The work's rhetorical structure is designed to give access to the narrator's certain knowledge, and Proust's rhetorical ploys take on their complete meaning when they are considered as part of his narrator's epistemic quest aiming at a certainty science cannot offer. The center for this certainty is the knowing subject in the novel, the first-person narrator. Proust's first-person narration is told by a self-observer whose scope is limited to the world of his, the narrator's, subjectivity (with the notable exception of the nearly omniscient narration, about a time before the narrator's birth, that he offers in *Un Amour de Swan*). The narrator self-consciously knows he can deal only with what I call the narrator's own inertial reference frame: the narrating self is the framework of reference for all that happens in the novel. This framework determines how time and space are perceived in the work. Temporality is an absolute for Newtonian cosmology, and for the realm of contingent truths that rely upon that cosmology, but the novel's subjective time and space exist relative to the narrator. The effect of the rhetorical structure is to remove the narrator's subjective space from the realm of objectivity so that subjectivity is separate from the realm wherein science and its laws rule supreme.

The first pages of the novel work to "delocalize" the narrator. He is often sleeping, or present in chambers, in which space is uncertain. The boundary lines separating dream, aesthetic perception, and perception of reality are blurred as the narrator wanders in memory. From the out-set, the narrator is situated so that there is no absolute narrative space that can be called the present space of narration. All dynamics in the novel, and all development therein, is recorded and measured in a space that is defined strictly relative to the narrator: he is the only framework for viewing the novelistic world. Yet, as many students have com-plained, it is never clear where he may be located. The net effect of this separation of narrative voice from the world is that even time recalled exists finally as a function of the self outside of the coordinates of space and time. This is the sense of the narrator's dictum when he says that a man who sleeps holds in a circle about himself the thread of the hours, the order of years and of worlds (1:5). Proust is willing ascribe absolute time to science's domain, the domain of laws that destroy the body, but he reserves for his narrator's epistemic realm another version of time, the time in which the narrator functions in a space defined by the nar-rator's sensations.

The temporality of the work's rhetorical structure is grounded in Proust's use of verb tenses. For example, the first sentence in the novel gives us a narrator who says, rather bizarrely, that he has gone to bed early for a long time—"Longtemps, je me suis couché de bonne heure." In this opening sentence, the composed past tense functions somewhat like the English present perfect tense in that it seems to relate a past act to the present moment, or the fictional present in which the novel is nar-rated. The past is thus situated relative to a present moment that is the present moment of the fiction's enunciation. Logically, it is only in the present moment that the narrator can narrate his past life unfolding in the imperfect tense, the tense of the repetition of acts carried out in the past. The imperfect tense, the French *imparfait,* is the tense the narrator often uses to describe the mechanical unfolding of repetitive events, when the events are not clearly unique events narrated in the literary past tense, the *passé simple.* At times he also uses the imperfect for events that seem logically to have been unique occurrences, but the imperfect endows them with a sense of repetition that transforms them into eter-nally repeating acts of memory. In this way the novel's temporal frame-work is polarized between the unnamed present moment of narration and the imperfect tense that describes the past for a narrator who is sit-uated outside that past. In a sense, the present-tense narrator, who is never situated in the novel, is outside the temporal flow governed by the laws of time ruling over objective reality. The reader only knows, or vaguely feels, that the narrator is narrating in a present moment because the *passé composé,* or composed past, is used by the narrator, albeit only a few times in the course of the novel. This tense, each time it is used, situates the narrator in a present moment, a moment of dreaming or awakening, lying outside the temporal flow of ordinary experience. This tense thus contrasts with what is usually narrated in the imperfect tense, though sometimes in the literary past tense, the tenses used for those contingencies that can be described by the laws of time, the laws that bring matter to dissolution. The *passé composé* relates a past to a transcendental present moment of narration.

The *passé composé* is the tense, at the beginning of the novel, first used to recall all of Combray and the narrator's childhood in their complete fullness. This recall is effected through the images re-creating the sensations of the past after the narrator finds, through the sensual associations sparked by a pastry and a linden tea, that his childhood past has been restored to him. He then declares, using the *passé composé,* "tout Combray et ses environs, tout cela qui prend forme et solidité, est sorti, ville et jardins, de ma tasse de thé" [all of Combray and its surroundings, all of that which can acquire form and solidity, the city and the gardens, *has arisen/arose* from my cup of tea] (my emphasis, 1:48). Combray is restored in all its fullness and, therewith, the narrator can entertain the certain knowledge of his past re-created as a present—in the form of the narration called "Combray." However, the act of narration itself never coincides with what is narrated, and the narrator never coincides with himself as the character who, in the novel's past experience, is subject to the laws governing the novel's unfolding. The past can explode into the present moment of narration, but it never ceases being a past that unfolded according to the laws of time.

To recapitulate, the goal of Proust's narrator is to shape a work of art that respects and, indeed, uses the laws of time and reality, the laws of physics and physiology, at the same time that the narrator seeks a perception offering certain truth. Since certainty cannot exist in the realm of contingent laws, certain truth must exist in a realm where these laws hold no sway. Many indifferent laws can be invoked to describe the world that is essentially underdetermined, as Poincaré's epistemology describes it. This is the world of the aleatory that Mallarmé deplored and from which Baudelaire sought escape. Opposed to this domain is that unnamed realm inhabited by the narrator-observer who looks from his narrative framework upon the world and, in so doing, finds a perspective that is not subject to contingency—for he discovers that his perceptions cannot be inscribed in any deterministic matrix that would reduce them to some expression of a scientific model. At this point, the narrator can say that contingency is transformed into necessity. Contingent impressions can be converted into a realm characterized by necessary knowledge, at least when the artist successfully embodies his or her random sensations or perception into a work of art. The work of art is a realm of necessity because it is unique to that artist and to that subjective framework of reference that is different from all others. This knowledge is certain knowledge, because it can have no other status. In its uniqueness it defies contingency. Memory of the two ways at Combray, or of the church at the center of the village, gives knowledge of necessity as it offers a revelation of the subject's world, one that necessarily can be no other than what it is, or rather was.

Hopefully these remarks throw light on the idea that Poincaré's epistemological theory parallels the belief in the artist's unique perception in other, important ways. For the grounds for the belief that the artist can escape the deterministic laws of the universe, as described by classical physics and physiology, are strongly implied by Poincaré's general epistemology. This epistemology was crucial in the demise of the belief in determinism, and with the demise of the belief in Laplacian totalizing determinism, the artist could feel justified in the belief that there might be realms sheltered from the iron hand of deterministic laws. Specifically, the loss of belief in determinism resulted in large part from the interpretation of work in physics undertaken by Poincaré on the three body problem, or the unsolved problem of how to determine the mutual gravitation attraction of more than two bodies. As I shall presently elaborate, there are reasons to believe that Proust was quite attentive to the implications of the three body problem. The unsuccessful attempt to work out the dynamics of the attraction among three bodies was generally taken to signify the end of the theoretical possibility of prediction granted by a total determinism. By the end of the nineteenth century, the problem was already a long outstanding one, for work on the three body problem had begun a century earlier. After Newton's laws of motion had successfully described the attraction between two bodies, the next step in celestial mechanics was to try to find equations that could account for the motions of three bodies, but the complexity of the problem defied resolution.

Belief in determinism depended very much on successfully resolving this problem: extrapolations from Newtonian mechanics had allowed Laplace to claim that, if a sufficiently powerful mind were to know the position of every atom in the universe, then this mind could calculate the future of the entire cosmos. Laplacian hubris foundered not on the infinite number of equations needed for these predictions, but rather on what could be said about three bodies. The historian of mathematics Morris Kline has shown that a loss of certainty came to afflict mathematics as well as physics when the mathematics necessary for three mutually attracting bodies proved intractable. In commenting on how the three body problem affected the very ontology of mathematics, Kline points out that it also severely eroded the foundations of determinism: "The core of this problem is the question of the mutual gravitational effect of three bodies on each other. If one could devise a procedure to determine the perturbing effect of a third body, this procedure could be used to determine the perturbing effect of a fourth body, and so on. However, exact solution of the general problem of the motion of even three bodies has not been obtained even today."[8] Proust does not entirely reject Laplacian claims for determinism, at least not for the ordinary world of objective reality for which his narrator offers numerous examples of deterministic laws that rule over the body and society. But he is certainly willing to accept as an epistemic principle that determinism has its limits.

My minimum claim here, then, is that the underdeterminism formulated by Poincaré, and by his contemporary epistemologists like Mach and Duhem, provided some of the motivation that led Proust to postulate a realm in which determinism does not hold sway. This is the subjective realm to which objective reality is always relative in its representation in a work of art, or the inertial framework of the artist's self, the framework provided by the limited perception of Proust's narrator-artist. Underdeterminism cuts in two directions, however, for there are limits of which one must be aware to understand Proust's strategy. In a sense, it affirms that the subjective realm is primary because, in the determination of what we know, the subject has the power to opt for an in-

8. Kline, *Mathematics: The Loss of Certainty,* 61–62.

definite number of models and laws with which we chose to describe reality. What the subject cannot opt for, what the subject must accept as a necessity, is the subject's own unique world of sensation and perception once the subject has experienced that world.

For Proust and his conception of the novel, the following aspect of Poincaré's type of epistemology is perhaps most important: with his sense of relativity, Poincaré went so far as to deny that perception was determined by any geometry intrinsic to the nature of things in space. If we think the world exists in three dimensions, this is an effect of habit, or that "law" of psychology that Proust, after Poincaré, made into the dominant law of mind. But, as Poincaré states, we could live in two dimensions, or four dimensions—those four dimensions that Proust's narrator found in the church at Combray. Perception itself is radically underdetermined by Poincaré. This claim parallels Proust's affirmation that the artist's perception offers a unique truth that escapes from the rule of law. Poincaré proposes a comparable vision of the freedom of perception, in "Space and Geometry," when he says that there are no laws intrinsic to the nature of perception: "[the association of ideas] . . . is the result of a *habit*; this habit itself results from very numerous *experiences*; without any doubt, if the education of our senses had been accomplished in a different environment, where we should have been subjected to different impressions, contrary habits would have arisen and our muscular sensations would have been associated according to other laws."[9] At this point, Poincaré argues, we could use either Euclidian or non-Euclidian geometries to describe or even to perceive the real. It is a question of habit. Proust translates this notion in radical fashion by allowing his narrator to escape from habit in his own subjective realm where, at the novel's outset, he is situated outside of the ordinary world of space and time. It is in this context escaping context that the narrator makes the claim that, as a sleeping man, he escapes the empirical laws and patterns that habit usually accepts, for, to use Moncrief's translation, he "has in a circle round him the chain of the hours, the sequence of the years, the order of the heavenly host." Conventional laws governing matter and perception no longer necessarily hold, no more than do the metric conventions that habit accepts for ordering the perception of space and time.

9. Poincaré, *The Foundations of Science*, 69.

In brief, Proust's strategy is to use a classical scientific model to talk about a deterministic world exterior to the narrator, but a relativist and conventionalist model to talk about the subjective world of the narrator's unique perception. He applies the lessons he learned from Balzac, Flaubert, and Zola for fashioning the laws of history and society, but he calls upon Baudelaire and Mallarmé for rhetoric and concepts that illuminate the world of subjectivity. This mix corresponds, interestingly, to Baudelaire's idea that a novel is a mixed genre, containing, in Proust's case, objective truth and self-sufficient poetic correspondences. In the wake of Baudelaire, but with more epistemological rigor and considerably less irony, Proust staked out the realm that Baudelaire demanded for the realm of poetic self-sufficiency. Finally, might we not see that in creating his world of unique impressions, Proust arrived at the "idea" that Flaubert despaired of ever finding in the world of mechanical phenomena, the fallen world of viscera driven by laws that only science seemed capable of describing?

Poetic self-sufficiency derives from the writer's impressions, for they are the unique material that forms the truth of the narrator's world and hence the certain truth of art as found in the novel. These impressions are not contingent, though they owe their existence to chance. But once they are given to the narrator, they are his necessary material for certain truths. This material is a necessity in the sense that the narrator should find the entire first section of the novel, "Combray," in a fortuitous encounter when he tastes a bit of pastry that he has dipped into a cup of linden tea. In this chance encounter, the narrator overcomes all the contingencies of ordinary existence, which is to say that this experience cannot be explained by those deterministic paradigms that, unfortunately, condemn us to death. Moreover, the experience born of linden tea is a direct translation, from poetry to fiction, of Baudelaire's doctrine of correspondances, but one occurring as an epistemic experience contrasting with the world of laws. The narrator's present sensations coincide with sensations he experienced in the past, and, through the correspondence between the two, the past is resurrected in the present. All of Combray surges forth as the living paradise of the narrator's youth. In this moment "Combray" is, for the narrator, a form of necessity that escapes contingency.

Proust thus begins his novel with a demonstration of the certain truths of Combray that the narrator must then later recover, having lived himself through the years of experience that constitute the novel, with its portrayal of characters and society that begins in a time before the narrator's childhood and unfolds until some time after World War I. At the end of this period, after the War, the narrator discovers the meaning of artistic experience in the context of the novel itself in discoveries that take place many years after the episode with the *madeleine.* At the end of the novel, he discovers what the episode with the *madeleine* meant, as the reader sees in the long analysis that the narrator proposes in *Le Temps retrouvé,* wherein the narrator explains that he has discovered that subjective life is too complex to be described by deterministic law. Interestingly for our argument, this analysis takes place after the narrator realizes that art is analogous to science in their common study of relations. In a moment of self-reflection, he thinks about the music of the composer Vinteuil. At the same time, he reflects upon what he calls the materialist hypothesis—"celle du néant"—or the hypothetical nothingness to which we, as material beings, are destined by the laws of physiology and physics that govern our bodies.

The narrator wonders if Vinteuil's musical phrases were the expression of certain inner states analogous to what he had experienced in tasting the *madeleine* dipped in linden tea in "Combray." What in these states, he asks, made them different from any other experiential state? The simple fact that Vinteuil's musical phrases resist analysis does not necessarily mean that there is something more real in them than in ordinary reality, the "material" reality that the mind encounters everywhere. The spirit of doubt, he says, suggests rather that the states produced by the musical phrases cannot be analyzed precisely because they place in action too many forces: "ils mettent en jeu trop de forces dont nous ne nous sommes pas encore rendu compte" (3:381). In speaking of the analysis of forces, Proust suggests that the reduction of artistic states to component elements is too complex to be resolved—a complexity to be understood on the order of the three body problem. There can thus be no deterministic resolutions of the forces that would allow them to be described by some contingent law. But this is not surprising: artistic states arise from a subject's inner world, and this subjective realm is where one also finds the origins of the choice of a deterministic model. It is the subject's choice to use a given deterministic model that, then imposed through force of habit, grants the knowing subject its operational power—something the narrator suggests at the novel's beginning when he wonders if the immobility of the things around us is forced on them by our conviction that they are themselves and not anything else. The subject's inner world must therefore lie outside the realm of simple determinism. Poincaré's type of conventionalism seems evident here, for the knowing subject determines epistemic conventions—and not the contrary.

At the end of the novel, the narrator returns from a long absence he spent in a sanatorium. This is when he finally understands the nature of art, for, upon returning to society, he experiences a revelation analogous to the one he had experienced at the novel's beginning with the linden tea and the *petite madeleine*. Going to a social gathering, he is crossing the Guermantes's courtyard when he unexpectedly undergoes a series of epiphanies in which various present sensations recall their exact equivalent that occurred once in his past. After this renewed experience of the resurrection of a living past, after this contingent encounter with his own unique reality, the narrator can now analyze the artist's task to escape from contingency. By understanding this task, he can understand why he has failed to be a writer, and why, throughout the course of the novel, he has been able only fruitlessly to ponder upon his desire to be a writer. Before the epiphanies in the courtyard, he had already realized that he could not be a true artist if he merely registers in his work general essences (3:718), or if he is content simply to describe general laws (3:719). Saying that intellectual performances, typical of the naturalist novel, and such as are undertaken by the Goncourt Brothers, offer only sterile joys, the narrator offers a muted critique of naturalism. In this critique, he translates Baudelaire's attitude toward intellection and objective truths, for these truths of science are not essential to the goals of art—and this in spite of the fact that *A la Recherche* has just devoted nearly three thousand pages to these truths.

After the experience in the courtyard, the narrator comes to the full realization that the realm of artistic experience is a unique reality: it cannot be analyzed using the Kantian coordinates of space and time, the metric province of classical analysis. Now facing the prospect of death after a long period of illness, he discovers that his task as a successful novelist would be the re-creation of the perceived real. And so he sees that for the remainder of time that he has yet to live, he must undertake the exploration of the reality of multiple sensations that are too complex to be reduced by analysis. These sensations must be freed from the patterns imposed by conventional perception and habit and laid bare as the realm of a unique and necessary truth outside the ken of science. This revelation is nonetheless an epistemic endeavor, though different from the discovery of relations that science undertakes.

The question is open as to whether the narrator will be able to write a novel, or if in fact he has achieved his task precisely with the novel *A la Recherche* that we readers have in hand. It is tempting to say, and many have said, that the novel is circular and narrates its own coming into being, but there is nothing in the novel that says this is case—or that this is not the case. The fiction of the narrator's presence outside of time suggests in fact that the novel's narrated events never coincide with the space of narration. It stretches our imagination to conceive that the narrator is an epistemic quester outside the realm circumscribed by time and space, and thus outside the deterministic realm of conventional science. But it does appear that Proust intended that the novel's recall of the narrator's unique experience be experienced as the fiction of something like a nontranscendental transcendence. For only in fiction does it appear that we can find that noncontingent realm wherein are found those unique truths the narrator likens to essences, and which are more like the contrary of any Platonic essence. Only in fiction, as Mallarmé's example proposed, can one find the enactment of a unique truth that is necessary, as necessary as the narrator's subjective fiction that discovers noncontingent truth in a contingent world.

The nature of artistic truth, as the narrator sees it, is perplexing. Sensation in this world is the point of departure for the creation of what Proust's narrator calls extra-temporal essences (3:871). These are not Platonic ideas or abstract essences located outside of temporal experience. Rather, they are the unique states that contain within them the temporality of the (fictional) moment of perception. This notion is perhaps best illustrated when the narrator says, about his recalled perceptions of the church at the center of Combray, that time is its fourth dimension. Proust's essences are in fact quite anti-Platonic, if by Platonic we mean an essence devoid of temporality. Proust's essences are also the antithesis of what the classical scientist describes when he uses some metric framework that situates the real in terms of absolute time and space. The only frame of reference for these essences is the artistic self that must find some appropriate language for communicating them— literary, musical, or painterly. Once this language is found, once a framework is established, then, to quote Montcrief's translation, the artist can "reestablish the significance of even the slightest signs by which the artist is surrounded" (2:1014), for every aspect of the artist's unique experience can be converted into noncontingent meaning and certain truth. This is the realm of transcendence, and it is not as paradoxical as I may have implied, if we are willing to grant to the ontology of art a space that is not contingent.

In his analysis of his future task as a writer, the narrator says that the artist's work is symmetrical to the scientist's research. With this comparison, the narrator calls to mind Poincaré's description of the model-making work of the scientific mind, though really with reverse symmetry. Rather than with the objective demonstration of invariant reality that scientists seek in an experiment, artists must start with the only reality they immediately possess—the reality of their subjective perception. The artist's objective intelligence can intervene only after he or she has found a realm of truth in subjective experience:

> Seule l'impression, si chétive qu'en semble la matière, si insaisissable la trace, est un critérium de vérité, et à cause de cela mérite seule d'être appréhendée par l'esprit, car elle est seule capable, s'il sait en dégager cette vérité, de l'amener à une plus grande perfection et de lui donner une pure joie. L'impression est pour l'écrivain ce qu'est l'expérimentation pour le savant, avec cette différence que chez le savant le travail de l'intelligence précède et chez l'écrivain vient après. (3:880)

> [Only the subjective impression, however inferior the material may seem to be and however improbable the outline, is a criterion of truth and for that reason it alone merits being apprehended by the mind, for it alone is able, if the mind can extract this truth, to lead the mind to a greater perfection and impart to it a pure joy. The subjective impression is for the writer what experimentation is for the scientist, but with this difference, that with the scientist the work of the intelligence precedes, and with the writer it comes afterwards.] (trans. Montcrief, 1001–2)

The comparison also suggests another way in which scientist and writer are united, for if the artist, like the scientist, is not constrained by any absolute system of reference, nonetheless constraints exist by the very nature of research. The comparison obliges one to recognize that both artist and scientist are subject to constraints. The mind is not free to choose its world, whatever be the conventions chosen to explain this world. Once the artist has chosen the area to explore, the world imposes its limits. These limits are immediately encountered when the narrator makes his own decision to write: "Ainsi j'étais déjà arrivé à cette conclusion que nous ne sommes nullement libres devant l'oeuvre d'art, que nous ne la faisons pas à notre gré, mais que, préexistant à nous, nous devons, à la fois parce qu'elle est nécessaire et cachée, et comme nous ferions pour une loi de la nature, la découvrir" (3:881) [Thus I had already come to the conclusion that we are not at all free in the presence of the work of art to be created, that we do not do it as we ourselves please, but that it existed prior to us and we should seek to discover it as we would a natural law because it is both necessary and hidden] (trans. Montcrief, 2:1002). The material for art awaits to be discovered before the artist turns to discovery. The artist makes a discovery in that what he or she finds is always already there, in the artist, as the necessary world hidden from the immediately conscious realm of the present moment.

With this affirmation, we touch again on the seemingly dichotomous nature of modern scientific epistemology that Proust embodies in his novel. This epistemology oscillates between being realist and antirealist. In its antirealism, it says that phenomena are underdetermined. In its realism, it declares limits of reality that cannot be transgressed. Antirealism allows that there can be as many laws and models, or theories and worlds, as there are scientists and artists. But realism points out that the world imposes a limit, specifically the invariant relations that, in spite of being invariant, may be assumed and used by different models or modes of explanation. Poincaré affirms these limits when he states, for example, that the principle of the conservation of energy is a "limit imposed on our freedom" to chose the physical models that seem best to fit our purposes.[10] Proust affirms the same when he recognizes that the artist must accept the world that is given to him, even though it is randomly imposed by the artist's chance experience. In this random encounter, the artist encounters the unique laws of unique experience.

In accepting what the mind finds as a limit to its freedom, in accepting what is imposed upon it, the mind finds certainty within itself. This

10. Poincaré, *The Foundations of Science*, 158.

viewpoint is as true of Poincaré's epistemology of mathematics as of Proust's vision of the artist's certainty. Poincaré recognizes that scientific truth is largely a product of reasoning through recurrence. In fact, in *La Science et l'hypothèse*, he describes both empirical statements and mathematical statements as products of induction. Empirical induction can only result in contingent statements—uncertain because they are about the exterior world so that "they rest upon a belief in a general order of the Universe, an order that is outside of us."[11] But mathematical induction imposes itself as a form of certitude because, faced with the infinite recurrence that characterizes mathematical propositions, the mind recognizes, in direct intuition, its own power to make such infinite extensions. The certainty that mathematics offers is a property of the mind, and the fact that the world allows mathematics to be used is a tribute to the mind. One sees finally how close Poincaré's philosophy of mathematics is to Proust's vision of the novel when one considers that Poincaré says that the material world is there to allow us to become conscious of the mind's power (30). Mathematical certainty arises from the mind's own structure, an idea that the mathematician pointedly affirms: "Mathematical induction, which is to say, demonstration through recurrence, imposes itself . . . because it is simply an affirmation of a property of mind itself" (31). Analogously, we have seen that the Proustian narrator discovers that his artistic truths are endowed with certainty because they are part of mind itself, the artistic mind that finds its own truths to be certainties because they are properties of that mind.

Both at the novel's beginning and at its end, the narrator's reflections upon his discovery of his past contain a meditation upon mind. In the narrator's own mind he discovers the past that is first resurrected by the accidental encounter with the pastry and a cup of herbal tea. Or as he says after tasting the *petite madelaine*, "Je pose la tasse et me tourne vers mon esprit. C'est à lui de trouver la vérité. Mais comment? Grave incertitude, toute les fois que l'esprit se sent dépassé par lui-même; quand lui, le chercheur, est tout ensemble le pays obscur où il doit chercher et où tout son bagage ne lui sera de rien" [I put down my cup and turn toward my mind. It is the mind's task to find truth. But how to do this? Great incertitude, every time that the mind feels itself outreached by itself; when he, the seeker, is altogether the dark country where he must

11. Poincaré, *La Science et l'hypothèse*, 30.

undertake his search and in which all his mental baggage will be of no use] (45). This is what the narrator defines as creation: the search by the mind within the mind itself for those relations of experience that are now properties of the mind that undertakes the search. The symmetry with science, or at least with Poincaré's science, is inverse, since the artist's mind seeks the certainty of the particular, rather than the general law of recursion. But, as Valéry had early proposed in comparing art with Poincaré's recursive reasoning, the production of certainty is the same: through the mind's seizure of its own procedures.

Proust's demonstration of the artist's task seems especially close to Poincaré's description of the scientist's work in yet another important respect. The narrator makes a critique of literary realism that is analogous to Poincaré's critique of epistemological naïveté. Poincaré frequently stressed that science does not describe things in themselves: all one can know, as Valéry also echoed in describing epistemic relations, are the relations between things. Comparably, toward the end of the novel, Proust's narrator rejects the "sad realism" that tries to give a "miserable account sheet" (3:885) of the lines and surfaces of things in themselves. He maintains that the artist's task is analogous to the scientist's search for relations, since artistic truth begins only when the artist takes two objects and posits a relationship between them. The unique truth of the artist's experience is rendered through the description of relations, and in Proust it is usually metaphor that produces artistic truth by describing, from the artist's viewpoint, what Poincaré repeatedly calls "les rapports entre les choses"—the relations between things.

The narrator's theory of art is fully articulated at the end of the novel, but it is consciously demonstrated largely at the novel's beginning, especially in the use of images and metaphors in the creation of the narrator's childhood in the village Combray. I recall that this recollection of the plenitude of a unique childhood springs from the experience that the *madeleine* once gave the narrator when he was already an adult, but before he had come to understand fully his task as a writer. Notwithstanding the mature narrator's supposed lack of comprehension, the opening section, called "Combray," gives the reader the most glorious concrete demonstration of the theory that the narrator finally elaborates in the novel's conclusion, *Le Temps retrouvé*. In "Combray," the reader finds the creation of the fullness of the time that the narrator experi-

enced himself as an adult in the act of remembering, and which the narrator then narrates from a fictional transcendental standpoint that escapes time. In re-creating—or recalling—the fullness of the past, Proust
calls upon the lesson of symbolism, for the narrator's recall of the specific quality of this past experience is achieved by the use of metaphor
and analogy. Not only can metaphor re-create the sensual qualities of
the past as the child lived it, but metaphor presents the analogies that
also describe, when they do not create, the relations that exist among
sensations whose uniqueness is, or was, the uniqueness of the past.
Metaphor brings about knowledge of the unique event. In this sense,
each metaphor is an epistemic event.

Perhaps the most intriguing example of re-creation of the past in
"Combray" is found in the remembrance of the young narrator's first
attempt at writing. His writing can be quoted, and with this quoting in
the text itself the narrator restores the past through the reproduction of
past writing that perforce is enunciated in the present moment. In his
youthful writing, the narrator describes three church steeples seen in the
distance one day during an excursion in a carriage. The choice of three
bodies does not seem fortuitous. It is quite plausible that the description
of three churches is Proust's oblique way of paying homage to Poincaré's work on the three body problem—and Proust can be as recondite
in his allusions as the narrator's great aunts when they pay cryptic com-
pliments to Swann. An allusion to the scientist seems implicit in the rel-
ativistic way that Proust's narrator describes the motion of these three
steeples changing their position relative to the continuous motion of the
carriage in which the young narrator found himself as he began to write
a description of them. Moreover, at this moment in his youth, when he
decides to describe his impressions of the three steeples, the narrator anticipates, through the act of writing, his later ideas about writing. The
literal quotation of his youthful writing allows the older narrator to offer a metaphorical description that is also a demonstration of a discovery of the unique truth of the past that metaphor can bring about.

Calling the steeples "flowers," and then "three maidens of legend,"
the youthful narrator describes how the steeples change position,
though of course their movement only reflects the relative position of
the moving observer. As the narrator's position changes, the steeples
"move" metaphorically about, "timidly seeking their way, and, after
some awkward, stumbling movements of their noble silhouettes, draw-

ing close to one another, slipping one behind another, shewing nothing more, now, against the still rosy sky than a single dusky form, charming and resigned, so vanishing in the night" (trans. Montcrief, 1:182) ["je les vis timidement chercher leur chemin et, après quelques gauches trébuchements de leurs nobles silhouettes, se serrer les uns contre les autres, glisser l'un derrière l'autre, ne plus faire sur le ciel encore rose qu'une seule forme noire, charmante et résignée, et s'effacer dans la nuit"] (1:140). With these metaphorical motions, the three bodies have danced out their relations in a ballet that successfully describes the unique truth of that moment for a youthful narrator who is suddenly very happy—for could one not say that, with these metaphors, the boy narrator solved, artistically and with certainty, the three body problem? He has resolved it through the web of metaphors that relate three bodies in their mutual metaphorical attraction.

With this "solution" to the problem of knowledge in art, with this demonstration of the necessity of the artist's truth, Proust brought to a closure the epistemic rivalry with science that novelists, throughout the nineteenth century, had felt with tremulous anxiety. Proust's modernist solution for the rivalry closed a chapter in literary history, though Proust proposed a solution that relatively few writers have sought to imitate. If Balzac, Flaubert, and Zola have had an untold number of imitators, Proust's work is, by its own epistemic declaration, unique. Perhaps few subsequent writers have felt that they could rival science by incorporating science and then going beyond it to offer an epistemic realm that escapes the realm of contingent truths. The history of twentieth century literature and its relation to science is quite heterogeneous. On the one hand, as exemplified by Sartre's ferocious parody in *La Nausée* (*Nausea*) of Proust's escape from contingency, a later generation of French writers no longer felt that an epistemic encounter with science was a viable issue for the novel. Or as one might infer from the savage satire of scientific research written by the doctor who signed Céline to his first novel, *Voyage au bout de la nuit* (*Journey to the End of the Night*), many later writers have been actively hostile to science. On the other hand, without any feeling of rivalry, many twentieth-century French writers have drawn upon science as a source of intellectual renewal. Queneau's constant use of science for his own thought experiments in fiction are a telling example, as is Robbe-Grillet's justification of his experimentation by reference to post-Heisenberg epistemology. In any case, few writers of later generations in France seem interested in, or are perhaps capable of, rivaling science on its own terms. And if one surveys the European literary landscape, perhaps only the Austrian Robert Musil stands out as a writer who, shortly after Proust, sought to liberate literature from any feelings of subordination toward science by transforming the novel into an epistemological instrument second to none. Or at least Musil tried.

To conclude, we might speculate that Proust brought the rivalry to a close for another, more generous reason, and one that many find quite valid today. To use a notion presented at the outset of this study, let us entertain the idea that Proust restores a separation of literature and science that goes back at least to the seventeenth century, the one first described when Pascal set forth the opposition between *l'esprit de finesse* and *l'esprit de géométrie*. The former, the mind knowing through *finesse* or intuition, has to deal with an infinite number of principles, and thus can easily go astray; whereas the latter, or the mind knowing through mathematics, will rarely go astray if it follows the simple reasoning involved in deductive chains of thought. Mathematical and scientific reasoning owes its strength to the narrowness of its field, whereas knowledge of humanistic issues is more difficult because it is more diffuse. In rejecting the claims of analysis against subjectivity and its complexity, Proust restored a modernist version of Pascal's *esprit de finesse* to its position as an epistemic equal to the scientific mind, and, in so doing, freed the writer from envy of the "mere geometric mind"—as Pascal had phrased it. I offer this comparison to help understand why fiction in the twentieth century has avoided the head-on collision with science that one finds in Balzac and Zola, and, in a sense, in Proust himself. In *A la Recherche du temps perdu*, Proust has recourse to a doctrine of "two cultures," to borrow C. P. Snow's famous coinage, in which literature and science share a certain mutual responsibility for offering two different types of knowledge of the world. On the one hand, science has its varied protocols for truth, many of which turn upon quantification. On the other hand, mind, for most of its operations, does not function according to some algorithm, as Pascal might have said, and which a contemporary physicist like Roger Penrose often does say. The conclusion then imposes itself that, as Proust argued, literature as knowledge of the mind offers unique knowledge that can be had in no other way. For, in principle, and not just in practice, there is no quantification that can offer knowledge of the self when the self is the locus for all epistemic operations. Knowledge of the self can only be had in the immediate seizure of the self's multiple certainties, and, for this, literature is a privileged tool. Of course, we have always known that literature grants us knowledge of ourselves and others, but it is reassuring to have the greatest modernist novel show us that we have garnered knowledge from it, and about it, and hence about ourselves, that we could get nowhere else.

BIBLIOGRAPHY

Except where otherwise noted, all translations in the text are my own from the cited edition. After the first footnote, all subsequent references are noted parenthetically in the text.

Auerbach, Eric. *Mimesis.* Trans. Willard Trask. Garden City, N.Y.: Anchor Doubleday, 1957.

Baguley, David, "The Nature of Naturalism." In *Naturalism in the European Novel,* ed. Brian Nelson. New York/Oxford: Berg, 1992.

Balzac, Honoré de. *La Comédie humaine.* Ed. Pierre-Georges Castex. Paris: Editions de la Pléiade, 1976–1981.

———. "Discours sur l'immortalité de l'âme. In *Oeuvres diverses,* ed. Pierre-Georges Castex. Paris: Editions de la Pléiade,1990.

———. *Le Lys dans la vallée.* Paris: Editions Garnier-Flammarion, 1972.

———. *Oeuvres complètes.* Paris: Club de l'honnête homme, 1956.

———. *La Recherche de l'absolu.* Introduction by Raymond Abellio. Paris: Le Livre de Poche, 1967.

———. *Le Père Goriot.* Preface by Félicien Marceau. Paris: Editions Folio, 1971.

Baudelaire, Charles. *Oeuvres complètes.* Ed. Y.-G. Le Dantec. Paris: Editions de la Pléiade, 1961.

Bernard, Claude. *An Introduction to the Study of Experimental Medicine.* New York: Dover Publications, 1957.

Blavier, André. *Les Fous littéraires.* Paris: H. Veyrier, 1984.

Bonfantini, Mario. *Stendhal e il realismo.* Milan: Feltrinelli, 1958.

Brock, Norton. *The Norton History of Chemistry.* New York: W. W. Norton, 1992.

Burtt, Edwin A. *The Metaphysical Foundations of Modern Physical Science.* Garden City, N.Y.: Doubleday, 1954.

Byynum, W. F., E. J. Browne, and Roy Porter, eds. *Dictionary of the History of Science.* Princeton: The Princeton University Press, 1985.

Carnot, Sadi. *Reflections on the Motor Power of Fire.* Ed. E. Mendoza. New York: Dover, 1960.

Cassedy, Steven. "Mallarmé and Andrej Belyj: Mathematics and the Phenomenality of the Literary Object." *MLN* 96, no. 5 (December 1981), 1066–83.

Cassirer, Ernst. *La Philosophie des lumières.* Trans. Pierre Quillet. Paris: Fayard, 1966. [*Die Philosophie der Aufklärung.* Tubingen: Morh, 1932.]

Condorcet. *Selected Writings.* Indianapolis: The Bobbs-Merrill Co., 1976.

Daston, Lorraine. *Classical Probability in the Enlightenment.* Princeton: Princeton University Press, 1988.

Descharmes, René. *Autour de "Bouvard et Pécuchet."* Paris: Librairie de France, 1921.

Dethloff, Uwe. *Balzac: "Le Père Goriot": Honoré de Balzacs Gesellschaftsdarstellung im Kontext der Realismus Debatte.* Tubingen: Francke Verlag, 1989.

Edelman, Gerard. *Bright Air, Brilliant Fire: On the Matter of Mind.* New York: Basic Books, 1992.

Fargeaud-Ambrière, Madeleine. "Balzac, Homme de science(s)." In *Balzac, L'invention du roman,* ed. Claude Duchet. Paris: Pierre Belfond, 1982.

Habermas, Jurgen. *Erkenntnis und Interesse.* Frankfurt: Suhrkamp, 1968.

Flaubert, Gustave. *Bouvard et Pécuchet.* Preface by Raymond Queneau. Paris: Le Livre de poche, 1959.

———. *Correspondance.* Ed. Jean Bruneau. Paris: Editions de la Pléiade, 1973–1980.

———. *La Tentation de Saint Antoine,* preface by Michel Foucault. Paris: Le Livre de Poche, 1971.

———. *L'Education sentimentale.* Paris: Editions Garnier Frères, 1964.

———. *Madame Bovary.* Paris: Editions Garnier-Flammarion, 1966.

Gaillard, Françoise. "L'En-signement [*sic*] du réel." In *Production du sens chez Flaubert,* ed. Claudine Gothot-Mersch. Paris: Editions 10 / 18, 1975.

Gardner, Martin. *The Relativity Explosion.* New York: Vintage Books, 1976.

Genette, Gérard. *Figures.* Vol. 1. Paris: Editions du Seuil, 1966.

Geoffroy Saint-Hilaire, Etienne. *Philosophie anatomique.* Paris: Mequig-non-Marvis, 1812–1815.

Gershman, Herbert S., and Kernan B. Whitworth, eds. *Anthologie des préfaces de romans français.* Paris: Julliard, 1964.

Grant, Eliot. *Zola.* New York: Twayne World Author Series, 1966.

Hacking, Ian. *The Emergence of Probability.* Cambridge: Cambridge University Press, 1975.

Hawking, Stephen. *A Brief History of Time.* New York: Bantam Books, 1988.

Henderson, Linda. *The Fourth Dimension and Non-Euclidean Geometry in Modern Art.* Princeton: Princeton University Press, 1983.

Horvath, R. A. "Les idées de Quételet sur la formation d'une discipline statistique moderne sur le rôle de la théories des probabilités." In *Quételet et la Statistique de son époque,* ed. Robert A. Horvath. Szeged: Acta Universitatis Szegediensis, 1976, Tomus 23, Fasciculus 3.

Jacob, François. *La Logique du vivant: Une histoire de l'hérédité.* Paris: Gallimard, 1970.

Jacobs, Alphonse, ed. *Gustave Flaubert-George Sand: Correspondance.* Paris: Flammarion, 1981.

Jeter, Dieter. *Geschichte der Medizin.* Stuttgart: Georg Thieme Verlag, 1992.

Kant, Immanuel. *Foundations of the Metaphysics of Morals* and *What Is Enlightenment?* Trans. Lewis White Beck. New York: Liberal Arts Press, 1959. In Kant, *Werke.* Vol. 6. Frankfurt: Insel, 1964.

Kavanagh, Thomas. *Enlightenment and the Shadows of Chance.* Baltimore: Johns Hopkins University Press, 1993.

Kenner, Hugh. *Flaubert, Joyce, Beckett: The Stoic Comedians.* Boston: Beacon Press, 1962.

Kline, Morris. *Mathematics: The Loss of Certainty.* Oxford: Oxford University Press, 1980.

Laidler, Kenneth. *The World of Physical Chemistry.* Oxford: Oxford University Press, 1993.

Lamarck, Jean-Baptiste Pierre Antoine de Monet de. *Philosophie zoologique.* Paris. New York: Hafner, 1960. [Paris: Dentu, 1809]

Laplace, Pierre Simon. *Essai philosophique sur les probabilités.* Brussels: Culture et Civilisation, 1967. [Reprint of 1814 edition.]

Le Yaquanc, Moise. *Nosographie de l'Humanité balzacienne.* Paris: Maloine, 1959.

Luckhurst, Nicola. *Science and Structure in Proust's "A la recherche."* Oxford: Oxford University Press, 2001.

Malinas, Y. *Zola et les hérédités imaginaires.* Paris: Expansion Scientifique Française, 1985.

Mallarmé, Stephane. *Oeuvres complètes.* Ed. Henri Mondor and G. Jean-Aubry. Paris: Editions de la Pléïade, 1945.

Mason, Stephen F. *A History of the Sciences,* rev. ed. New York: MacMillan, 1962.

Mayr, Ernst. *The Growth of Biological Thought: Diversity, Evolution, and Inheritance.* Cambridge: Harvard University Press, 1982.

Michelet, M. J. *Love.* Trans. J. W. Palmer, M.D. New York: Carleton, 1867.

Nadeau, Maurice. *Gustave Flaubert, écrivain.* Paris: Les lettres nouvelles, Denoel, 1969.

Newton, Sir Isaac. *Newton* [selected writings]. Ed. I. Bernard Cohen and Richard S. Westfall. New York: Norton and Co., 1995.

Nykrog, Per. *La Pensée de Balzac dans "La Comédie Humaine."* Copenhagen: Munksgaard, 1965.

Poincaré, Henri. *The Foundations of Science.* Trans. George Bruce Halsted. New York and Garrison, N.Y: The Science Press, 1913. [Includes three works by Poincaré: *Science and Hypothesis, The Value of Science,* and *Science and Method.*]

———. *La Science et l'hypothèse.* Paris: Editions de la Bohème, 1992.

Poulet, George. "La Pensée circulaire de Flaubert." In *Flaubert, Miroir de la critique,* ed. Raymonde Debray-Genette. Paris: Firmin-Didot, 1970.

Prigogine, Ilya, and Isabelle Stengers. *La nouvelle alliance.* Paris: Gallimard Folio, 1989.

Proust, Marcel. "A propos du style de Flaubert." In *Chroniques.* Paris: Gallimard, 1927. Also in *Flaubert, miroir de la critique,* ed. R. Debray-Genette. Paris: Didier, 1970.

———. *Contre Saint-Beuve.* Preface by Bernard de Fallois. Paris: Gallimard. 1954.

———. *A la Recherche du temps perdu.* Ed. Pierre Clarac and André Ferré. Paris: Editions de la Pléïade, 1954.

———. *Remembrance of Things Past.* Trans. C. K. Scott Montcrief. New York: Random House, 1932.

Queneau, Raymond. *Les Enfants de Limon*. Paris: Gallimard, 1938.

Rimbaud. *Oeuvres*. Ed. Suzanne Bernard. Paris: Garnier Frères, 1960.

Ripoll, Roger. *Réalité et mythe chez Zola*. Paris: Librairie Honoré Champion, 1981.

Schneer, Cecil J. *The Evolution of Physical Science*. New York: Grove Press, 1960.

Schwartz, Joseph. *The Creative Moment*. New York: HarperCollins, 1992.

Segrè, Emilio. *From Falling Bodies to Radio Waves: Classical Physicists and Their Discoveries*. New York: W. H. Freeman, 1984. [Also cited from *Die grossen Physiker und ihre Entdeckungen*, trans. into German by Hainer Kober. Munich: Piper, 1990.]

Serres, Michel. *Feux et signaux de Brume: Zola*. Paris: Bernard Grasset, 1975.

———. *Les Origines de la géometrie*. Paris: Flammarion, 1993.

Starr, Peter. "Science and Confusion: On Flaubert's *Temptation*." In *Gustave Flaubert: Modern Critical Views*, ed. Harold Bloom. New York and Philadelphia: Chelsea House Publishers, 1989.

Stratton, Buck. *Flaubert*. New York: Twayne Publishers, 1955.

Strickland, Geoffrey. *Stendhal: The Education of a Novelist*. Cambridge: Cambridge University Press, 1974.

Sypher, Wylie. *Literature and Technology*. New York: Vintage Books, 1971.

Theorides, Jean. *Stendhal du côté de la science*. Aran: Editions du Grand Chêne, 1972.

Valéry, Paul. *Oeuvres*. Ed. Jean Hytier. Paris: Editions de la Pléiade, 1957. [In this edition, *Introduction à la méthode de Léonard de Vinci* is part of *Variété*.]

Westfall, Richard. *The Construction of Modern Science*. Cambridge: Cambridge University Press, 1977.

Wittgenstein, Ludwig. *Philosophical Investigations*. Trans. G. E. M. Anscombe. New York: Macmillan, 1953.

———. *Tractatus logico-philosophicus*. Frankfurt: Suhrkamp, 1963.

Zola, Emile. *Le Docteur Pascal*. Paris: Collection Folio, 1993.

———. *Le Roman expérimental*. Paris: Charpentier, 1890.

———. *Les Rougon-Macquart*. Ed. Armand Lanoux and Henri Mitterand. Paris: Editions de la Pléiade, 1960–1967.

INDEX

Abbé Prévost, 32
Aesthetic ideal, in *Madame Bovary*,
     117–20, 124
Aesthetics, 9, 31
Agrippa von Nettesheim, 95–96
A la Recherche du temps perdu (*Remem-*
     brance of Things Past) (Proust), 169–
     70, 182, 184, 190–210
Aleatory models, 25, 195–96
Allegory, 40; of Balzac, 47–52; of
     Flaubert, 84; vs. the modern novel,
     7, 38; of Zola, 129, 158
Amour, L' (*Love*) (Michelet), 136
Ampère, André-Marie, 11, 41
Analogical reasoning, 17
Anger, 102, 104
Anthropology, 12
"A propos du style de Flaubert"
     (Proust), 169
Archeology, 86–87, 89
Aristotle, 24
Armance (Stendhal), 30
Art, 178, 186, 195, 201; knowledge in,
     180, 190; misuse in *Madame Bovary*,
     108–9, 117–18; relation to science,
     104–5, 109, 132–33, 169–70, 200;
     resemblance to science, 83, 94; as
     subjective realm, 197–98; truth of,
     199, 201–6
Artists, 196; compared to scientists,
     203–4, 206
Aspect-seeing, 48, 51
Assommoir, L' (*The Dram-Shop*) (Zola),
     145, 149
Astronomy, 5, 13
Atomism, 34, 44–45
Au Bonheur des Dames (*The Ladies'*

Paradise) (Zola), 145, 149, 154–
     55
Auerbach, Erich, 32–33, 35, 106

Baguley, David, 104
Balzac, Honoré de, 12, 137, 151; com-
     petition with science by, 39, 43–44,
     48, 54, 57; on energy, 49, 76, 78–80;
     on human society, 67–70, 72–73; in-
     fluence on Proust, 169, 199; influ-
     ences on, 40, 45, 56–57; on knowl-
     edge, 47–49, 62, 71; on knowledge
     and desire, 49–50, 52–53, 60, 74–
     75; nominalism of, 40, 65–66; and
     probability theory, 59, 72–73; real-
     ism of, 18, 40, 59, 62–63, 66–67, 79;
     satire of science by, 50–51; totaliza-
     tion in, 33, 35–36, 41, 46–47, 55–
     57, 61, 64–67, 79–80; and the unity
     of knowledge, 12, 56, 63–64, 70;
     use of mysticism by, 62–64; use of
     science by, 42–43, 46–47, 64, 67–69
Baudelaire, Charles, 176–84, 192–93,
     195, 199
Bayes's rule for conditional probabili-
     ty, 26, 59
Beauty, revealed through literature,
     177
Bergson, Henri, 188
Bernard, Claude, 85, 92, 94, 130; on
     determinism, 121–23; on develop-
     ment of physiology, 137–38; in
     Madame Bovary, 105–6
Bernoulli, Jacques, 24
Berzelius, Jöns Jakob, 45, 58
Bête humaine, La (*The Beast in Man*)
     (Zola), 145, 147

Beyle, Henri. *See* Stendhal
Bichat, Marie-François-Xavier, 20, 45, 116
Biology, 11, 39; and Balzac, 46, 69–70; development of, 5, 20–21, 45, 65; and Flaubert, 83, 92; individuals in, 36, 152; influence of Darwin on, 139–40; rejection of Platonism in, 15–16; and statistical mechanics, 140–41; vs. physics, 66, 156
Bohr, Niels, 6
Boltzmann, Ludwig Eduard, 140, 149–51
Boutroux, Étienne-Émile-Marie, 184
Bouvard et Pécuchet (Flaubert), 84, 95–103
Brief History of Time, A (Hawking), 157–58
Bright Air, Brilliant Fire (Edelman), 132
Brock, William H., 58
Broussais, François-Joseph-Victor, 51, 111, 137
Buffon, Georges-Louis Leclerc de, 13, 19, 20, 39, 47, 65
Burtt, Edwin A., 22

Calculus, 57; and common sense, 59–60; with Newtonian dynamics, 21, 23–24
Camus, Albert, 4–5
Capitalism, 146, 154–55
Carnot, Sadi, 41–42, 49, 75, 78–79, 151
Cassedy, Steven, 175
Cassirer, Ernst, 4
Cause: in Balzac's work, 59–60, 63, 73; in fiction, 42; in *Madame Bovary*, 121–24; and probability, 25–27, 73
Certainty, 193, 204–6; loss of, 186–87, 197; quest for, 174–76; vs. artistic truth, 188, 190; vs. contingent laws, 195–96
Cervantes, Miguel de, 12
Chance, vs. probability theory, 28
Chaos theory, Poincaré anticipating, 184–85
Chartreuse de Parme, La (*The charter-house of Parma*) (Stendhal), 32–33, 36
Chemistry, 11, 30, 39, 85; in Balzac's works, 57, 60–61; development

of, 20, 44, 137; in Flaubert's works, 97
"Cimetière marin, Le" (Valéry), 183
Classical dynamics: demise of, 131–32; and representations of reality, 13, 151
Classical Probability in the Enlighten-ment (Daston), 25
Clausius, Rudolf Julius Emanuel, 150–51
"Coeur simple, Un" (Flaubert), 103
"Combray" (Proust), 189, 191, 195, 199, 206–7
Comédie humaine, La (Balzac), 45, 48; "Avant-Propos" to, 65, 69
Complexity theory, 132
Comte, Auguste, 85
Condorcet, Marquis de, 8–9, 12, 26, 40
Consciousness, 106–7, 180
Contre Sainte-Beuve (Proust), 169
Conventionalism, in mathematics, 185–87, 201
Copernicus, 13
"Correspondances" (Baudelaire), 181
Cosmography, 21–22, 133
Cosmology, 61–62, 92, 133, 193
Cousine Bette, La (Balzac), 62
Creative Moment, The (Schwartz), 15
Cultural relativism, 8, 10
Culture, 8, 12, 25, 166; history of failed theories in, 42–43; individu-als and group dynamics in, 142–53; laws of, 190–91; and nature, 69–70; pathology in, 148–49; role of sci-ence in, 136–38; types of, 9–10, 209
Curé de Tours, Le (Balzac), 44, 78
Cuvier, Georges, 39, 68; debate with Geoffroy Saint-Hilaire, 48, 50; in development of biology, 21, 45; in-fluence on Balzac, 46–47, 56–57

Dalton, John, 44–45
Darwin, Charles, 68, 83, 134; Zola compared to, 138–41
Darwinian perspective, 128, 140–41, 154–55
Daston, Lorraine, 25–26
Davy, Sir Humphry, 58
Débâcle, La (Zola), 145, 149, 152–54; as conclusion of *Les Rougon-Macquart* series, 157, 166

De Fleury, Maurice, 138
Defoe, Daniel, 6
De incertitudine et vanitate scientiarum
   (*Of the Vanitie and Uncertaintie of
   Artes and Sciences*) (Agrippa), 95–
   96
De l'Amour (*On Love*) (Stendhal), 30–
   32
De Occulta Philosophia (Agrippa), 96
Descartes, René, 15, 22
Desire, 91, 147; and knowledge, 74–
   75; for knowledge, 57, 60–61, 71–
   74, 87–88; in *La Peau de chagrin,* 49–
   50, 52
Destruction, as theme in *La Recherche,*
   57
Determinism, 16, 32, 196–97; of
   Flaubert, 110, 121–24, 145; limits of,
   162, 200–201; of Proust, 191–92; of
   Zola, 136, 145–48, 162. *See also*
   Heredity
De Vries, 138
Dictionnaire des sciences médicales, 110
Dictionnaire philosophique (Voltaire),
   7–8
Diderot, Denis, 4–5
Differential equations, 16–17
Disorder: as most probable tendency,
   79, 102–4, 145, 153–54; in Zola's
   novels, 164–65
Docteur Pascal, Le (Zola), 133–34,
   156–66
Duhem, Pierre-Maurice-Marie, 197
Dupuytren, Guillaume, 114

Edelman, Gerard, 132
Education, 19, 40; Balzac on, 44, 55;
   futility of, 109–10
Education sentimentale, L' (Flaubert),
   103; influence on rhetoric of fiction,
   83–84; as naturalist novel, 104
Einstein, Albert, 6, 184, 188–90
Elective Affinities, The (Goethe), 5
Emancipation, as goal of Enlighten-
   ment, 10
Emergence of Probability, The (Hack-
   ing), 25
Empirical assessments, 6
Empiricism, 54, 91, 185. *See also* Ratio-
   nalist empiricism
Energy, 133; Balzac's conception of,

52, 74–76, 78; conservation of, 78–
   79, 151, 156–57; development of
   concept of, 49–50; theories about
   heat, 150–51; in Zola's novels,
   164–65
Engineering, 20
England: poetry of, 172; realism in
   fiction of, 6
Enlightenment, 5, 9, 26, 44; beliefs
   about knowledge in, 7–9, 24; goals
   of, 12, 63; unity of knowledge in,
   10, 39–40, 57; writers' awareness of
   science in, 3–4
*Enlightenment and the Shadows of
   Chance* (Kavanagh), 28
Entropy: in Balzac's work, 79; coun-
   tering through research, 160–61;
   development of concept, 78–80,
   151; in Flaubert's work, 102–4; irreversibility of, 140, 151; vs. increasing organization, 156–57, 165–66;
   in Zola's novels, 153–54, 156, 164–
   65
Epistemic discourses, 5, 7, 17, 84; by
   Balzac, 41, 67; composites, 72; diversity of, 12–13; hierarchy of, 190;
   history of, 16; influence of, 94; in
   natural philosophy, 4; novels as, 38,
   126–27; as quantitative vs. qualitative, 13, 14–15; science's dominance in, 10, 127; unity of, 131–32;
   vs. narrative discourse, 107; vs.
   novels, 121, 123; vs. practice, 115
Epistemology, 18; analytic, 9;
   Balzac's, 47, 58–59; of conventionalism, 185–87; of poetry and science, 173–74; Poincaré's, 190, 198;
   relations in, 206; science in, 184,
   204
Erasmus, Desiderius, 12
*Esquisse d'un tableau historique des pro-
   grès de l'esprit humain* (*Outlines of a
   Historical View of the Progess of the
   Human Mind*) (Condorcet), 8–9
Essai philosophique sur les probabilités
   (*A Philosophical Essay on Probabili-
   ties*) (Laplace), 26–27, 59
Essences, Proust's, 202
Ethics: and epistemology, 9, 12; universal, 13–14; vs. truth and beauty,
   177–78

Euclidean geometry. *See* Geometry

Europe: German romantics, 10–11; writers' awareness of science in, 3. *See also* France

Evolution, 156; Balzac's interest in, 67–68; and Darwin, 83, 134–35, 138–39; debates about, 45, 48; of open systems, 79–80; vs. entropy, 154–55, 165–66; Zola's theories on, 138–39

Evolutionary biology, 12

Evolution of Physical Science, The (Schneer), 79

Fargeaud-Ambrière, Madelaine, 68

Faust: imitation of, 86; references in *La Peau de chagrin*, 48–49, 52–53, 57

Faust (Goethe), similarity of *La Tentation de Saint Antoine* to, 85

Fermat, Pierre de, 24–25

Fichte, Johann Gottlieb, 56, 74

Fiction. *See* Novels

Fielding, 32

Flaubert, Gustave, 55; on aesthetic ideal, 118–20, 124; ambiguity about science, 83, 86–87, 93–94; determinism of, 121–24; on futility of knowledge, 96, 100–102, 109–16, 120; on increasing disorder, 103–4; on the infinite, 91–92; influence on Proust, 169, 199; and positivism, 83–86, 93, 108, 116; realism of, 18, 82, 104, 123; on relation of science and art, 104–5, 108–9, 123–24; rivalry with science, 84–86, 95, 101, 106, 123; satire of knowledge, 84, 88, 95–99, 117; significance of, 82–84, 104, 106–7; and Zola, 126, 144–45

Flaubert, Joyce, and Beckett: The Stoic Comedians (Kenner), 117

Fleurs du mal, Les (*Flowers of evil*) (Baudelaire), 179

Fontenelle, Bernard Le Bovier de, 5

Force, attempts to quantify, 76–77

Fortune des Rougon, La (Zola), 139, 142, 145

Foucault, Michel, 10, 101–2

Fourier, Jean-Baptiste-Joseph, 41

France, 19, 40, 168–69; peasant society in, 153; Second Empire of, 147–48, 156–58

Fresnel, Augustin, 41

Future, 186; ever-increasing knowledge in, 129–30, 161–62; predicting through probability, 26–27

Galen, 20

Galileo, 12–14

Gardner, Martin, 189

Gauss, Carl Friedrich, 64

Genette, Gérard, 107

Gensoul, Joseph, 114

Geoffroy Saint-Hilaire, Étienne, 39, 92; and Balzac, 46–47, 56–57, 69, 70; Cuvier's debate with, 48, 50; in development of biology, 21, 45

Geoffroy Saint-Hilaire, Isidore, 92

Geology, 11, 15, 39

Geometry, 8, 15; Balzac's use of, 74, 78; to describe reality, 16–17, 198; Euclidean, 23; non-Euclidean, 174, 176, 185, 189–90; of time and space, 22–23

Germany, romantics in, 10–11

Germinal (Zola), 145–46, 149, 153–54

Gibbs, Josiah Willard, 149

Goethe, Johann Wolfgang von, 4–5, 85

Goethe-envy, 85–86

Goldsmith, Oliver, 32

Grant, Eliot, 143

Growth of Biological Thought, The (Mayr), 15–16

Hacking, Ian, 25

Haeckel, Ernst Heinrich Philipp August, 83, 93

Hanska, Madame, 62

Hegel, Georg Wilhelm Friedrich, 33–35, 56

Helmholtz, Hermann Ludwig Ferdinand von, 156–57

Henderson, Linda, 185

Heredity, 138; laws of, 190–92; Renaissance belief in inherited signatures, 135–36; theories of Zola compared to Darwin, 138–41; in Zola's novels, 133–36, 141–48, 158–60, 162–64, 166

Hertz, Heinrich Rudolph, 76

Hippocrates, 20, 137

Histoire naturelle (Buffon), 47

Histology, 45
Historiography, 12–13
History, 12, 39, 94, 145, 156; changing
  conceptions of, 86–87; in Flaubert's
  novels, 85, 94, 113; and historical
  knowledge, 68, 75; of science, 136–
  38; as totalization, 35, 39; in Zola's
  novels, 156
Hugo, Victor, 178–79
Humanism / humanists, 2–3, 98, 132
Humanities, science estranged from,
  14

Ignorance, 60, 89–90, 102
Imponderables, 42–43, 54, 63–64, 76
Impossible, the, 24–25, 28–29
Improbable, the, 28–29
Individuals, 36, 141, 177, 180; in pop-
  ulation dynamics, 139–40, 150–55;
  relation to society, 142–53; and
  types, 68–69, 71–72; vs. popula-
  tions, 65–66
Industrialization, in *Madame Bovary*,
  117
Infinite, the, 64, 91–92; quest for, 74–
  75, 86
Intellect, 173–74, 182–84, 192
*Introduction à la méthode de Léonard da
  Vinci* (Valéry), 173–74
Irony, in *Madame Bovary*, 104–5, 117

Jacob, François, 140
James, Henry, 106
Jansenist background, 102

Kant, Immanuel: and primacy of time
  and space, 21–23; rationalism of,
  40, 177; and unity of knowledge,
  10, 13–14
Kantian metaphysics, 42, 185–86;
  Balzac's opposition to, 54, 61
Kavanagh, Thomas, 28
Kelvin, Lord, 157
Kenner, Hugh, 117
Kepler, Johannes, 12–13
Kline, Morris, 197
Knowing subject, 13–14, 23, 28, 49,
  162
Knowledge, 23, 107; access to, 84–85,
  170–71; in art, 190, 208; in Balzac's
  novels, 47–48; certainty in, 187,

190, 195–96; contingency of, 174–
  75, 195–96; desire for, 57, 60–61,
  166; as ever-increasing, 129–30,
  161–62; foundations of, 99–100,
  107; futility of, 96–97, 100, 109–10,
  115–16; futility of pursuit of, 86–
  87, 95–96; historical, 68, 75; history
  of, 16, 94; lack of, 110, 112–14; limits of, 52, 74–75, 176–77; nonintellectual, 180–81, 192–93; in poetry
  vs. science, 173–74, 183–84; and
  probability, 24, 27, 187; quantification of, 75–76, 111; quantitative vs.
  qualitative, 15, 19, 65–66, 68; resist-
  ing, 88–90; in rivalry of literature
  with science, 11–13, 84; science as
  arbiter of, 94, 158; search for, 55–
  56, 71–74, 92–93, 160–61; through
  literature, 32, 43–44, 188; total, 26–
  27, 157–58; types of, 13–14, 209–
  10; unity of, 7–10, 12–13, 56, 63–64,
  70, 131–32; uses of ideals, 118, 120.
  See also Totalization

Lagrange, Joseph-Louis, 16, 33
Lamarck, Jean-Baptiste Pierre Antoine de Monet de, 13, 20–21, 39,
  46
La Mettrie, Julien Offroy, 70
Language, 193; of art, 181, 202–3;
  limitations of, 112–13. *See also*
  Rhetoric
Laplace, Pierre Simon, 11, 19; Newtonian worldview of, 23–24, 33;
  and probability theory, 24, 59–60;
  on total knowledge, 26–27, 33–34,
  55
Laplacian worldview, 41; and Balzac,
  44, 59, 63, 68; critiques of, 44, 46;
  demise of, 196–97
Lavoisier, Antoine-Laurent, 11, 20, 44,
  57–58
Laws, 36, 198; contingent, 195–96;
  describing reality through, 190–92;
  deterministic, 197; discovering
  through science, 160–63, 171
Laws of motion, Newton's, 16–17,
  41–42, 78. *See also* Newtonian dynamics
Légende des siècles, La (Hugo), 179
Lesage, Alain-René, 32

Lettres provinciales (Pascal), 25
Life, in *Le Docteur Pascal,* 165–66
Linnaeus, Carolus, 39
Literary history, 43
Literature, 38, 55, 173; emergence of, 5; and knowledge, 7, 34, 180–81, 188; misused in *Madame Bovary,* 108, 118. *See also* Epistemic discourses; Novels; Poetry
Literature and Technology (Sypher), 172
Livre, Le (Mallarmé), 175–76, 193
Lockean nominalism, Balzac's, 40, 63
Louis Lambert (Balzac), 54–57
Lubbock, Percy, 106
Lucas, Prosper, 135–36, 143–44
Lucien Leuwen (Stendhal), 30, 32, 36
Luckhurst, Nicola, 188
Lys dans da vallée, Le (*The Lily of the Valley*) (Balzac), 44

Mach, Ernst, 197
Mach-Duhem-Poincaré hypothesis, 18
Madame Bovary (Flaubert), 103; on aesthetic ideal, 117–20; determinism in, 121–24; influence of, 83–84, 126, 169; as satire of science, 108–17; science and art in, 104–7, 109
Magendie, François, 20, 51
Magnetism, 46, 54; as imponderable force, 43, 63–64
Malinas, Y., 138
Mallarmé, Stéphane, 21, 183, 193, 195, 199; attitude toward science, 172–76
Marx, Karl Heinrich, 33–35, 56, 76
Materialism, 60, 200; Balzac's, 63–64, 70; Baudelaire's, 183; Flaubert's, 93, 118; Zola's, 166
Mathematics, 17, 186; and Balzac, 64, 68; Balzac's use of, 40, 75; and certainty, 174–76, 187, 197, 205; critique of, 19, 44; desire for moral equivalent, 57; foundations of, 185–87; hyper-evaluation of, 14–16; metaphors from, 75, 178; and science, 15–17, 23; in theories of heredity, 133–34
Maxwell, James Clerk, 150–51, 157, 171–72
Mayr, Ernst, 15–16, 65, 139–40

Mechanical models, 16, 26, 41, 149; rejection of, 19–20, 131; and thermodynamics, 79, 151
Medécine experimentale, La (Bernard), 123
Medicine, 83; development of, 5, 19–20, 41, 45, 137; in Flaubert's works, 87, 93–94, 97–98, 110–16; hopes for, 39, 158; laws of, 190–92; positivism in, 85, 93–94; satire of, 51, 110–11; status as art or science, 132–33; Zola portraying pathology, 148–49
Mendel, Gregor Johann, 138
Mesmerism, 46
Metaepistemology, of Balzac, 47, 54
Metaphors: escape from time through, 207–8; from mathematics, 178; in nonscientific realm, 180; from sciences, 31–32, 148–49
Metaphysical Foundations of Modern Physical Science, The (Burtt), 22
Metaphysics: of Balzac, 41, 54; of Kant, 21–22, 54, 185; of Newton, 21–22; romantic, 61; 19th century, 35; as totalizing, 34, 39
Michelet, M. J., 136
Mind, 185; and art vs. science, 204–6; autonomy of, 174; types of, 2–3, 9, 209
Mineralogy, 31–32
Modernism: development of, 168–69; probability vs. certainty in, 187
Montesquieu, Baron de La Brède et de, 12–13, 36
Moraliste tradition, 30–31
Morality, 63, 65, 77
Moralizing, in novels, 6, 40–41
Musil, Robert, 209
Mysticism, 61–62, 136–37
Myth, 61, 129, 134–35
Myth of Sisyphus, The (Camus), 5

Nadeau, Maurice, 93
Nana (Zola), 145, 148–49, 152
Narrators: in *A la Recherche,* 174, 187, 189–95, 198–208; in *Madame Bovary,* 104–9, 113–15, 120–21
Natural history, 19, 20, 41, 47, 136; and Balzac, 46, 50–51, 56, 69–70; as totalizing discourse, 39, 65

Naturalism, 168; critique of, 201; Flaubert's, 104; Zola's, 129, 152
Naturalist novels, 126, 129, 141
Natural philosophy, 4
Nature: society's resemblance to, 69–70; unity of, 46–48, 92–93
Naturphilosophie, 56
Nausée, La (Nausea) (Sartre), 208
Neoplatonism, 14
Neveu de Rameau, Le (Diderot), 6
Newton, Sir Isaac, 5, 11–12, 15, 23
Newtonian dynamics, 4–5, 33, 42, 74, 186; Balzac's respect for, 67–68; critiques of, 19, 23, 44, 46, 54, 63, 179, 189; problems with, 134, 171–72, 177, 196–97; used to explain everything, 21, 27, 39, 55, 64. *See also* Laws of motion, Newton's
Newtonian revolution, 11, 13, 20, 22
Nietzsche, Friedrich Wilhelm, 89–90, 99–100
Nodier, Charles, 53–54, 62
Nominalism, 19, 40, 63, 65–66
Normal/abnormal, 92, 128
Norton History of Chemistry, The (Brock), 58
Nouvelle alliance, La (Prigogine and Stengers), 140
Novels, 18; Balzac's goals in, 43–45, 58, 62, 65–67; Balzac's use of science in, 69–70, 77, 151; Baudelaire's intentions in, 178–79; determinism in, 122; development of, 6–7, 12–13, 25–26, 72–73, 79; ending rivalry with science, 169–70, 208–10; Flaubert's goals in, 82, 106; Flaubert's rhetoric in, 82, 106–7; having realms science cannot rival, 176–77, 179–80, 184; incorporating science in, 39, 66–67, 94; modernism in, 168; naturalist, 104, 126, 129, 141, 168; Proust's, 169, 198; Proust's goals in, 170, 193, 201–2; realism of, 18–19, 66–67; relation to science, 2–6, 16–17, 29–36, 86, 99–101, 141; relation to science in Flaubert's, 83, 99–101, 121; rivalry with science, 7–8, 11–13, 17, 168, 170, 188; rivalry with science in Balzac's, 39, 45, 48, 56, 67, 79; rivalry with science in Flaubert's, 82–

85, 106, 123–24; rivalry with science in Zola's, 144, 155–56, 161; totalization in, 34; and truth, 99, 177; uses of, 38, 60, 175–76; Zola's goals in, 126–31, 138, 161–62

Objectivity, in *Madame Bovary,* 104–6, 108–9, 113
Oeuvre, L' (The Masterpiece) (Zola), 126–28
Open systems, evolution of, 79–80
Origines de la géométrie, Les (The origins of geometry) (Serres), 8
Overdetermination, 77, 104, 120

Paleontology, development of, 39, 47
Paradigm shifts, 43
Paré, Ambroise, 113
"Parfum, La" (Baudelaire), 181–82
Paris, 55; as center of scientific debate, 42, 45–46; as center of surgical knowledge, 114
Parisian Commune, in *La Débâcle,* 153
Pascal, Blaise, 2, 24–25, 92, 209
Peasant society, in *La Terre,* 153
Peau de chagrin, La (The Magic Skin) (Balzac), 41, 47–54, 66, 77, 87, 92
Penrose, Roger, 209
Perception, 36, 202; in *Madame Bovary,* 106–7; and parameters of reality, 23, 198; subjectivity of, 198, 203
Père Goriot, Le (Balzac), 41, 67–68, 70–77; realism of, 44, 62
Philosophical Investigations (Wittgenstein), 34
Philosophy, 9, 19, 38; positivism in, 85, 171
Physics, 15, 76, 171, 186, 196–97; abandonment of Aristotelian, 22, 137; Baudelaire's escape from world of, 179–80; development of, 20, 26, 137, 156; explanations of phenomena by, 11, 64; Laplacian, 19, 55; positivism in, 85; and representations of reality, 13, 23; and totalization, 34, 55; vs. literature, 64, 178–79; in Zola's novels, 133–34, 149–51
Physiology, 39, 41, 83; development of, 20, 94, 137; laws of, 190–92; as

Physiology (*cont.*)
　model for scientific discourses,
　132–33
Pinel, Philippe, 20, 51
Plague, The (Camus), 5
Planck, Max, 171–72
Plato, 3
Platonism, 14–15, 23, 202
Poe, Edgar Allan, 172–73
Poetry, 180; beauty revealed through,
　177–78; language of, 181; Proust
　using, 170–71; revelation through,
　175–76; self-sufficiency of, 199;
　transcendence through, 176–77,
　183–84; vs. science, 172–74
Poincaré, Henri, 172; analogies to
　work of, 173, 188; conventionalism
　of, 184–87, 201; epistemology of,
　174–75, 195–96, 198, 204–6; influ-
　ence on Proust, 174, 188–90
Poisson, Siméon-Denis, 26
Positivism, 116, 158, 171, 185, 190; in
　Flaubert's works, 93–94, 109; sci-
　ence's explanations, 83, 85–86; in
　Zola's works, 131
Poulet, Georges, 106
Prigogine, Ilya, 140
Principia (Newton), 15
Probability theory, 40, 151, 187; and
　Balzac, 59, 67, 72–73; development
　of, 25–26; in heredity, 142, 144; for
　individuals vs. populations, 142,
　150–52; influence of, 6, 27, 28, 134;
　and limits of knowledge, 24–26
Proust, Marcel: on absolute time, 180,
　202; on certain knowledge, 176,
　186–88, 190, 193, 195–96, 199, 204–
　5; combining literature and science,
　169, 171, 179; conception of the
　novel, 174, 178–79, 184, 198, 205;
　on determinism, 190–92, 196–97,
　200–201; goals in novels, 170, 193,
　195, 198; influences on, 169, 172,
　187–91, 198–99; on laws of reality,
　190–92, 198, 200; modernism of,
　169, 187, 208; and realism, 204, 206;
　on realms of literature vs. science,
　169–73, 181, 184, 188, 201–4, 207–
　10; rhetoric of, 181–82, 193–95; sig-
　nificance of, 170, 208–9; techniques
　of, 174, 193–95, 199, 206–7; on

three body problem, 196–97, 200,
　207–8
Psychology, 36, 41
Public, scientists not writing for, 14–
　15

Queneau, Raymond, 17, 98, 208
Quételet, Adolphe Lambert, 150

Rabelais, François, 12
Rational empiricism: defining cate-
　gories of, 24–25; and probability, 26
Rationalism, 9, 98; in *Madame Bovary*,
　111; opposition to, 54, 177; quest
　for, 76; of Stendhal, 29
Rationalist empiricism: knowing sub-
　ject vs. reality in, 13–14; primacy of
　mathematical descriptions in, 17
Real: descriptions of, 17, 44, 76; ratio-
　nal as, 98; science as arbiter of, 94
Realism, 6, 33; Balzac's, 47, 58, 60,
　62–63, 68, 70–77; bound to empiri-
　cism, 17–18; Flaubert's, 82, 84, 104;
　influence of probability theory on,
　25–26; intentions of, 11–12; in nov-
　els, 18–19, 40, 62–63; Proust's, 169;
　of scientific epistemology, 204;
　Stendhal's, 29, 32; vs. conventional-
　ism, 186; vs. the improbable and
　impossible, 28–29
Reality, 35; access to, 39, 42, 178–79,
　190; in Balzac's fiction, 66–67; de-
　scriptions of, 21–22, 53–54, 197–98;
　interpretations of, 13, 24, 151; pa-
　rameters of, 23, 75, 176–77; types
　of, 27, 201; underdetermination of,
　18, 186, 198
Recherche de l'absolu, La (*The Quest of
　the Absolute*) (Balzac), 44, 48, 57–61,
　77
*Reflexions sur la puissance motrice du
　feu* (Carnot), 79
Relativism, vs. universalism, 12
Relativity, 184, 207–8; development
　of concept, 189–90; of knowledge,
　48, 53–54
Religion, 70; science replacing, 84,
　88–90, 93–94; in *Séraphita*, 61–62,
　64; vs. science, 159–60
Renaissance, 12, 96, 135–36
Republic, The (Plato), 3

Rhetoric: Flaubert's, 82–84, 106–7, 169; Proust's, 181–82, 193–95

Ripoll, Roger, 164

Robbe-Grillet, Alain, 208

Roman expérimental, Le (Zola), 130–32, 161

Romanticism, 11, 24, 40, 61, 120, 172; of Balzac, 74; in *Madame Bovary*, 109, 118; of Stendhal, 29

Rouge et le noir, Le (*The Red and the Black*) (Stendhal), 32, 35–36

Rougon-Macquart, Les (Zola), 156; conclusions of, 157, 166; entropy in, 164–66; heredity in, 138–39, 141–47; physics applied to individuals and groups in, 149–52; as scientific novel, 126–28, 133–34, 141. *See also* specific titles within series

Rousseau, Jean-Jacques, 32

Saint-Simon, Claude Henri de Rouvroy, 32

Salammbô (Flaubert), 85

Sand, George, 83

Sartre, Jean-Paul, 208

Satire: of knowledge, 84, 88, 95–99, 117; of science, 50–51, 72, 108–11; vs. the modern novel, 6

Schelling, Felix Emanuel, 33, 56

Schiller, Johan Cristoph Friedrich von, 32

Schneer, Cecil J., 79, 151

Schwartz, Joseph, 15

Science, 11, 14, 38, 63, 96, 158–59, 187, 209; as arbiter of knowledge and reality, 94, 158, 178–79; art's relation to, 109, 169–70, 200; Balzac incorporating into fiction, 66–67; Balzac's criticisms of, 44, 53–54, 61–62; conventionalism in, 186; definitions of, 173; developments of, 44–46, 97, 170, 184; and education, 19, 44, 55; and ever-increasing knowledge, 161–62; in Flaubert's novels, 96–98, 104, 108, 111–12, 115–16; history of, 43, 136–37; hopes for, 21, 147; influence of Darwinian perspective on, 140–41; magical views mixed with, 135–36; and mathematics, 15, 19; modernity of, 20, 140; observation vs. experimentation, 123–24; power to replace religion, 84, 88–90, 93–94; primacy of, 10, 87; questions asked in fiction and, 187–88; rejection of, 95–96, 158–60, 164, 171–72; respect for, 158–60, 164, 184; scientists' attitude toward, 171–72; structures of, 19; and truth, 101, 192, 201–6; Zola's model of, 128–29, 142

Science and Structure in Proust's "A la recherche" (Luckhurst), 188

Science et l'hypothèse, La (*Science and Hypothesis*) (Poincaré), 188–89, 205

Scientific revolution, Kant codifying, 13–14

Scientists: Poincaré as model of, 185; vs. artists, 203–4, 206; vs. humanists, 2–3

Segrè, Emilio, 151

Self-objectification, 31

Self-reflexivity, 146–48, 160–62, 173

Sensations, 198; in *A la Recherche*, 195, 199, 201–2; in *Madame Bovary*, 122–23; as outside realm of intellect, 182–84; truth via, 192–93

Séraphita (Balzac), 41, 48, 61–67

Serres, Michel, 8, 133–34

Sleep, as outside time and space, 53–54

Space: primacy in describing reality, 21–22, 53–54; in Proust's work, 189–90, 193–94; realms outside, 201–2; restrictions of reality by, 56, 63

"Space and Geometry" (Proust), 198

Spinoza, Baruch, 91

Starr, Peter, 88

Statistical mechanics, 152; linked with thermodynamics, 149–51; parallels with evolution, 140–41

Statistical models, 149

Statistical reasoning, 26, 28, 156

Stendhal, 29–36, 40

Stengers, Isabelle, 140

Stochastic models, 25–26

Stranger, The (Camus), 5

Strickland, Geoffrey, 35–36

Structuralism, 19

Subject, knowledge through lens of, 91

Subjectivity, 197–99, 203

Swift, Jonathan, 5
Sypher, Wylie, 172–73

Tale of a Tub, The (Swift), 5
Taxonomy, 65, 69; in Balzac's novels, 46, 72–73
Temps retrouvé, Le (Proust), 200, 206
Tentation de Saint Antoine, La (Flaubert), 84–91
Terre, La (*The Earth*) (Zola), 153
Thermodynamics, 26; development of laws, 78–79; influence on *Bouvard et Pécuchet*, 102–3; and statistical mechanics, 149–51; in Zola's novels, 133–34, 149–51, 156–57, 165–66
Thought experiments, 5–6, 175, 208
Three body problem, 196–97, 207–8
Time: Baudelaire's escape from, 179–80; laws of, 140, 192; primacy of to describe reality, 21–22, 53–54; in Proust's work, 188–90, 193–95, 207; realms outside, 201–2; restrictions of reality by, 56, 63
Totalization, 21–22, 26–27, 33–36, 65, 128, 197; in Balzac's novels, 38–39, 43–44, 46–47, 51–53, 55–56, 60–61, 66; effects of entropy concept on, 79–80; in Flaubert's novels, 91, 111–12; of knowledge, 43–44, 157–58; satire of, 111–12; search for, 55–57, 102, 174–75; vs. the infinite, 91–92; Zola's faith in, 131–32
Tractatus (Wittgenstein), 34
Traité de l'hérédité naturelle (Lucas), 143
Transcendence, 203; modernist, 168–69; through poetry, 170–71, 176, 183
Truth, 186; of art vs. science, 188, 199, 201–6; joy through, 89–90; sources of, 93, 107, 192, 195; through poetry not science, 176–79, 183–84
Truth claims, 99, 101

Underdetermination, 18, 186, 197–98, 204
United States, writers' separation from science in, 3
Universalism, 7–8, 12
Universities, science vs. humanism in, 3

Valéry, Paul, 206; attitude toward science, 172–74; on knowledge through poetry, 183–84
Van Helmont, Jan Baptista, 51, 87
Vectors, Balzac's conceptions of, 76–78
Verisimilitude, 25
Vie de Henry Brulard (Stendhal), 30
Virchow, Rudolf, 93
Vitalism, 19–20; in Flaubert, 87; influence of, 116; in Stendhal, 32; vs. conservation of energy, 157; vs. mechanicalism, 41
Voltaire, 4, 5, 32; historical thinking of, 12–13; on unity of knowledge, 7–8
Voyage au bout de la nuit (*Journey to the End of the Night*) (Céline), 208

War, in *La Débâcle,* 152–54
Watt, Ian, 6, 25
Westfall, Richard, 23
"What Is Enlightenment?" (Kant), 10
Wittgenstein, Ludwig, 34
Writers, 3, 12, 201–2, 206, 207; Goethe-envy of, 85–86; relation with science, 11–13, 208–9; scientists compared to, 17, 203–4, 206; total knowledge of, 27, 34; use of probability and possibility, 24, 28. *See also* Literature; Novels; specific authors

Zola, Émile, 12, 18, 28; compared to Darwin, 134, 138–41; desire for totalizing knowledge, 33, 35, 128–32, 158; on entropy vs. increasing organization, 156–57, 164–66; future epistemology of, 129, 162, 186; goal of writing scientific novel, 126–29, 132–33, 138, 141; goals in novels, 141–42, 161–62, 166; heredity in novels, 133–36, 138, 141–48, 157–60, 162–64, 166; on individuals vs. group dynamics, 139, 141, 149–55; influence on Proust, 169, 191, 199; influences on, 126, 130, 137; and naturalism, 129, 168; and positivism, 131, 158; rivalry with science, 127–28, 148, 155, 161; unity of science for, 130–31